The 2,000 Percent Solution

Free Your Organization From "Stalled" Thinking to Achieve Exponential Success

Donald Mitchell
Carol Coles
Robert Metz

AMACOM
American Management Association
New York • Atlanta • Boston • Chicago • Kansas City • San Francisco • Washington, D.C.
Brussels • Mexico City • Tokyo • Toronto

This publication is designed to provide accurate and authoritative information in regard to the subject matter covered. It is sold with the understanding that the publisher is not engaged in rendering legal, accounting, or other professional service. If legal advice or other expert assistance is required, the services of a competent professional person should be sought.

Library of Congress Cataloging-in-Publication Data
Mitchell, Donald
    The 2,000 percent solution : free your organization from "stalled" thinking to achieve exponential success / Donald Mitchell, Carol Coles, and Robert Metz.
       p.   cm.
    Includes index.
    ISBN 0-8144-0476-6
    1. Creative ability in business.   2. Organizational change.
  3. Management.   I. Coles, Carol. II. Metz, Robert. III. Title.
HD53.M58   1999
658.4'063—dc21   98-40541
                                                  CIP

Original illustrations, images by artist Tobi Kahn: 12 images from the series PYM-CADAH © Tobi Kahn. All rights reserved by the artist.

Printing number
10 9 8 7 6 5 4 3 2 1

To our spouses, parents, and children for inspiring
us to want to improve the world for everyone

Contents

Foreword

How to Get the Most Value
From This Book

Unlike most business books, *The 2,000 Percent Solution* is primarily about *what* to do differently rather than *how* to do something better than you do it today. Its purpose is to focus your attention on important tasks that your organization should be, but probably is not, working on now.

The book's fundamental premise is that no matter how successful your organization is, it is performing way below its easily achievable potential. If your organization is like most, it is probably functioning below average in many important activities. For example, if yours is a public company, the price of your stock may have grown more slowly than the Standard & Poor's 500 stock average in the last five years—an average that you can easily exceed by adopting actions that stockholders strongly prefer and that make sense for your company.

Complacency is the primary reason for this frequent, significant gap between potential and achievement. Here are three reasons why:

1. At best, complacency causes you to be satisfied with far less than your personal and organizational best. If your company is not accelerating its rate of improvement, you are probably resting on your laurels—something that often occurs when compensation and promotion are associated with easy-to-beat budgets.
2. Complacency also keeps you from seeing and acting on your organization's best opportunities. You may achieve gains by measuring costs that involve spending money, but if you neglect to measure what happens when you do not pursue certain large,

excellent opportunities, the reduced results may offset the former gains. For example, Walt Disney's accounting records indicate how much it costs to operate its theme parks, but they say
nothing about lost profits as a result of not opening more parks
or by having allowed another company to develop the Japanese
version of Disneyland.

3. At worst, complacency fools you into falling behind others, trig-
gering predictable crises. However, those crises may cause you
to act to restore your organization's effectiveness and vitality to
a portion of its former competitive level. For example, IBM
once dominated the market for all kinds of computers. That
dominance slipped, and for years little effective action was
taken until profits, cash flow, and the balance sheet were really
in trouble. Then the company began to take meaningful action
to improve itself under Lou Gerstner's leadership.

The 2,000 Percent Solution is easy and fun to read, with many more
anecdotes than most books. Hopefully, you will see yourself in the examples. But don't let the anecdotes tempt you to read it as a discussion
about how successful companies got that way. Use them as examples of
new things *you* must do, and be encouraged as you see the types of
results that can follow from asking the right questions.

*This book has a serious and important purpose: to make you and
your organization vastly more successful by having you ask and answer
new questions.* The authors are trying to shock you out of your complacency—to get you to think and to act effectively on the basis of these
new thoughts—and we ask you four new questions that are critical to
your organization's future:

1. Of all the things you do now, how do you know what works for
you?
2. Where is complacency costing you the most in light of what you
could accomplish?
3. What do you need to know and do that is different from and
more successful than what you know and do now?
4. No matter how successful you are in what you do, how can you
improve a lot where it will be worth a great deal?

Ernest Hemingway's famous novel *The Old Man and the Sea*
(Scribner 1952) can be read from several different perspectives. For

some it is merely an adventure story about catching a fish. For others it is also about "mankind versus nature." For still others, the novel is about mankind's indomitable spirit.

Similarly, *The 2,000 Percent Solution* can be read in many different ways, each of them rewarding. There are six ways you can and should read this book to benefit you and your organization. The book offers:

1. Stories of problems that many have found difficult to overcome
2. Stories of solutions to these same problems, located later in the same chapter, called stall erasers
3. "How to" steps to implement solutions for these problems in your organization, at the ends of the chapters, called stallbusters
4. A call to set objectives and plans to achieve well beyond the best of what someone will soon implement as tomorrow's best practice for your key activities
5. A call to go for the maximum result that can be achieved in your most important activities with reasonable risk and resources— always much greater than merely exceeding tomorrow's best practice
6. A way to create economic relations between your organization and your customers, employees, suppliers, partners, shareholders, and the communities in which the organization operates that will create much more effective and affluent results for all these stakeholders

To make it easier for you to appreciate and see all the perspectives, you will find a few sentences at the beginning of each chapter that put the material you are about to read into one or more of these perspectives. This material is printed in italics to remind you that they serve as road signs to the meaning of the material that follows.

The 2,000 Percent Solution has another important meaning for you and your organization. It contains a new thought process to help you achieve large benefits that can be applied to a broad range of issues, both organizational and personal. In essence, you have an opportunity to adopt a way of thinking that can help you in everything you do. Instead of adding specialized thinking that fragments your organization, *The 2,000 Percent Solution* will add valuable thinking that will unify and direct your organization into new and more effective ways of operating.

Be sure to read the Afterword. In it, you will find a call to action that will focus you on what you must do now.

Acknowledgments

The 2,000 Percent Solution was improved by assistance from many hundreds of people, and space does not permit us to thank each of you individually. We hope that they will know we appreciate and care about them and are indebted to them for what they did for this book. We believe that those we acknowledge here should receive praise for their contributions. Responsibility for any errors or missed opportunities to improve the book are ours alone.

Mitchell and Company's clients over the last twenty-one years deserve first mention and thanks, because they provided the opportunity to develop the insights in the book. In many cases, they also served as examples, usually anonymously. We thank them for providing for the success of our firm, as well, so that we had the time and resources to devote to the project. Many dozens of client executives also took time to provide useful comments that were used to rewrite the book in the way that you read it today.

Some of the original members of the Twenty Times Progress Steering Committee went out of their way to provide useful comments and guidance that proved critical to our final result. We want to especially recognize the assistance we received from Robert L. Guyett, Robert P. Kanee, Richard E. Koch, and Michael A. Sharp.

During the drafting of the book, thousands of executives and many academics took the time to consider our words. The comments and ideas we received from the following people proved to be essential to the book you are about to read: C. Michael Armstrong, chairman and CEO of AT&T; Norman R. Augustine, former chairman and CEO of Lockheed Martin; Robert B. Catell, chairman and CEO of KeySpan Energy; Dr. Peter F. Drucker; Brian D. Frenzel, president and CEO of Centaur Pharmaceuticals; James M. Kilts, president and CEO of Nabisco Brands; Robert Rock, chairman and publisher of *Directors & Boards*; Dr. Kenneth L. Lay, chairman and CEO of Enron; Ronald Y. Oberlander, operating chairman of Abitibi Consolidated; Gerald E.

Schultz, former chairman and CEO of Bell & Howell; Glenn Schaeffer, president of Circus Circus Enterprises; Orin R. Smith, chairman and CEO of Engelhard; and James A. Sutton, former chairman and CEO of UGI.

Joseph McClendon of the Anthony Robbins Companies offered many suggestions for how to improve the manuscript to add understanding and emotional impact.

Tobi Kahn worked for several months on dozens of potential images for this book based on his careful study of the book's content, and originally suggested twelve drawings as candidates for helping you better understand the book. We are grateful that he and our publisher permitted us to use all twelve. His world-class art helps make the book a better solution for you.

At Mitchell and Company, Joan Henson was a key resource, providing invaluable help with facts, editing, and facilitating communications between the authors and our publisher, AMACOM Books. Early in the project, Jason Breyan worked closely with all three coauthors in developing stall theory. Sarah Christopher, Kim Loomis, and Phyllis Smalls also pitched in to help in many ways too numerous to mention.

Pam Ellsworth helped us with her many useful comments, questions, research, fact checking, and aid in locating and obtaining permissions for illustrations.

We also wish to thank Norman A. Augustine for introducing us to AMACOM, and helping us find our wonderful publisher. The authors particularly appreciate the commitment that AMACOM made to producing this book in the fastest possible time so that you could read it sooner.

At AMACOM, we especially appreciate the wholehearted and knowledgeable support that we received from our editor, Adrienne Hickey. She always tried to find a way to say yes to us. On the editing side, we acknowledge and appreciate the contributions made by Kate Pferdner and Jacquie Flynn, and we benefited greatly from the copyediting done by Bernice Pettinato of Beehive Production Services.

Don Mitchell had a teacher (now deceased) who inspired him to be his best and to love to write. Without the encouragement of Verna L. Reynolds, of Pacific High School in San Bernardino, California, this book might not have happened.

Finally, we would like to thank each other for the great support and many contributions each made during the book's development.

The
2,000
Percent
Solution

Becoming an effective stallbuster (someone who eliminates stalls that block rapid organizational progress) requires seeing many sides to any given situation. This drawing is the first of many that will provide you with practice in that skill. If you are like most people, you will at first see only one image. For some, that image will be footsteps in the sand approaching the water. For others, it will be an aerial view of three islands and some coastline. Still others may see a mysterious horned figure in a white cloak with three holes in the front. This drawing was designed to stimulate you to see dozens of images. How many can you find? (Here's a tip: Rotate the page.) The more you see, the more likely you will be to notice important things around you that cause stalls and ways you can eliminate them. In daily life, our ideas about what we "should" see prevent us from seeing what is actually in front of us.

Introduction

There's gold in them thar hills.

—Forty-Niner Expression

The Introduction defines and explains "stalls," frames of mind and thought processes that are the sources of complacency and that delay progress; "stallbusting," weighing your choices consciously and effectively to overcome complacency; and "2,000 percent solutions," ways to accomplish twenty times as much, or the same results twenty times faster, after banishing complacency. Each of these new concepts will be used to describe what you should be doing now in order to achieve the best ongoing organizational results.

Have you ever fallen behind the competition? Wondered why great opportunities for your organization remain untapped? Wanted to add new strengths to your organization, but could not? Grown frustrated by persistent problems that have been around for decades in your company? If so, this is the book for you. It focuses on the bad habits, what we call "stalls," that cause these problems and tells how to overcome them. Whether you are a leader, problem solver, trainer, or educator, you will find answers in *The 2,000 Percent Solution.*

What Is a Stall? The Pavlovian Imperative for Self-Sabotage

Habits, good and bad, are formed when our brains develop consistent patterns of behavior based on our response to stimuli, in much the same way Pavlov's dogs did in associating food with the sound of a bell. As a result, we can perform many activities with little conscious thought.

Unfortunately, though, our mental associations are often seriously limiting.

We all have habits that prevent us from being fully effective in our work and at home. On a personal level, most of us have some little thing we do as a kind of psychological security blanket. Some of us won't go out the door before checking the teakettle to be sure the range is turned off. Well and good. But some will check a second, third, and fourth time. When such behavior is repeated irrationally so that it unnecessarily delays our progress, it becomes a stall. In business, irrational mindsets also hobble progress so that full potential remains unrealized.

In fact, stalls, those habitual actions based on ways of thinking that impede progress, keep individuals, organizations, businesses, and even civilizations from realizing their full potential. Life is good? It could be far better for all of us if we eliminated the monumental stalls that dog us in all of our activities. Consider, for example, the talented prolificness of Leonardo da Vinci, who generated so many ideas that lots of them never saw the light of day in his time. The ones he did pursue often were abandoned before they were complete. Dozens of his innovations could have significantly benefited his royal employers, who frequently preferred to keep him occupied playing music and telling jokes for their amusement. Had these more important ideas been developed sooner, much of the knowledge and technology of today could have been in place at least a hundred years ago.

Organizations are mostly unaware of how much their activities are influenced by stalls, so relatively little improvement occurs. Meantime, each repetition of the stalling behavior increases the likelihood that change will not occur. The universal craving for elevated self-esteem can encourage you to take comfort in being stalled, just as a company that does everything for itself becomes smug, feeling that it is making good use of its many competencies.

What Is Stallbusting? Weigh Your Choices Consciously Where It Counts

Learning not to give in to stalls creates the opposite result. The potential for progress, personal and professional, can be astonishing when we apply better habits of thinking. With conscious thought to challenge our habits, we can eliminate stalled thinking and move on to opportunities that have major payoffs, opportunities that our habits have been steering us away from.

In your own organization, there may be dozens of powerful ideas or bits of knowledge that could create exponential future success. But many of these ideas are not pursued because people are pressed for time. Imagine what you and your company could accomplish if only you could stop the clock. One chief financial officer of a leading company masterminded the pesky annual budgeting process in only three days and avoided conflict with fellow officers to boot. The result: He spent the time he saved working on operating changes that made the company tens of millions of dollars annually. His was a 2,000 percent solution.

What Is a 2,000 Percent Solution? Shoot for the Moon When It Counts

We often do a task the way we always have even though a vastly better alternative is available to us. And often that better way is a 2,000 percent solution. For example, a semiconductor manufacturer spends seven months designing its own chips. But a supplier can design the chips more than twenty times faster, in less than ten days. This is an enormous benefit to the manufacturer because having new products available to its customers sooner is worth millions in extra sales and profits. Using the outside supplier here is a 2,000 percent solution, which simply means creating twenty times more benefit or doing something twenty times faster than the manufacturer's normal, 100 percent solution. In this example, the outsourcing alternative is both twenty times (2,000 percent) more beneficial and faster for the semiconductor manufacturer.

A 100 percent solution can fall far below the actual best practice (the best anyone anywhere is doing now with the same process), as we see in this example. The future best practice (what will be the best anyone anywhere is doing by the time you can establish your new process) is estimated by the outside supplier to take only three days to design. The theoretical best practice (the most effective process that can possibly be accomplished by anyone) is to use artificial intelligence software (that has yet to be written) to do the chip design in only a few minutes.

The semiconductor manufacturer in our example has been so focused on doing everything for itself that it missed the potential benefits of collaborating with others outside the organization, whether in tracking market trends, developing new technologies, improving management processes, or shifting its attention to developing customer needs.

These internally focused habits limit the semiconductor company's progress dramatically.

You owe it to yourself to look for the 2,000 percent solutions for your own organization. You may not always hit the magic 2,000 percent mark, but improvements will still be exponential.

What Is the Key to Exponential Success? Focus Like a Laser

How can you organize to identify easily achievable opportunities for your organization's exponential progress? To us, the answer seems obvious. Yet executives and their organizations cannot see the opportunities because they continue to devote almost all their time to historically time-consuming, low-payoff issues. But like the CFOs who spend months on a job that needs just three days of their personal attention because they do not delegate much of the task to their controllers, you may be assuming that all sorts of things can only be done by you. This book shows you how to successfully overcome that assumption.

Organizations are bedeviled by dozens of major stalls. Overcoming them requires shifting time and attention from the least productive to the most productive areas. For example, you can discover how those you do not have as customers see both you and your competitors, with the goal of ferreting out potential high-profit customers. You can look at your compensation system and how it can be changed to stop encouraging behavior that hurts your organization. You can recognize opportunities that will cost your organization dearly if you do not pursue them quickly.

The basic problem that every organization faces is how to decide what to pay attention to and what to spurn. As a culture, we suffer from information overload. At any particular moment, individuals and organizations automatically ignore 99 percent of the data that are being sensed. It is a curious fact that the information we need is always out there somewhere, but mind-set stalls cause us to ignore or dismiss the pertinent information needed for the 2,000 percent solution. By reading *The 2,000 Percent Solution,* you will learn the stallbuster's approach to uncovering the major opportunities being delayed unnecessarily by stalled thinking, and thus discover the key to exponential success.

Each 2,000 percent solution will generate more skill, time, resources, and effectiveness to look for the next 2,000 percent solution.

In a sense, each 2,000 percent solution is a step in the process of creating ever greater exponential success for your organization.

How to Use This Book: Follow the Recipes for Exponential Success and Tell Others

In *The 2,000 Percent Solution,* we address the stall mind-set and the most commonly encountered organizational stalls in the first part of the book. You get a chapter-by-chapter look at the role of some specific stalls that abound in many organizations that give in to multigenerational habits (the tradition stall), lack of experience (the disbelief stall), misunderstanding the facts (the misconception stall), letting surface appearances repel us (the unattractiveness stall), poor listening and sending of messages (the communications stall), red tape (the bureaucratic stall), and putting off action too long for our own good (the procrastination stall). In fact, some of the world's major stalls have persisted for hundreds of years. For centuries, China refused to trade with the West, a tradition stall that denied both cultures the benefits of cross-fertilization, one of the most effective ways of improving thinking. Companies lose out this way, too.

Chapters 1 through 8 include organizational and personal examples and sample solutions that you will be able to use to explain to others in your organization what its problems are, what stalls are, and how you can overcome them. Each chapter can be read as a stand-alone essay and also includes stallbusters, or action guides, at the end to help you apply the lessons to your organization. First review the chapters applicable to your own important issues. Then visit the other chapters for additional ingrained stalls that you may not yet perceive.

Part Two presents an eight-step process that lays out an even better way to overcome the obstacles and caused by stalls and to solve these problems to the 2,000 percent level by establishing a new set of habits built around asking and answering new and better questions. The easiest way to retrain the mind is to teach it to ask better questions and in the right order, and to develop skill in answering the same questions over and over again, like an athlete practicing his or her sport daily. By repeating the process, you can build your organization's skill at bypassing stalls.

Although the chapters in Part Two can be read and used as individual essays too, you will get more out of the section if you read and use

Chapters 9 through 16 together. The ideas build on each other to take you to a more valuable result, in the same way that the stories of a building take you to a higher elevation and a better view. Each chapter also has an action guide, called Stallbusters.

The Epilogue provides a brief case history of how one company used several elements of the stall-busting approach to cut costs, double its market share, and make many of its shareholders wealthy.

Throughout, you will read about opportunities for cultures, countries, organizations, and individuals to share more ideas with each other. Many of these stories are meant to stimulate your imagination about what may be possible in your own situation. Keep in mind that the examples are not intended to be critical of or favor one group of people over another. Stalls exist on all sides. Some are encouraged by physical limits, such as long distances, while others are solely mind-set habits, such as assuming that the other side is of less worth (a common assumption in the absence of compelling evidence to the contrary).

You can rewrite your own story and that of your organization by seeing stalls for what they are and by effectively acting on your opportunities, using stall-busting techniques to achieve 2,000 percent solutions for exponential success.

Part One
Free Your Organization From Mind-Forged Manacles

. . . the mind-forged manacles I hear.
—William Blake, *London*

Part One investigates the causes for ways of thinking that most often "stall" organizations, describes "stall-busting" methods that organizations have used successfully to overcome these stalls, and details methods for overcoming stalls in your organization. You will get the most from this part of the book if you assume that your organization may now have each of these stalls in your most important activities. This part allows you to experience the book's messages through the first three of six perspectives discussed in the Foreword.

The trickiest part about overcoming stalls is to recognize them as such, both in your own personal habits and in organizational cultures. Habits become ingrained so that you may forfeit your ability to make the best use of your time. Bad habits become embedded in organizational traditions. They limit your insight into your future potential. Misconceptions, deeply held aversions, and a tendency to be too timid in setting goals are progress-limiting. You may also wallow in communications gaps, in bureaucracy, and in procrastination. In this section, we give

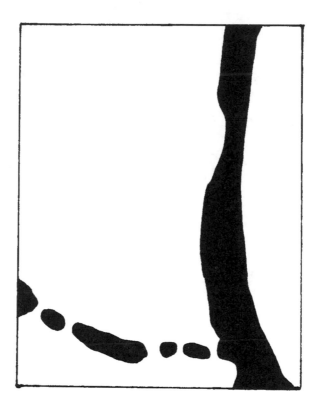

After practicing with the first illustration, you should have improved at seeing many images in any picture (and, hopefully, seeing more potential in every situation you encounter). This drawing is more challenging than the first because it's a little more abstract. Here are a couple of clues: For the first interpretation, imagine that you're looking at an aerial view again and the vertical dark swatch is a black sand beach in Hawaii. To the right is an inlet of the sea. At the bottom left are volcanic rocks sticking out of the ocean. For another interpretation, imagine that you're looking at the sun through a high-powered telescope that allows you to see the corona. The white part at the right is the sun. The black section next to it is part of the corona. The black fragments at the bottom left are part of a solar flare emerging from a sunspot. What else do you see?

you practical information concerning how habits, both helpful and harmful, are established so that you can develop skill in leading your organization to more beneficial habits. In addition, we provide you with practical advice for defeating key stalls that keep you from discovering the 2,000 percent solutions for achieving exponential success.

Chapter 1

Like a Mosquito in Amber, Suspended in Time
The Stall Mind-Set

Chapter 1 explains how powerful thinking habits are formed that stall organizational progress. The purpose of this chapter is to make you aware of how your stalls were formed so that you can be more aware of this stall-formation process in the future and then intercede, when appropriate, in order to achieve more conscious thinking through "stall-busting."

A mind-set is simply the way we organize our thinking, consciously or unconsciously. As discussed in the Introduction, one way we do this is to let our subconscious mind direct most of our actions to repeat what we have done before. Often, we repeat that pattern with our conscious mind in a new situation. When we do decide to seek a new action, that search will often also follow a predictable pattern. Some will wait until they have the facts and have discussed them with everyone involved, weighed the alternatives quantitatively, and reviewed the choices with experts before deciding. Others will look only to what the best solution is that anyone has found before. Still others may rely on an emotional feeling of comfort with some solutions over others.

Organizations develop their own mind-sets through rules, processes, and rituals, as well as the mind-sets of those who work in them. In an organization where the individuals seldom leave and few are added, these organizational mind-sets will receive very powerful reinforcement through repetition and will become very difficult to change.

We can make changes more easily in our personal lives than we can in the organizations we serve. So to lay the groundwork for understanding corporate stalls, let's begin with individuals.

The Individual Stall Mind-Set

Daydreaming is something that occupies a lot of time. We shift our attention from some boring or irrelevant activity to something far more exciting or charming, especially in long meetings and when we are driving or waiting. During those intervals, we often miss chances to seize important opportunities, such as making the meeting shorter and more relevant, listening to instructional tapes while driving, or solving problems (including how to shorten our wait).

When we arrive home, many of us spend dozens of hours weekly letting our minds be directed by the entertainment and information offered on television shows. This activity (if you want to call it that) creates certain ways of thinking and encourages us to be passive (unless we happen to perform aerobics with a television-based instructor).

Since you probably feel that you are already too busy to take on any new challenges, you should use this section to help you see in how many ways you can free up your time and resources to accomplish more. This will also help build your confidence to change other habits and create more benefits for yourself and those you care about.

The Tradition Stall

A bridegroom sits down to enjoy his first Sunday dinner with his new wife. He notices that she has cut off the ends of the roast beef, his favorite part. When he asks why, she replies defensively, "That's how you cook a roast—everybody knows that." But the next day she calls to see if her mother can explain. Together they call grandma to find out why *she* did it. Grandma answers matter-of-factly, "It's because my roasting pan was too short to take a whole roast."

This often-told story is a good example of a mind-set rooted in tradition. Too often we live by such traditions, the origins of which escape us. You do certain things simply because that's the way they've always been done. Such automatic thinking and behavior create personal stalls that keep you from getting the most out of life.

Consider the stall mind-set that keeps you in line waiting for a service. For example, you're in line at the airport when it's announced that your flight is canceled or delayed. Instead of staying in line as habit would have you do, step out of line and head for a pay phone (or get out your cellular phone). Call the airline's 800 number or your travel agent. You'll get an alternate flight or routing a whole lot faster than will those waiting for the agent at the gate. He's facing 150 fuming customers, all with the same problem. You've found a 2,000 percent solution by busting your stalled mind-set.

The Complacency Stall

There are all manner of stalls that impede progress. Among them is complacency. Here's an example of how one famous newspaper publisher dealt with the tendency most of us share to become satisfied with our personal status quo. According to reporter John Sibley, who wrote for Scripps Howard's *Cleveland Post,* the impeccably attired *Post* publisher, Louis Seltzer, once entered the newsroom trailed by his uniformed chauffeur replete with jodhpurs and polished leather knee boots. The chauffeur walked to the center of the room and placed a crate of oranges on a desk. Seltzer calmly reached in for the oranges and began pelting reporters with them. The reporters stood speechless for a while but then threw the oranges back at Seltzer, and soon the newsroom was awash in orange juice. Then Seltzer walked out, Florsheims squishing, to await brighter copy. He was confident that his reporting staff had been shaken out of complacency. This worked so well, he did it repeatedly.

The moral of this story is that the publisher was sending a message by his actions that he wanted people who worked in the newsroom to be unconventional, to challenge established practices, and to have more fun with their work. The physical and emotional experience of pelting and being pelted by the publisher made a large impact on the memories of those involved. You can do similar "mind-expanding" things to yourself in order to provide your own wake-up call.

The Easy-Path Stall

On a personal level, stalls can lead to a lifetime of bad habits that can affect our health and our enjoyment of life. Individually, we waste too much time on the wrong paths. Early on we lose our childlike idealism. That's why some writer wanna-bes never sit down to write their novels. Other jaded workers stay in dead-end jobs. They avoid career changes that would bring happiness and fulfillment. They are stalled in inertia.

For many, easy-path stall psychology is strongly reinforced with career choice. At a law school reunion, there was a discussion group led by people who had changed jobs more than four times since graduation. A number of them were still casting about and had not found something they enjoyed doing. Everyone in the audience was asked were they to do it over again, would they be doing the same job today. Most, well over 80 percent, said they had chosen the wrong career and were very unhappy with their work. They were next asked why they took those jobs. Most said they took jobs offered by the scouts who showed up at the law school recruiting office in the spring before they graduated. Prestige was a factor. Or the alum wanted to please parents or spouse. "Oh, you work at Sullivan and Cromwell! Isn't that wonderful!" They were next asked why they didn't give up lawyering if they didn't enjoy it, like a former corporate lawyer who is happy owning and piloting a ferry boat on the American River in Sacramento? Responses were limp.

Suppose that before they committed, these heartsick lawyers had shelled out around $20 for a standard test to help them learn in which careers they would be happy and successful? Fewer in this group would have chosen law school—and, no doubt, more of them would be happier today. They might instead have done what they loved. We know that if you do what you love, you can do it better. Some who do that earn more money. Even if you don't earn more, you get more satisfaction. (Two of our authors are "reformed" lawyers.)

Imagine yourself when you are quite elderly looking back on your life. Ask yourself: "What did I accomplish?" Typically, the answer goes like this: "I supported myself. I worked hard. I raised a family. I was a good person." But many do all this by rote. Throughout life we make mindless choices that take us along sterile paths.

The You-Can't-Get-There-From-Here Stall

Many people dream about travel abroad but often put it off indefinitely. Some create travel stalls even before they marry and settle down. Let's assume, for example, that you have always wanted to go to Paris. Let's also assume you are saddled with student loans. But you are eager to catch the Gallic flavor of the City of Light. In fact, the flavor of France may be closer than the airport. Should you rent *Les Miserables* from the video store? Should you go to dinner at a French bistro down the street, close your eyes, and love Paris vicariously? These are poor substitutes. Here's an upbeat approach: Borrow language tapes from the library. Learn to speak French so that you'll have more pleasure when you do get to Paris.

Meantime, you can probably afford a drive to Montreal where you can practice your *parlez-vous.* Some students with no money for travel actually visit Paris at little or no cost. They work as assistant tour guides, directing people in and out of hotels and onto the right buses. Whatever the obstacle to your dreams, jump over the stall by doing what can be done now or begin to build on achieving the dream soon.

And it's never too late to turn dreams into reality: Begin to live the life you crave. After retiring, Colonel Sanders refused to be stalled by a lack of capital when he wanted to go into business. He used his Social Security checks to set up a restaurant featuring his finger-licking-good chicken. He then decided to grow the business by licensing his special recipe. Sanders traveled from town to town, living in his car where he kept his white suits neatly folded in the back-seat. He visited dozens of restaurants and got nowhere. Owners either said no, or, if they wanted the recipe, refused to track the chicken they served in order to pay the royalty. Keeping a running record was an inconvenience, even though the price at 5 cents a head of chicken served was acceptable. So Sanders developed a homespun stall-busting answer to their tracking dilemma.

He said, "Don't write me a monthly check. Just throw a nickel in a jar. When the jar is full, send the nickels to me." That broke the logjam. Soon, scores of restaurants were filling jars with nickels to pay the royalty for Kentucky Fried Chicken.

John Y. Brown, a lawyer, overheard an overworked mailman complain that Colonel Sanders got hundreds of pounds of mail. "Why?" "He gets all those nickels." Brown was entranced. He eventually bought the business from the Colonel with the understanding that Sanders would stay on as a company spokesman. With his stall-busting approach to royalties, Sanders's future included far more than just a small Social Security check.

The One-Dimensional-Thinking Stall

> *A Melancholy actor complained to his psychiatrist:*
> *A: I can't sing, I can't dance and I can't act.*
> *P: So why don't you get out of show business?*
> *A: Oh, I couldn't do that . . . I'm a star!*
>   —Widely told joke

As you read on, you'll discover that, all too frequently, stalls develop because of thinking that is too narrow or too conventional. Consider the stall that prevented oil men from getting more oil and gas out of their production wells.

Since the first drilling find in 1859 by Edwin L. Drake near Titusville, Pennsylvania, oil wells were drilled straight down. When drillers struck a zone in which oil did not flow, they ran an explosive charge down the shaft and used it to crack the rock formation to free some of the oil in the perimeter of the shaft itself. Some years ago, thoughtful petroleum engineers got a new slant on this problem. If an oil formation was discovered to range in a lateral direction, the drillers would bore at an angle and more oil was recovered. Drillers can go just as far sideways as straight down. This solution is like the progress a sailboat captain makes by tacking left and right to move forward.

The No-Star-to-Guide-Me Stall

In a similar vein, sometimes the market for a key product collapses abruptly. A classic case in nineteenth-century history was the fate of the buggy whip after automobiles became popular. One buggy whip producer closed his Indianapolis plant and studied law. (His son, who tells the story, also became a lawyer.) This was one way to beat going down with the surrey. Another might have been to manufacture saddles and other tack. Horses didn't disappear. Today, in fact, there are more horses in North America than ever before in history. Or perhaps the buggy whip manufacturers could have broadened the original business definition to one of being in the "vehicle acceleration industry." They could have become manufacturers of parts for cars or locomotives.

You need not stop thinking just because your market peaks or slows, or your original approach is keeping you from maximum benefit.

The stall-busting individual can always find ways to alter thought processes and change bad habits to move forward.

The Organizational Stall Mind-Set

Since the advent of military organizations, the goal of many groups of people has been to focus and direct each person's attention to a narrow, predictable path. Since communication used to be almost impossible in large organizations, there was little choice but to try to do little in order to accomplish anything. Such groups are now called command-and-control-style organizations.

Today's fast-changing world is filled with much better educated individuals and more ways to communicate, so organizations can aspire to be very responsive by having those who first notice a problem or opportunity move quickly to take appropriate action. This works better if each individual knows that this should be done and develops her or his ability to notice problems and opportunities and to take appropriate, timely action.

Too often, however, the habits of command and control are carried over intentionally or unintentionally into a free-form world that most closely resembles a fast-break opportunity in NBA basketball. In this section, we will look at some group behaviors that are harmful to organizations.

The Monday-Go-to-Meeting Stall

In an effort to save time, executives often make ill-advised decisions that backfire. We have all been stalled by meetings that drone on forever. One executive was so frustrated by long meetings with individual staff members that he substituted a single Monday morning meeting for everyone who reported directly to him. Alas, the unfortunate result of this decision was a Monday morning stall.

There was so much discussion that the staff meeting ate up even more time than all the individual meetings put together. An outside adviser pointed this out, suggesting that staff meetings be eliminated entirely. Instead, the executive should encourage those with problems to immediately seek out the person who could actually help solve the problem. The executive would get involved only if a solution could not be found within a week. The executive was delighted with the idea. But his actual response indicated that he was still subject to the stall. He said, "I'm going to bring up that idea at the very next Monday staff meeting!"

The Accounting Stall

Some of the stalls we must deal with relate to rules that have little if anything to do with a company's quest for future profits. Accounting makes many assumptions that are very helpful for accountants, but not very helpful for decision makers. To a surprising degree, accounting rules can blind us and stall our progress. Consider the balance sheet, for example. These documents purport to capture the financial health of the organization, and in some ways they do. They can tell you how much your company owes other people compared to how much others owe you. But what about deadbeats? The balance sheet may not accurately expose doubtful accounts. You need to keep in focus how likely you are to get paid. Otherwise, you may be stalled when the money you need does not materialize.

While you are at it, check the assets that are carried on the balance sheet. The assets are listed in terms of their original cost, minus charges such as depreciation, depletion, goodwill amortization, and charge-offs. These stated values are unlikely to be today's real values, unless you are looking at the value listed for the company's current checking account balance. Old assets may, in fact, be worthless; others are priceless. Many items of value are not even reflected on the balance sheet. Very clearly the name, Coca-Cola, is extremely valuable. No sensible person would disagree with that idea, but accountants assign no value to brand names except in acquisitions.

Hostile takeovers are often pursued because of imprecise accounting stalls thinking on the part of the target company's management: It doesn't realize the worth of all of its assets and does too little to expand its share price.

The Forget-About-It Stall

Humans and organizations have a wonderful talent for snatching defeat from the jaws of victory. During the Q and A session at a meeting of top executives of a premier packaged goods company, several executives mentioned problems in connection with key product lines. The speaker was incredulous. He had worked with other executives to resolve these very same issues at this very same packaged goods company years earlier. At the time, profits and share price had soared. Now it was obvious that current management knew nothing of the earlier work nor of the methodology that was developed to set the issues to rest. The lessons were clearly forgotten. At this point, they were tyros again, landing the space shuttle for the first time in a violent windstorm. Profits were static and the stock had tanked.

A company that forgets is destined to be stalled as managers spend valuable resources solving the same problems over and over. We know of a low-margin food business that looked at one easily resolvable issue seventeen times in fifteen years. Much later, we heard that the CEO had assigned a group to review the same question again! What a waste.

The Protocol Stall

It can be hard to break a stall mind-set, but to do so can be crucial in a corporate setting. Consider, for example, the story of a top executive with a large firm who was worried about sagging morale. The lack of motivation had such a serious impact on profits that workers had to be laid off. This action exacerbated already tense labor–management relations. The executive became convinced his managers-in-suits did not understand the problems of workers in open-collar shirts and blue jeans. His question to his management team was, How can you find out what is going on in the company unless you mingle—get to know the workers and their concerns? Gamely, this savvy executive was determined to learn why workers were shirking duties.

Just as in the army, where officers do not mingle with enlisted men, in business, executives don't normally mingle with laborers. So every week or two, the executive would dress as a laborer and work in a company facility. Sometimes he dressed as a janitor and manned a broom on the night shift. Or he would work as a package delivery person. As a result, he learned what was actually going on and what employees thought was happening at headquarters. The changes he made were reflected in the working environment. They were noticed.

For months no one recognized him, but eventually the word spread. People started to look for the new "worker." The employees loved the attention. They could see that someone in a position to help really cared about them. Morale rose and workers started to seek out other executives. They would talk about issues they had and suggest new approaches to problems. The executive soon discovered that some of the company's problems that were viewed as knotty at the executive level were actually easy to correct, often without cost. By breaking the protocol stall, this thoughtful, frequently suitless man resolved key labor issues and restored high profits.

The Gatekeeper Stall

The gatekeeper stall is commonplace in the business world, the gatekeeper being the aide to an important executive who is so protective of the boss that even top team members have trouble getting to see him or her. The gatekeeper stall, like so many stalls, is inexplicable. It is hard to believe it can even exist uncorrected. The only thing worse would be a firehouse company with arson stall: "We have this fireman who likes to burn down a building now and then. But he's the only guy on the squad who knows how to drive the truck."

Stalls are destructive habits. They sap profits and waste time and resources. You should strive to identify and eliminate them. Be a stall-buster: Advance your company, your career, and your personal satisfactions.

Stall Erasers

Consider some stalls that have plagued great companies, in these cases, IBM during the early 1990s and Eastman Kodak. The stalls herein are hardly definitive of the overall problems at these two corporations-in-transition, but they offer you added insight into the organizational stall mind-set.

Big Blue

Stalls may strike you as characteristic of the also-ran company, but stalls are endemic in our society. No company is immune from their profit-sapping effects. Take IBM. Founder Tom Watson is widely believed to have set up the greatest firm in history. Curiously, IBM's mainframe computers were never the most advanced available, but IBM service, a critical element in this highly technical field, was unparalleled. In time, IBM was to dominate the mainframe computer market and to earn near-monopoly profits. And Big Blue got a reputation for invincibility. The word among data processing managers and purchasing agents: Nobody ever got fired for buying IBM equipment. Investors even left wills instructing heirs that under no conditions were their IBM shares to be sold.

But despite IBM's seeming omnipotence, stalls of all sorts were at work. Powerful smaller computers—"minis"—were introduced by Digital Equipment Corporation. Minis were only the first of a series of ever-more-powerful, ever-smaller computers. Each series in turn was to eat into IBM's once dominant position in the computer world. This trend was to continue until desktop units, with power rivaling that of IBM mainframe computers of the 1960s, became the workhorse of American business.

The most seductive source of stalls is the siren song of success. People are attracted to companies like IBM, hoping to share in their unprecedented success. (Young writers seek jobs at *The New York Times*. Software programmers flock to Microsoft, and young MBAs vie for analyst jobs at Goldman Sachs.) But latecomers to top companies like IBM don't always perceive the actual source of success, which, in this case, was IBM's unsurpassed service. The company itself forgot its groundings as conditions changed. IBM began to take its market primacy for granted. Service deteriorated and, after 1970, IBM's markets eroded, too. Eventually, IBM's vaunted "Premium Price for Premium Service" boast turned into a stall. As tough competitors entered the marketplace, IBM's service people were unable to outdo the work of its more aggressive rivals. All that remained of the Premium Price/Service model was the premium price.

Another key to IBM's success had been its close ties to CEOs. This was enormously useful; the CEO as the key decision maker could say yes to IBM. But over time, Big Blue salespeople focused more and more on lower-level executives and managers, such as purchasing agents, not the CEOs. It was clear that drastic measures were called for to save the company from a slide into the ranks of second-rate companies. Big Blue needed a stallbuster and totally fresh thinking to break the complacency stall and the bad habits complacency had helped create over the years. Enter Lou Gerstner, who was no doubt picked in part for an outsider's perspective. He had run RJR Nabisco and played troubleshooting roles at other firms. It is clear that Big Blue's board felt an outsider would be better equipped to break the stall mind-set that threatened IBM's very existence as a leading company. Because executives in the top echelons of the company had helped create the bad habits and major stalls, stallbusters were needed to address the problems with fresh eyes. They needed to be unfettered by parochial ties, willing to cut through the existing corporate culture and set it to rights.

Gerstner soon reestablished CEO contacts for IBM by his personal example, and he created a new pricing model based on fair value for the price charged. This model usually meant a competitive price with similar or slightly better service. These and many other sensible changes helped put IBM on the road to recovery, a path it is still following. But the stallbusting needs to continue.

Eastman Kodak

CEOs talk about getting back to basics after a period of poor financial performance. But which basics are the right ones to get back to? If the CEO winds up reinforcing the basics that are in fact stalls, things will just get worse. Kodak's long, slow decline as a still film producer was a result of repeatedly getting back to the wrong basics. It focused on cutting costs, hoping that by reducing overhead, profits would rise, but that tactic did not work. As Kodak cut operations and reduced the head count, profits refused to go up. Recently, a savvy observer wrote that one reason for Kodak's decades-long slide in film market share was undoubtedly related to the decision to deemphasize high-performance film for professional photographers. This product was in fact a "basic" that had once helped Kodak achieve its market primacy.

Professional-quality film is a paramount issue for all avid shutterbugs. The quality of Kodak film came to be considered no better than that of its arch rival, Fuji Film. Fuji gobbled up Kodak's lunch in this vital market. Finally, Kodak is again catering to professionals with a super fast film that needs less light. It was developed for the professional market, but, happily for Kodak, amateurs are paying up, too. Once again, Kodak film is perceived to be superior to Fuji's by more and more camera users. As Kodak learned, it is easy to address the wrong issue and develop a stall around it.

Become a Stallbuster

Now you should have a better understanding of what a stall is. You know stalls exist both in your personal life and in your organization, and that you can do things to correct them. And you know it is important to do so. In the chapters that follow, you will read about major stalls in organizations and touch on hundreds of others. You will learn to spot stalls on your own and to become part of the 2,000 percent solution.

You may doubt that human beings can change mind-sets and become vastly more productive in fairly short periods of time, but such quick change may be easier than you think. "Necessity is the mother of invention," so the saying goes, and it appears to apply even to physical evolution. Physical evolution normally takes place over thousands of years, but recent work with Darwin's finches, which the famed British scientist studied in the Galápagos Islands and detailed in Jonathan Weiner's *The Beak of the Finch: A Story of Evolution in Our Time* (Knopf 1996), suggests that survivors of an embattled species can physically adapt to a fundamental change in environment in a single generation. In 1977, a prolonged drought hit the Galápagos, and small seeds became scarce. Small seeds are the mainstay diet of *Geospiza Fortis*, a small ground-dwelling finch found on the tiny Daphne Major. Tough, spiky seeds were about all that was left and the shells of those seeds resisted the *Geospizas'* small beaks. Most of the *Geospizas* died (1,020 out of 1,200), but those that survived possessed the thickest beaks and were thus best able to crack big, spiked seeds (see Exhibit 1-1 for examples of beak variation among different types of Darwin's finches). Mere survival of the fittest, you'd say. But wait. Chicks of the survivors developed beaks 4 to 5 percent larger than those of their parents. In the hatch of an egg, then, *Geospizas* were no longer quite the same creatures as before. This occurrence constitutes astonishing instant evolution, physical change of a sort normally believed to require hundreds of thousands of years. Can humankind adjust as fast as *Geospiza* bird beaks did? Stallbusters can!

Stallbusters

Identifying our stalls and overcoming them is challenging at the beginning. This section is designed to give you basic training in identifying

Exhibit 1-1   Beaks of Darwin's Finches.

From Jonathan Weiner, *The Beak of the Finch: A Story of Evolution in Our Time* (New York: Knopf, 1996), page 18. Reprinted by permission of Alfred A. Knopf, Inc.

your own habits and those of your organization, deciding when those habits operate as stalls, and learning how to change them. You do this by looking at stalls from several perspectives: what you do today, how others influence you, and how you influence others.

Be Aware of Your Habits

Habits are the things we do automatically. These habits help us when they reinforce what we need to do, like stop at red lights. But even good habits may have less meaning in certain circumstances, such as when a pedestrian breaks the law, dashing across the street against the light to rescue a child who has wandered into traffic.

If you are like most people, you are much better at identifying the habits of others, especially when they are different from your own, than identifying your own. A good way to overcome this natural bias is to check your own habits with the people who spend the most time with you. They will be very helpful in pointing out things of which you may not be very aware. Then keep a diary to see what you do in your personal and working life without much thought. Next, review what you have learned and think about the patterns. When would you have been better off changing these patterns?

With this perspective, we also suggest that you redesign how you spend your time to reflect a more useful path to your goals and what makes you happy. If you have not recently developed personal goals, this would be a good time to do so. Be sure to update these in writing every six months or so.

Be Aware of Your Organization's Habits

For the next week, notice everything that your company or organization does without much thought. Write it down. Pay particular attention to how problems are addressed. If your organization is like most, you will find that one approach will almost always be used, even if there is no formal policy on the issue. For example, if a customer calls up and is angry about some problem that is clearly your organization's fault, what is said and done about the problem? Does anything different happen when the problem may not be your organization's fault? How about when the customer is probably wrong? Before going further, are these responses in the best interest of your organization? For example, regardless of who is right or wrong, do you want to have a good relationship with the customer in the future? If so, what response is most likely to ensure that good relationship? Can you afford this response? If not, is there another good response that you can afford?

Consider the items on your list and ask yourself the following questions:

Why are these things done? In many cases, there will be no apparent reason other than they have always been done that way. Ask around, just in case you have missed something. For example, some organizations check every single item of every single product while other organizations just check a random sample. If your organization makes few errors and the checking process can actually cause errors to occur, random sampling may make sense. (If you do not understand how a random sample can be adequate for that purpose, ask someone who has studied statistics to explain this to you.) On the other hand, if you check everything and make few errors, the checking process may simply be a leftover from when the organization did make a lot of errors. Or perhaps no one involved in checking understands how to design a random sample. Keep asking until you have pinned down the circumstances behind the habit to your satisfaction, as validated by what the people involved perceive.

What is the benefit? In the example of checking for errors, the complete checking process probably picks up some errors that would otherwise be missed and may also encourage everyone to work a little more rapidly because they know that any errors are likely to be caught before a customer is affected.

When are these habits harmful? If complete checking causes people to become careless, then checking actually increases the error rate and makes more work for the error checkers. If error checking also accidentally destroys some products, that also increases costs. If repairing the errors once they are caught is expensive, then this error-checking process is potentially very expensive because of all the increased errors it creates.

When might these habits stall progress? A stall could result from error checking if everyone relies more on error checking to solve a problem than on determining and correcting the causes of the error.

How should the habits be changed? If you find that any of the potential error-checking issues actually arise in your situation, then you will want to change the organization's error-checking habit. You obviously do not want to do this in ways that mean that customers will receive faulty products. The change that is required is to lower the error rate itself so that small-scale random checks will be adequate. Alternatively, you can redesign your products to test themselves and report what is learned. For some, you may be able to redesign the products in such a way that they can actually correct their own errors through software changes (such as rerouting around damaged portions of an integrated circuit).

Does the company or organization have an effective method for making the needed change? For many organizations, this will be the proverbial $64 question. If such a method is not available, you will have to develop one. A good way to begin is to find the best practices for making such changes, a subject we explore in detail in Chapters 11–14.

Be Aware of How the Habits of Others in Your Organization Affect You

Many employees who work with the organization's CEO soon begin to sound, look, and think like the CEO—down to the last cadence and phrase of speech. The more you think about habits, the more you will notice them and create the necessary adjustments. Answering the following questions provides another perspective:

What habits do people in your company pick up from the CEO? A good way to think about the answer to this question is to consider what habits did not exist under the prior CEO. If you did not work for the organization at that time, you can still learn the answers by interviewing people who did.

What are the benefits? Let's say that your CEO believes in acting immediately, rather than procrastinating. A benefit of that habit is to be timely in responding to new information, problems, and opportunities. Another benefit can be to avoid studying things to death that need little consideration. Further, your organization may attract opportunities ahead of others because of a reputation for being able to make a decision and act.

When are these habits harmful? When quick action happens, sometimes it ends up being the wrong action (some people call this circumstance "Fire, Ready, Aim"). Another problem can come into play when actions should be sequenced in some way. By acting quickly in one area, your organization may miss the chance to act first in another area that should come first, if possible. For example, customers may be happier if you give them some warning before you raise prices so that they can purchase items at the lower prices; therefore, contacting them before raising prices should be the first act for many organizations.

When might these habits stall progress? If quick action is the wrong action, you may slide backward. For example, if a quick bid on a project ends up being poorly constructed because of time constraints, you may lose the business . . . or get the business on a basis where you will lose lots of money and obtain no benefit from the quick action. If you are always so busy acting, there may be little time to consider alternatives that might work better. Some companies will automatically assume that existing technology should be in the next generation of products. Yet if the technology is about to change, you may end up creating only obsolete products, as is happening now with people producing analog-technology cellular telephones.

How should the habits be changed? Obviously, a bias for action is a wonderful habit to have. Perhaps the only change we should consider is stopping to think about whether there is a strong likelihood of losing large benefits by acting *too* quickly.

Be Aware of How Your Habits Affect Others in Your Organization

Habits can come from being with anyone. In fact, you are creating quite a few of them in others yourself. Because you are the source, such habits will be easier to change than the others we describe in this section. To increase your awareness of the situation, ask yourself the following questions:

What habits do people in your company pick up from you? You may find this a hard question to answer. Others you work with may also have trouble with this question. You can do better by asking those you work with to describe one another's habits and considering that they may be picking them up from you. It is much easier to see others objectively than to see ourselves.

What are the benefits? Because you are reading this book, we will assume that a good habit they are picking up from you is your interest in better ways to manage your organization. Some of the benefits that flow from that interest are spotting ways to improve, making the job easier and faster to do, and creating an environment where everyone feels like they have a stake in making the organization a better place for all.

When are these habits harmful? Like most good habits, this one becomes harmful when taken to extremes. For example, if each of you spends the bulk of your time studying new ways to improve, at some point you will be having problems getting your existing responsibilities done. Also, if you do not consider the new ideas carefully enough, you may be using ideas that do not work very well for your activity or organization. That circumstance could leave you worse off than you were. Others in the organization may not share your interests, which could lead to making communications more difficult. This can occur because you have changed the way you think about the organization, but because you have not communicated well, others do not yet understand your new perspective.

When might these habits stall progress? Continuing with the example, this habit of focusing on organizational improvement could divert attention from pressing issues that are not related to organizational improvement. Taken to an extreme, the result could also be a loss of credibility with the rest of the organization so that ideas coming from you and your colleagues are viewed suspiciously.

How should the habits be changed? As described, you want to keep this interest in balance with all of your other responsibilities in the organization, relevant to your organization's needs, and pursued in a way that furthers communication and credibility with other parts of your company or organization.

Improve Self-Examination and Change Skills

If you find that many habits need to be changed, set a higher frequency of review. Many people find that after a few times, they become more aware of bad habits. You also need to practice helping others in your company or organization to change habits. Having a schedule for repeating the exercise of answering the following questions is a good idea:

What habits have been changed recently by your organization? Many such changes do not affect everyone, so you will want to pick ones that have been more widespread and effective. If you cannot find any that affect the entire organization, look at parts of the organization for examples. If none are evident, consider places where partial changes have occurred.

How were those habits changed? You should be cautious about assuming that you know the answer to this question. Remember the adage, "Success has a 1,000 fathers while failure has none." Speaking with those who experienced the change is a good place to start. Ask people what they changed, why, and how. Their answers will give you clues about which changed programs and activities the organization used were the most effective ones. For example, if everyone mentions that they did not want to change until they had experience with the new way of doing business, you should focus on what was involved in getting each person this experience.

How could that change process have been improved? Everyone likes to be a critic, so you will probably get lots of help answering this question. Using our example, people may have preferred getting the experience sooner, in ways more relevant to their own work, and in ways that took less time.

What habits is your company having trouble changing? Simply ask people what bad habits the company or organization had five years ago, and read about the programs that the company initiated since then. These are usually in the company newsletter to employees, the annual report's CEO letter, other shareholder communications, and press releases. Match up the programs to the bad habits.

How could these habits be changed more effectively? A good place to start is to ask those who experienced the unsuccessful programs what they did not like about the programs. Compare those programs to the successful ones that you studied in answering the preceding question.

Practice Soaring Like an Eagle

Most impassable barriers to progress occur only in the mind. In reality, there is usually another way around (over, through, or away from the barriers) that will work just fine. To get better at seeing past your habitual ways of thinking, you need a success with doing something that is seemingly impossible. Pick a business objective that is seemingly impossible to you and then address the following questions. An example might be to sell more of your company's products at a higher price with less marketing, and have a higher profit margin. That does sound tough, doesn't it? Use your answers to the following questions to find out how tough it is:

What would have to happen for this to be possible? One way to achieve such a positive result would be to greatly improve the products so that they needed less marketing and could command a higher price. The improvements would probably have to be ones that are exceptionally valuable to customers and easy for them to understand. Another way might be to sell the product through a different channel of distribution, which could afford to pay a higher price. Michael Dell did this at Dell Computer Corporation by selling direct and manufacturing his products to order.

If the company had all the resources in the world, could it be done? The answer to this question should almost always be yes. If you are having trouble getting to that answer, involve someone else who can help you think it through. Ideally, this should be an optimistic, can-do sort of person. In the case of our example, having all the resources in the world makes it fairly easy to design better products and enter new distribution channels.

What would it be worth to accomplish this objective? You will have to answer this for yourself, but Michael Dell's answer was worth billions to shareholders in 1998.

How much could the company realistically afford to spend in order to reach the objective? You should probably assume that you would be willing to spend between 10 and 25 percent of the benefit. Check with your financial people for a better answer. Since the benefits come after the costs have been incurred, you have to get more back to reflect the time period during which the funds were invested and no benefit was yet received. Also, you should want to have some earnings return on your investment.

Do other people see this objective as being impossible, or, rather, do they see it as difficult or inconvenient? If you do not know about alternative distribution channels, you may be in the first category. Someone who does will be in one of the other two categories. That person might have to be someone with experience in the other distribution channels and may not now be in your organization.

Assuming for the moment that you could know how to reach the objective of selling more of your company's products at a higher price

with less marketing and a higher profit margin, what is the answer?
Many people have trouble getting started with finding a solution for this
type of objective. A good way to remove a negative mind-set stalling
progress is to assume that you already know the answer and to ask yourself what that answer is, which is what the preceding question does for
you. Solving the challenge in the example is worth vastly more than it
would cost to achieve, so you should go ahead as soon as you are convinced that you have a viable, working answer. You will have to make
your own evaluation by especially being careful to take into account the
risk that many of the approaches will fail, cost a lot of money, and provide no benefits. That's when soaring like an eagle becomes more like
laying a rotten egg. Naturally, you should expect that some setbacks will
occur, but try to be realistic in pursuing paths that are more likely to get
you to the eagle's nest in the mountains, the objective of your flight.

Chapter 2
Knucklebusters and Sawdust
The Tradition Stall

This chapter looks at the most powerful cause of complacency: the un-questioning certainty that nothing will change or should be changed, which is brought on by repetition over many years and possibly even generations. You will learn how to understand when tradition should be challenged and abandoned for the good of the organization.

Tradition: The Way It Was

If It Ain't Broke, Don't Fix It

A motorist asks a farmer for a glass of water. The farmer obliges, using a hand pump to draw water from a well. The pump handle is close to a board and the farmer curses as he scrapes his knuckles on it. Motorist: "Why not move that board? It serves no purpose."

Farmer: "It's been there since my father's time. If it was good enough for him, it is good enough for me."

This answer seemed ridiculous, of course. But the motorist later realized he too had long ignored a similar, senseless tradition. His house had a large knob on the outside door that was too close to the doorjamb. He usually twisted the handle to the right and cleared the jamb. Occasionally, though, he twisted the knob to the left and scraped *his* knuckles on the molding.

The Level Playing Field

As stalls of tradition go, knucklebumping is small potatoes. But serious tradition stalls are sometimes allowed to exist for decades, even centuries. For generations, sawyers' helpers were blinded by sawdust. Manning the end of a two-handled lumberman's saw, the helper worked at a lower level than his boss. The sawdust floated down into the helper's eyes.

The sawyers' helpers could have used Frederick Taylor, who leveled a different playing field. Taylor, a pioneer in measuring work processes, might have extended and improved many lives had he lived hundreds of years ago. In fact, he did his experiments only a century ago. After watching bricklayers routinely heave heavy materials above their heads, Taylor used scaffolding to put man, brick, and mortar at optimum levels for minimum effort by the workers. Until Taylor defied tradition, bricklayers became crippled or disabled after a few years. With his new approach, an able-bodied man could work the job for a lifetime.

In the business world today, employers are, in many ways, more attuned to workplace hazards. Most make serious attempts to limit obvious hazards to life and limb. More insidious than such hazards are the stalls that occur because a harmless tradition becomes subverted due to circumstances that have changed markedly. The resulting tradition stall may be more nuisance than travesty, but, even so, the stall can lead to low morale, reduced production, and lower earnings. Consider the next anecdote.

Aping Human Beings

Imagine a cage containing five apes. In the cage, hang a banana on a string and put stairs under it. Before long, so the story goes, an ape will go to the stairs and start to climb toward the banana. As soon as it touches the stairs, spray all the apes with cold water. After a while, another ape makes an attempt with the same result: All the apes are sprayed with cold water. Do this repeatedly and then just watch when another ape later tries to climb the stairs. The other apes will try to prevent it even though no water sprays them. Now, remove one ape from the cage and replace it with a new one. The new ape sees the banana and wants to climb the stairs. To its horror, all of the other apes attack. After another attempt and attack, it knows that if it tries to climb the stairs, it will be assaulted. Next, remove another of the original five apes and replace it with a new one. The newcomer goes to the stairs and is attacked. The previous newcomer takes part in the punishment with enthusiasm although it has no idea why it was not permitted to climb the stairs. After replacing the third, fourth, and fifth original apes, all the apes that had been sprayed with cold water have been replaced. Nevertheless, no ape ever again approaches the stairs. Why not? "Because that's the way it's always been around here." Sound familiar?

Traditional Ways to Toe the Line

The Pecking-Order Tradition: After You, Alphonse . . .

Imagine that you were asked to speak to the top thirty executives of a very large company. The meeting runs late, and so the food has been sitting on the buffet table long past the lunch hour. Everyone is hungry and needs a break from the intense discussions of the morning session. The breather arrives at last and you, as the honored guest, are escorted through the buffet line first. Then, by company tradition, the CEO goes through the buffet line followed by each executive in the pecking order by descending rank. The most junior executives line up last. But there is a problem: This CEO is a fast eater.

Within ten minutes, the CEO has gulped down his last bite. He promptly states that everyone might as well get back to work because there is a lot left to be done. He either does not notice or, having noticed, does not care that only he has finished eating. (A few juniors in the line haven't even filled their plates yet. You are ruefully pleased that you ate fast, too.)

After the meeting, you ask the corporate planner what that was all about. The corporate planner explains that the pecking-order tradition was begun under the prior CEO, a slow eater who needed more time to finish than everyone else. The practice had become a tradition and was continued without challenge when the CEO who wolfed his food came on board.

The Hazing Tradition: Get Down!

In the 1970s, working conditions at the Kentucky Fried Chicken restaurants were hard. To help new executives understand the problems faced by the workers "in the trenches," the new managers were assigned all the dirty jobs in a given restaurant for a day. Eventually, this custom was transformed into a grand tradition of executive hazing. True, the executives became suitably impressed with the hard conditions the workers had to deal with, but they became so embroiled in the hazing aspect of the tradition that they missed key opportunities to address the problems. Mesmerized by a mindless tradition that emphasized hard work in tough conditions instead of imagination and initiative, the corporate culture delayed important improvements for many years. KFC should have been redesigning equipment and restaurant layouts to improve their efficiency and safety instead of merely subjecting the executive to hazing.

The Necessity Tradition: When Gillette Was a Young Blade

The habit of institutionalizing practices so they become stalls affects all companies. By tradition, formidable Gillette had always introduced new shaving products in the United States first, and then slowly introduced the same new product in its markets around the world on a piecemeal basis. Decades would pass before the new product reached the last country. Finally someone questioned the wisdom of the tradition. It was found to reflect Gillette's limited financial, marketing, and personnel resources in an earlier period. Finally realizing that it was losing sales by sticking with an outdated tradition, Gillette began to introduce new products more or less simultaneously around the world. Sales and profits immediately soared far above the historic level.

The Time-Is-Money Tradition: How Much Is This Conversation Going to Cost Me?

A company we know of has a tradition of not letting the CEO meet potential investors until the investor relations executive has met with those investors. While this tradition freed the CEO for other important tasks, the company's shares were shunned by that most important group of potential shareholders: the institutions, such as pension funds and mutual funds. Few of these institutional investors were prepared to invest millions of dollars in this company without first meeting the CEO. You can be sure they want the CEO's door to be wide open to them before and after they open their checkbooks. This company has failed to build a list of high-powered shareholders who can enhance its future. The more investors a company brings into the fold, the higher the potential for the price of its stock. When a company's shares go higher, money can be raised at a significantly lower cost.

The Isolation Tradition: Solitary Confinement for Learning Development

Harmful traditions have lasted for centuries in the past to the great detriment of the originators of the tradition. For hundreds of years, the tradition-bound Japanese refused trade access to foreign vessels, except for a small contingent of Dutch who were confined to a tiny plot of Japanese soil. Both Japan and its reclusive neighbor, China, built their societies around the idea that theirs were superior cultures, and they were unwilling to share their knowledge with the outside world. But for this tradition stall in Japan and China, the spectacular successes Japan won in the late twentieth century, for example, might have occurred hundreds of years earlier.

Ironically, after centuries of isolationism, Japan in the post–World War II period has bought up many American innovations and profited greatly. Item: The Sony Trinitron television picture tube was invented by American physicist, Edmund Lawrence, who tried in vain to sell his superior color tube to U.S. concerns. In an isolationism of our own, company engineers are often so eager to create their own innovations they shun those brought to the company by outsiders. It is the not-invented-here hang-up, one of capitalism's isolation shortcomings.

The Inertia Tradition: Fur on Ice

Without innovation, traditions can freeze and clog business arteries. Think about the pioneering Hudson's Bay Company, one of the world's oldest corporations. The company dominated the fur trade in Canada. Furs are a natural resource business. Canada, with its vast riches in oil and gas, gold and other precious metals, and minerals, is a natural resource treasure-house. So it seems it would have been natural for the Hudson's Bay Company to branch out to become a leader in the natural resource business world. But company leaders failed to recognize this logical extension of the business model that might have made the company a preeminent enterprise worldwide. By defining itself as a fur trader rather than a natural resource company, Hudson's Bay Company missed out on huge potential profits in mining and in oil and gas. Instead, it wound up as a department store chain, a Canadian business of modest success.

Stall Erasers

Before you can separate the tradition stalls from your good practices, you need to challenge current methods. A good approach is to imagine doing things in quite different ways. If new ideas must be approved by the boss first, consider what would happen if new ideas were tested before the boss saw them. Some might fail. Some might become better in the testing. Having learned from that experience, you can move in lots of new directions. To whet your appetite, read on to learn about cases in which a nontraditional approach, a total change of direction, worked much better than the traditional approach.

Good-Bye Memory Chip!

Intel's chairman, Andrew Grove, wrote a book in 1996 entitled *Only the Paranoid Survive* (Currency Doubleday). In it he describes strategic "inflection points" that call for a fundamental change in the business plan on pain of compromising the business's viability. He also says that inflection points bring to bear forces ten times the norm in business.

Intel faced an inflection point with the potential to ruin the company in the early 1980s. It was then a major producer of commodity memory chips. By contrast, microprocessors, the electronic brains that drive desktop computers, were a very small part of Intel's business in that same period. That's when large Japanese manufacturers set out to dominate the memory chip market. The Japanese made huge investments. Their capital costs were subsidized by low Japanese interest rates, which gave them a major competitive advantage over Intel and other American companies. Grove knew that many Intel customers believed the Japanese chips were superior to those that Intel made, which was even more alarming. By 1984 Japanese memory chips flooded the market and Intel was reeling. So Grove (then president) and his then CEO, Gordon Moore, chose a radical departure for the business. They jettisoned the memory chip and focused on the remaining part of their line, the microprocessor. In effect, they completely changed the business that Intel was in.

In 1985, Intel introduced the 386 chip, followed by the 486, and then by the Pentium chip and its successors, all of which became standards for the industry. The company has dominated the microprocessor market ever since. In fact, it has become the world's largest microchip manufacturer. So important are the chips today to computer users that computer builders' ads feature the words "Intel Inside."

Delegate, Delegate

Sit in for a moment at a meeting of some of North America's most successful and respected chief financial officers. They are seeking ways to be more effective. The consensus is that there are not enough hours in the day. It is clear that corporate budgeting is one of the biggest drains on virtually every CFO's time. In fact, one CFO reports that he used to spend more than 120 working days a year on this task. Now he has cut that time down to only three working days a year. This CFO usually works a normal day and gets everything done that needs doing. How, you wonder, is this possible?

What caused him to change was the realization that not only was he spending too much time on budgeting, he was so overinvolved with the operating executives that he was losing his clout with them. He had to find a way to get the budgeting done in less time and save his clout for other, more important issues. After a brief conversation, the other CFOs learned that the man's secret involved delegation of less important parts of the budgeting tasks to the controller and, at the same time, assigning an assistant controller to spend half of his time doing some of the controller's less sensitive work.

Interestingly, the CFO also appears to get better results for his company from his 3-day commitment than with the 120 days he had spent in the past. Why? Since the CFO has not been doing combat with the operating executives over the budgets, they are more inclined to pay attention when he raises questions about other important (and needlessly costly) decisions. As a result of careful training and coaching by the CFO himself, the controller learns to raise all of the issues that the CFO would have raised during the budgeting process. This CFO has truly found a 2,000 percent solution. By changing a process that tied him up unduly, the CFO helped move his company way beyond what the competition was accomplishing in the same time period.

Get Tanked: But Not on Concentrate

Hard-drinking W. C. Fields used to have a portable bar on the movie set with a fresh-made alcoholic drink he referred to as orange juice. One day an unwitting stagehand refreshed the comedian's drink. Fields took a long swig, looked startled, and cried, "Who put orange juice in my orange juice?!"

The thoughtful CFO who resolved the budgeting process in a novel way clearly had the uncommon ability to make leaps of imagination in circumstances hobbled by tradition. Imagination of this sort is golden. So is orange juice on the eastern seaboard, thousands of miles from the groves.

Most people would assume that all tankers steaming up the coast are carrying fuel of one sort or another. Tankers carrying crude oil are infamous for accidents that pollute our beaches. In the best of times, oil tankers are greasy and smelly. But imagine tankers with scrubbed decks and stainless steel compartments leaving orange juice docks loaded with squeezed juice. It is cost-effective to squeeze the juice near the groves, ship by tanker, and package the "not from concentrate" juice nearer the supermarkets in the Northeast.

The stall deriving from the traditional use for tanker ships could have been leaped years earlier. But first, someone had to ask whether the old way, extracting water and trucking the concentrate overland for the consumer to reconstitute at the other end, was the optimum approach. Someone had to surmise that it might be preferable to load whole juice in a sterile tanker for cost-effective transport on the high seas where enormous amounts of juice would be transferred inexpensively. Luckily for orange juice drinkers, someone did.

If Forward Does Not Work, Try Reverse

Some traditional stalls call for a great leap backwards. In what a medical conference referred to as a "daring experiment," stroke victims were treated by *reversing* the plumbing of the body's circulatory system. Veins were used to carry blood backwards to oxygen-starved parts of the brain following a stroke. Normally, veins carry the oxygen-depleted blood from the brain to the lungs. As we breathe, the blood vessels in the lungs soak up oxygen to feed arteries leading to the brain and to the other vital organs.

Strokes occur when a blood clot lodges in an artery that carries blood to the brain. Unless the clot breaks up fast—or doctors use clot-dissolving drugs—brain cells become oxygen starved and paralysis often results. Many stroke victims die.

When the "front door" to the brain is blocked by a clot, Dr. John G. Frazee, the neurosurgeon who invented the reverse-flow procedure, uses the "backdoor." He uses an external pump to push blood from an artery in the groin through a tube to large veins in the neck. From there, catheters are threaded through the veins to the back of the head. The catheters empty blood into the veins, which carry it to the brain. The veins give the entire brain a fresh blood supply, but the blood is drawn especially to the oxygen-starved area near the clot. Doctors must begin the process within seven hours of the stroke and keep the backwards flow going for several hours. The clot then either dissolves or is washed away by the pressure of the reverse-flowing blood.

The procedure was first used on six human patients following eight years of experiments with baboons. Four had virtually complete recoveries, escaping probable paralysis. The other two patients were not helped. One sixty-one-year-old California patient had a stroke that left his left leg and hip paralyzed. Frazee set up his experimental procedure within hours. The paralysis began to disappear and soon went away entirely. The patient walked out of the hospital five days later.

In a similar imaginative leap, savvy engineers in Chicago reportedly solved a serious problem of lake pollution by reversing the flow of the dirty Chicago River away from Lake Michigan and into the Mississippi River system. At first this may seem like merely sending the pollution to someone else. But pollution in a river system is reduced by the aeration that occurs due to the water's movement, something that does not happen in large lakes. So the pollution is reduced as well as redirected.

Sometimes, backwards is better.

No Experience Required

The traditional approach has been to fill organizations with people who are overqualified by education and then give them very little room to maneuver. A better solution is to observe the person who does a given job in the most expert manner, and then make that person's knowledge available to ordinary people so that they can make decisions and take actions reflecting the expert's savvy.

Let's say you call Sears because your overhead garage door is not working properly. Traditionally, Sears would arrange for a mechanic to visit your home, which often resulted in scheduling difficulties: Householders would take a day off work, but the mechanic would get stuck on another job and not show up. Call these days and the Sears representative will determine the model number of your overhead door, turn to the page in the repair manual for that model, and say, "Explain the problem." You tell her the chain that is supposed to raise the door does not move when the opener is used, though the gear cogs are clearly intact. The motor runs, but it makes an awful racket.

You are startled when the woman tells you the worm gear, to which the cog gear was attached, is shot. She offers a new worm gear assembly ($27.98) and an optional tune-up kit for a total cost of $35.70 including taxes.

"Expect delivery in fifteen days," she says. The parts arrive on schedule and the repair is straightforward. She has solved the problem. Has she ever installed a worm gear for an overhead door? Maybe it was part of her training, but it does not matter even if she has not because she can read her expert directions.

Likewise, NCR (National Cash Register), which was part of the computer business spun off by AT&T, has also jumped on the call-in bandwagon. In the 1990s, NCR has specialized in bank, retail, and airline reservation computers. NCR's repair approach is so direct that a high school dropout could field calls. The technician will ask, "Is the screen light or dark?" "Dark." "Is the equipment plugged in? Someone at the computer site may have knocked the cord loose, say, in vacuuming." During the call-in process, the technician can address dozens of common and telephone-addressable problems. In fact, NCR satisfies 90 percent of such cases by phone. Problems solved over the phone cost NCR about $10 each. Clearly, it is more cost-effective to deal with the unplugged cord and other obvious problems by telephone. Sending an engineer to the work site, the common approach in the good old days, cost NCR ten times that, over $100 per visit. NCR can save its experts for situations in which they are really needed.

The telephone solution clearly represents a trend as more and more companies discover this low-cost process can be expedited by alert, nontechnical people with a major, positive impact on the company's bottom line.

Trust Thy Customer

Once the expensive tradition of sending mechanics was challenged, manufacturers looked for better ways of serving customers who needed to return defective merchandise. Usually, you must return the item first. Then, if the item is found to be defective, your manufacturer will either replace it or return your money. The whole process may take a month or more. Not a nice prospect in a vacation setting.

Consider the golfer who thought he faced a bleak vacation on Hilton Head Island when he took a swing on the golf tee and watched the head of his Callaway Big Bertha driver leave the shaft and chase the ball down the fairway.

When the golfer arrived at the clubhouse, the golf pro told him, "If you call Callaway right now, this afternoon, they will airfreight you a new one and you will get it in time to tee off again late tomorrow morning."

The Callaway clerk who answered the phone said, "Send back the broken club in the box the new one comes in, along with a service number I'll give you." To the golfer it seemed that Callaway was too trusting. What was to keep a golfer from falsely declaring that his club was broken? He could order a new club and keep the old one, assuming he wasn't a con artist who didn't even own a Callaway Big Bertha golf club. Then the woman on the Callaway end said, "I'll need a credit card number so you can pay for shipping." This was Callaway's insurance policy. Had the golfer not returned an old club, Callaway could bill the new club to the credit card number.

Perhaps this stall of tradition could have ended half a century ago. The American Express card has been around for fifty years, and the U.S. Postal Service offered special delivery in 1885. It may have taken two days then. The golfer would have lost only one more day of golf without his golf club. Powerful solutions can be devised beyond what we, because of our mindless adherence to tradition, can imagine today.

Callaway found a 2,000 percent solution by figuring out a new way of organizing the process, turning the traditional manufacturer-comes-first equation upside down. This is powerful medicine, since it puts the customer first, in a way that has a trivial impact on the company's business routines and, we can definitely assume, in a way that has a positive impact on sales over time, since Callaway has enjoyed rising sales for many years.

Stallbusters

This section will help you to locate the benefits of and problems with traditions that are now part of your organization, to create better traditions for serving your organization's purposes, and to introduce new empowering traditions. The result will be to make your organization's habits more beneficial for all.

Identify Your Organization's Traditions and Their Original Purposes

Many traditions do start with a purpose, but others start by accident. Before changing something, you should find out if the tradition still serves some useful purpose. Consider the following questions:

What traditions does the company have that slow down or increase the cost of accomplishing important results? For example, many companies have a tradition of making new products available in a sequential way around the world that delays product availability by months or even years. Is such a delay absolutely needed, or simply a stall?

What benefits do these traditions provide the company? A benefit of a slow expansion for a new product is that if there are early errors, those errors can be corrected before the product's reputation is sullied with most potential users.

What values were intended to be served by the traditions? Slow expansion can be a reflection of caring about customer satisfaction, a desire to avoid errors, wanting to provide regular growth in earnings for investors, and a wish to reduce pressure for fast performance on employees.

What problems are created by the traditions? The slow introduction will usually provide competitors with more time to respond and disrupt the product's success. If customers will be greatly benefited by the new product, then they are required to wait for those improvements. The company can develop an image of being stodgy that will discourage some talented people from wanting to join and stay at the company. Investors may also pay a higher multiple to buy stock in competitors that move more quickly. Companies that place a priority on availability based on the economic development of a country may be viewed as being discriminatory.

Identify Empowering Traditions You Can Use to Improve Performance

Traditions are extremely powerful management tools for reinforcing good habits. A tradition has the potential to be helpful or harmful, depending on its relevance for what a company needs to accomplish. Most people are very uncomfortable with dropping or changing traditions because of the psychological sense of security that the routine provides. When thinking about improving on or substituting traditions, you will find that people in your organization will be more receptive to change if they can understand that a new practice you want to turn into a tradition has been validated elsewhere.

The best way to locate these alternative traditions is to begin by examining organizations that perform better than yours in ways that are important. Using the example of new product introductions, ask yourself who does these rapidly and well. A good next step is to have a telephone conversation with those who are responsible for such introductions to understand the values and traditions that lead to such rapid, successful expansions. Listen carefully for traditions that seem the most compatible with what you do now so that the need to change perceptions can be minimized. Companies and organizations often use value statements (either existing or newly created) as a touchstone for establishing a new tradition. Be sure to ask which value statements have been used in conjunction with the traditions you are interested in adopting.

The following questions will help you identify empowering traditions you can use:

What traditions do other companies have that speed up progress, make the results better, and reduce costs? For new products, an empowering tradition is to be the leading source of innovation in the industry and always be first to provide the new product to each and every customer around the world. A related tradition could be to constantly improve the way that new products are developed so that they are rapidly and thoroughly tested to a low level of errors before being broadly distributed. Motorola, with its paging products, could be a model in this area.

Which of these traditions are consistent with your company's values? In the be-first tradition, the values probably include a commitment to innovation, adding value for customers, excellence, error-free operations, constant improvement, and timely action. Are these values in conflict with your company's current values, complementary to the values, or overlapping?

How could the traditions be made more consistent with and supportive of your company's values? For example, if your company has a strong value favoring extreme customer satisfaction, you might amend the be-first tradition to include a variety of ways to please customers when an error occurs with a new product (or any product), such as offering triple-your-money back and a free product that does not have the error. You might also consider a tradition of rapidly advancing the careers of those who find the most errors before they reach customers.

Which aspects of these traditions are exciting and fun for people in your company or organization? People often translate a tradition into part of their self-image. For example, those who pursue slow expansions may see themselves as wise and caring adults. The faster new product expansion proponents could be characterized as being more like Santa Claus bringing goodies at Christmas: You have a bagful of toys and everyone will get one tonight. Most people think it is more fun to play Santa Claus than to be a wise and caring adult, so you can merge the two to become a wise and caring Santa Claus.

Establish New or Amended Traditions

What aspects of your business do you want to have on automatic pilot for all employees? One of the best examples of automatic response is a tradition at Ritz Carlton hotels that whenever an employee notices or is told by a quest about a problem, he or she has the responsibility to fix the problem immediately. That tradition ensures that guests receive quick, courteous solutions while feeling encouraged to bring problems to the attention of the hotel staff.

Use your answers to the following questions to create or change traditions in your organization:

What are the three most useful traditions your company or organization could have?

How can the new traditions be established so that everyone will be delighted with them?

How can you combine elements of existing traditions with useful elements of these new traditions?

What has been the best way that your organization has launched traditions in the past? Companies often try to launch new directions, hoping they will become traditions, and fail. Other efforts succeed. Take the strongest new traditions you have (ideally those that have occurred in the prior two years) and reconstruct how these were launched internally.

This drawing can provide you with the chance to see some humorous images. You'll find that locating humor in stalled situations can provide a lot of encouragement to you and others in busting those stalls. One image that some people see right away is a silly-looking moose's head facing right, against the background of a tree trunk on the left. You could also see this as a self-satisfied person who is wearing a very unusual hat on top of a very funny hairdo, sniffing in the air about how superior he or she is. What humorous images can you find?

Chapter 3
You've Got to Be Kidding!
The Disbelief Stall

Wonderful though your gadget may be, Mr. Fahrenheit, you'll have to admit that people know they need coats in the winter and that they don't need them in the springtime!
—Anonymous

Organizations usually fail to perceive the potential of the most important new information, technology, and ways of operating. This occurs because the new piece of information or resource unexpectedly makes untrue what has been true in the past. This chapter focuses on your opportunity to seize advantages by appreciating the implications of critical new areas you know about today but are incorrectly discounting as unimportant to your future.

Disbelief: Limited Imagination and Blind Spots

The disbelief stall is based on a valid experience, lack of relevant experience, or a previously established reality that no longer pertains. In the horse and buggy age, the thought of going sixty miles an hour for extended periods of time was beyond belief. Yet soon after the automobile was introduced at the turn of the century, such speeds were attained in races.

There is a strong tendency in the business world to react with disbelief to any important change. The most revolutionary changes meet with the most skepticism and are less likely to succeed initially, in part because capital sources are conservative. The bigger the idea, the more likely it will boggle the minds of those who are needed to bring the idea to fruition. Consider this: One hundred years ago, Alexander Graham Bell supposedly offered his ailing telephone business to the then king of communications, Western Union, for $100,000. Western Union's boss scoffed at the idea, disparaging Bell with the words, "What use could our company make of an electrical toy?"

The man's reaction is not surprising. In the last century, technology grew slowly. And even today, as we have seen, it is not easy to leap into the future with a novel idea that challenges present methods. Thomas Kuhn, a Harvard-trained philosophic scientist, uses the term "paradigm shift" to tell what must happen in a person's mind-set before a novel development can be understood. We are forced to fundamentally challenge the status quo before we can develop new ways of looking at things.

New Paradigms for Old

Thomas Kuhn's book, *The Structure of Scientific Revolutions* (University of Chicago Press 1962), sets forth his paradigm concept in detail. He states that those who break through to invent a new paradigm are almost always either very young or very new to the field whose paradigm they change. He wrote that the more flexible younger innovators, being little committed to prior practice and to the traditional rules of normal science, are particularly likely to see that those rules no longer define a playable game and to conceive of another set that can replace them.

As a real-life example, consider the experience of Solar Box Cookers International. In the poor areas of Africa and India where 100 degrees Fahrenheit is an everyday condition, cardboard boxes lined with 10 cents worth of foil are offered as solar ovens. These ovens may well free millions of women and children from the all-consuming daily task of gathering twigs or cow dung to fuel the hearth for supper. Solar Box Cookers International found that it was the children, not the adults, who were eager to use it. Even after the children cooked dinner with the solar oven, it was still quite difficult to overcome the disbelief stall in their own parents.

Kuhn's disciple, Joel Barker, in *Paradigms: The Business of Discovering the Future* (HarperBusiness 1993), says a paradigm is a theory or dogma that establishes boundaries and regulations. Paradigms filter data and can prevent discovery of new developments from outside the paradigm. Barker asks us to assume that the impossible in our business could, in fact, be done. He asks, "Would that change fundamentally what you do?" This is crucial to understanding his "going back to zero" rule: When a paradigm shifts, everyone goes back to zero; that is, past success guarantees nothing. The Swiss did, in fact, invent the quartz movement watch, but the hidebound among them snubbed it. They did not go back to zero in their thinking. Past success had blinded them to the new future of watch-making.

Barker's book and video set forth examples of paradigm shift: the airplane, the telephone, the radio, the photocopier. Their developers were open to new concepts—to new ways of looking at the world. Those who say it cannot be done should get out of the way of those who are doing it, Barker concludes.

Why Would Anyone Need a Phone?

Bell wasn't really thinking big initially; he wasn't moving to a totally new paradigm. He just thought he had a way to improve on the town crier. He expected to use the phone as a news medium. With each new technical advance, would-be users and, yes, even the inventor (like Bell himself) may be stymied by clinging to the old ways. They figure that the new knowledge will be employed in the same way the old knowledge was.

For their part, householders wondered, "Why get a telephone when I can step outside and talk to my neighbor over the back fence?" In Bell's time, people rarely left their immediate neighborhoods. They could *walk* that far. Not having identified a need, they asked, "Why should we have a telephone."

Later, people were to react similarly to cell phones, asking, "Who needs it?" But when people get cell phones, they begin by calling friends to enthuse. Then they make far more calls than they expected as the usefulness of the device quickly becomes obvious. Husbands often buy cell phones for their wives who are at risk if the car suddenly breaks down at night. Forget minimum rates. New cell phone customers often use the devices so much they rarely qualify for minimum-use fees.

Who would have imagined in those early days of Bell's "electrical toy" that someone in Europe would someday pick up a phone not radically different from the one Bell invented to call a bank in, say, Singapore? Or that a homesick immigrant would pick up a Brooklyn telephone to call a relative in Crete?

Why Would Anyone Need a Computer?

The usefulness of electronic computers, created during World War II, was suspect even to their most avid supporter. Thomas J. Watson, Sr., who was to build IBM upon mainframe computers, was quoted in 1943 as saying there was probably a world market for only five of the monster machines.

The early computers were certainly formidable. These mainframes took up a major portion of an entire city block. There were no desktop personal computers or other small units back then. Processing with these lumbering giants was molasses slow relative to the lightning speed of our desktop PCs today. The early software engineers had to write programs that weighed every possible contingency because it took so long to run a program that users could not afford mistakes. It is no wonder no one believed computers would ever be widely marketable. Under the first computer science paradigm, it was believed all computer operators would have to be scientists, each one writing his or her own programs. But that notion dissipated as manufacturers developed ever smaller and more powerful chips to replace vacuum tubes and ferrite core memories.

Profiles in Disbelief

The Watch That Became a Dog

Skepticism follows naturally if an innovation is revolutionary. Consider the reaction that a tuning fork, offered as a timing device, got during the heyday of mechanical wristwatches. Those watches had a mainspring and a stem to wind them up. A series of tiny, precision gears were linked to hands on the face that registered the time. These watches were universal a generation ago. Even though jewels were employed as a means of reducing friction, watches were, by and large, inaccurate by today's standards. Most of the premium watches with so-called Swiss movements (many of the top watches were made in Switzerland) lost or gained a minute or more a day.

Predictably, at the annual watch industry exposition some thirty years ago, all the watchmakers' booths but one featured timepieces with Swiss movements. The one dissenter was dismissed as a maverick though he was about to strip the gears. His neglected display is said to have featured a remarkable timepiece equipped with a tuning fork and a tiny battery. The battery energized the fork, the tone of which was wedded to a timing mechanism that marked passing seconds, minutes, and hours. This tuning-fork watch was more accurate than most ticktock watches, and it redefined the playing field. Back at that exposition thirty years ago, the other participants could not imagine that these highly innovative watches would have a shattering impact on their trade. But the quartz crystal watches that rule today's market are the tuning-fork watch's direct descendants. Swiss movements have 10 percent of the wristwatch market, which is down from their 80 percent market share in 1969.

In hindsight, the threat to watches with Swiss movements is obvious. It isn't over yet. Time is such a key element in our lives that inventors keep finding better ways to measure it. Some of the old ways were novel, if somewhat rough-hewn. Early in this century when the horse and buggy were still in vogue, workers who could not afford clocks would tie a shoe to a nail, pushing the nail into a candle well below the wick. When the candle burned down far enough, the nail slipped through the hot wax, and the shoe would hit the floor with a "clunk." The sleeper awoke in time to go to work. Primitive? Certainly. But for its time, the device was an effective means of alerting people to the hour that mattered most. Today, we require mind-boggling accuracy in our timepieces. For example, without precise synchronization, achieved through atomic measures of radioactivity, communication on the Internet would quickly collapse.

I'm Not Listening

After the trade show ended, the master of the tuning-fork watch accomplished something few others with new ideas have: He was soon able to find an audience and take over the market. By contrast, a few years ago, a small American company, New Age Industries, created a revolutionary new way to transfer kinetic power, a potential replacement for gears found in transmissions and nearly every other mechanical device. This demonstrably superior system was based on computer-derived gearing designs precise enough to offer up to 30 percent energy savings in many applications. The company hoped to sweep the market like a second hand sweeps the face of a Swiss movement watch. All the company needed was a production partner. It conducted market research to see which industries and markets had a history of accepting and introducing new concepts successfully.

The research examined dozens of product categories and management processes. In every case, someplace other than North America was the most promising area in which to market a revolutionary business technology. In fact, the best leads came from Japan and other advanced Asian nations. But the super-gear company had no experience in the Far East. Sadly, the company was unable to complete the sale. It turned out that most gear makers and users were content with the status quo. They were not convinced that the proposed capital investment would pay off.

Ignore It and It Will Go Away

Sometimes the disbelief stall is colored by feelings about short-term self-interest. Suppose someone walks into your office to offer you a variation on your primary product that, due to new efficiencies of production, can sell for half the price your product now commands. You are likely to be more shocked than pleased, unless, of course, you anticipate that the dollar value of the market will grow much larger. Failing that, the adoption of the outsider's product will probably cause your profits to drop. You may bear the extra burden of replacing specialized equipment and people. Who needs this? Your mind may play tricks on you. For example, you decide the new product will, in fact, cost more to produce. The disbelief stall is taking hold. You drag your feet, hoping you will be promoted and someone else will have to decide. This stall is very destructive. The business world is dynamic: He who hesitates is lost.

Tunnel Vision Darkens the Big Picture

To a surprising degree, managers, both those who know computers and those who do not, tend to see them in terms of their existing, standard applications. Most managers can easily understand the computer as an engine of personal productivity or as a tracker of production. They could, for example, understand computers used to prepare accounting. But many do not realize they can embed software on a chip in their finished product to help improve service.

Let us assume a company buys a piece of capital equipment for the factory. If that machinery has embedded software, the customer can call the factory, connect to the equipment chip by modem, and learn what repairs it needs. Another application of this idea is the V-4 truck engine, the Rodi HTI-450, developed by a former Boeing engineer. It has such a chip along with a cell phone and modem for remote diagnostics. Similarly, Cadillac has a code system in a dashboard button that lets mechanics check the car's diagnostics and learn what needs fixing.

Stall Erasers

Creative People

You should seek out the help of people who enjoy creating new solutions. These types of people are eager for new challenges. You may also find these helpful hands among suppliers, new employees, customers, and outside experts, including academics. Their imagination can be supplemented with your own good leadership.

In the same way that no two people have identical kinds of curiosity, organizations have personalities that favor or disfavor various ways of looking for new solutions. Likewise, you can easily imagine that Intel, Microsoft, IBM, General Electric, and Disney would take quite different approaches to dealing with the same issue. You should examine your organization's personality and consider how it can be expanded in useful ways, perhaps by adding new partners and new competencies.

Positive Thinking Starts the Exponential Progress Engine

To overcome the disbelief stall, you need to have a positive outlook. You have to believe wonderful things are just around the corner, if only you look for them. You have heard the old debate about the glass being half empty or half full. People who see a half-empty glass tend to see potential problems wherever they look, which also encourages them to focus on avoiding loss. It makes more sense to imagine potential opportunities. Ask yourself a positive question about any situation that occurs.

Imagine you were being asked to use a computer for the first time. Instead of fighting this new responsibility, ask yourself how this would make it easier for you to get home on time. It is also good to adopt other new beliefs about what is going on around you, beliefs that help you grow and exploit more and better opportunities, such as a belief that 2,000 percent solutions abound for those who seek them.

View roadblocks as in disguise. For example, if you can find a way to solve an especially difficult problem, realize that you are solving it for others in your organization. This viewpoint can add to your ability to help your organization as well as your customers: When you solve a recurring problem, you save time again and again.

It is also helpful to believe that all things that happen have a purpose: to help you improve. Adopt the idea that large changes are fundamentally good *and* possible. If something is unacceptable, remind yourself that there is probably at least one way you can change it. Once you believe you can make a change, work on making it a change for the better. If something happens to you that has not happened to you before, ask yourself, "What am I supposed to learn from this?" This upbeat way of looking at things makes life much more interesting, especially when this point of view is applied to what first appears to be temporary adversity.

Using positive thinking about how a new technology can solve day-to-day problems is hard work, but this approach can be immensely rewarding. A useful thing for you to do is to make a list of things that your organization does now that make little sense, but that need a new solution before they can be improved. Then you can match new ideas and technologies as they are developed to solve these problems.

Back-to-Zero Goal Setting

Even those with progressive mind-sets can be captured by disbelief and lose the chance to grow exponentially. The feeling is widespread that 15 percent growth is high. But an organization that sets an ambitious goal to grow 15 percent per year may be ruling out more attractive choices. Curiously enough, there are situations in which growth targeted at 25 percent per year is in fact easier to achieve than 15 percent growth. With that surpassing goal of 25 percent growth, everyone in the organization realizes new thinking is required. The goal can also help attract imaginative people to the organization who like to think differently.

Stallbusters

This section focuses on your organization's blind spots, the places where you do not see what is happening or is about to happen. You will learn how to eliminate or compensate for these blind spots so that you will not lose important opportunities as a result.

Locate Blind Spots

At least some of the things you are not thinking about or not taking seriously are missed opportunities. A good rule of thumb is to be aware that the more often you have heard about something, the more significant it is likely to be. Ignoring new information one time will usually be okay (unless someone is warning you about a car that is about to run over you), but to ignore it more than once is risking being stalled by a blind spot. To help identify your company's blind spots, ask yourself the following questions in the context of what the feasible reactions might be:

What things are your competitors doing that you have decided to ignore? Maytag recently scored a remarkable coup in the washing machine business by producing a premium-quality, premium-price front-loading washing machine. Front-loading was a technical direction that had failed repeatedly in the past. Some of the problems included leaks around the door, insufficient cleaning, and wear on the washer parts. Maytag decided to revisit this form of washing machine because of its potential to reduce wear on the clothes being washed and lessen the amount of water needed. It was well known that Maytag was working on this approach, but competitors chose not to respond immediately because they assumed that the product would fail. Instead, the product enjoyed a wonderful reception, and Maytag's competitors are now years behind in responding. If you were one of Maytag's competitors, then you would have described Maytag's front-loading washing machine while the new Maytag product was under development.

What things are the communities you do business in talking about that you have ignored so far? Sticking with the washing machine example, more and more communities are having problems with treating wastewater. Insufficiently treated, wastewater from washing machines helps generate those disgusting bubbles that cover rivers, streams, and lakes in many parts of the United States. If you do not have a front-loading washing machine under development, then you may not be addressing the question of how to produce washing machines that create less wastewater. Notice, too, that creating a design that requires less detergent and other cleansing and whitening agents (like bleach-based products) would be very helpful for wastewater disposal.

Further, you could take another approach to solving the wastewater problem and create a machine that cleans and recycles its own water. If this approach were inexpensive enough, it would be a customer benefit as well because the householder would not have to buy so much water to wash and rinse clothes. If it's not yet economically feasible, perhaps you could find a way that the water could be treated well enough by your equipment so that the householder could reuse it to water the garden and save money that way.

But perhaps neither of these options is yet feasible, so you could consider designing a machine that could use laundry products that are much cheaper, faster, and easier to remove from wastewater. In fact, if you did this well enough, you might be able to sell custom laundry products for your equipment and have an additional source of profits. If it were more economical for someone else to manufacture and distribute these products for you, you could outsource those activities.

Better yet, how about a waterless washer? Sounds crazy, but such a technology was announced in late 1998.

What negative feedback do you get from employees that you have been receiving for at least two years? In the washing machine business, there are two concepts about what the future holds. Maytag recently sold its foreign operations based on a reported belief that the company does not have to be a worldwide competitor in order to succeed. Maytag's competitors are often pursuing just the opposite strategy, expanding throughout the globe with local manufacturing and products. Recently, some of this activity has created machine and parts commonality in some regions around the world as a way to reduce costs.

If you were one of Maytag's competitors, you would probably be hearing from employees that they are very much in fear for their jobs. Globalization has often meant the end of high-paying, low-skill union jobs in the United States. This circumstance can distract employees from working on ways to improve operations and create a hostile labor environment, including difficult strikes. General Motors experienced just this circumstance with regard to outsourcing the manufacture of auto parts in 1998.

We can safely assume that there will always be a need for washing machines in the United States. Will there always be a need to manufacture those washing machines in the United States?

Many companies have found that the United States is a wonderful place to manufacture products that benefit from a highly educated, flexible, and well-trained labor force. If you retrained your labor force to be more like this, how could that help your manufacturing capability? One possibility is that you could switch to a different approach to manufacturing so that the washing machines are assembled and shipped within minutes of receiving the order. This could provide lots of additional sales by providing rapid response to changes in consumer buying patterns. Your customers (wholesalers and retailers) would be more profitable because they could carry less inventory, and you might be able to charge a little higher price for this service. Plus, your own inventories would be at least a little smaller, saving investment capital otherwise tied up in working capital.

What are the perceptions held about your company and your industry that you are not addressing? The washing machine business is hardly a high flyer. Those who follow these companies usually assume that nothing will happen. That is a very interesting environment to do business in. One reason that Maytag was able to surprise everyone with its new washing machine was that the new CEO was felt by many to be someone who would launch few changes, both because he was a carefully groomed internal candidate with a financial background and because there appeared to be few changes that a new CEO could make. Observers were then quite surprised when he quickly sold the European washing machine operations at a loss and successfully launched the new front-loading product line. For Maytag, it was a good time to question all of its assumptions because observers and competitors alike were probably asleep, so there was room to move without inviting an immediate response.

Evaluate the Implications of the Blind Spots

Once you have compiled your list of blind spots, or even a partial one, ask yourself the following questions to help you evaluate their implications:

Which blind spots are in areas where your organization's actions can improve or worsen your situation? At least some element of every issue that was raised in the Maytag example could be addressed fully or in part by developing new ways of designing and manufacturing washing machines. To the extent that a Maytag competitor did not address other customer, user, and community issues (unknown to us, but likely known to the Maytag CEO), these other issues too may point toward opportunities for new products and other manufacturing processes.

Let us assume that this observation in the prior paragraph about the development potential for new products and manufacturing is correct for now. How could new product development help? Obviously, to the extent that the new product development efforts focused on eliminating these blind spots by serving the unmet customer, user, and community needs described in the Maytag example, the company would be better off, all other things being equal. How could this get offtrack? One possibility is that the new design efforts produced products that worked well initially, but that failed in the long run because of design errors (the parts wear out prematurely, the seals leak water, or the clothes are damaged rather than just being cleaned). Disgruntled customers would be swearing never to buy your products again, your warranty costs to repair or replace the machines would be enormous, and the negative publicity would scare off investors and potential customers. Another problem that could occur with new products is that it would take a long time to solve the problems identified in these blind spots discussed earlier in this paragraph. If such delays occurred and too many resources went into new designs, the company might find itself with too few new models, and ones that did not offer any particular advantages other than new colors and shapes.

When would you need to act to get most of the benefit or avoid most of the harm? The answer to this question is always a somewhat relative one. As long as you arrive at the solution before anyone else, you have the opportunity to seize much of the advantage from having the initiative. In the relatively sleepy washing machine industry, there may be little time pressure. However, Maytag's very success with its new model could change that.

Many companies now realize that advances in computer-aided design of machinery allow problems to be solved quickly that earlier could not have been solved at all. Seeing someone accomplish that positive result in a previously difficult area such as front-loading washing machines may encourage aggressive companies like Whirlpool and General Electric to accelerate their new product development into previously unproductive areas. If each company immediately expands its new product focus, the fallout of the Maytag success may be to greatly reduce the amount of time available to obtain competitive advantages, making blind spots even more dangerous to your success as a Maytag competitor.

Maytag's decision to exit the global washing machine business raises especially interesting questions about timing. If Maytag is wrong in that decision, the company may have little time to recover from its decision to pull back because its competitors are rapidly expanding in this direction and seeking worldwide cost-reduction benefits from having globalized their businesses. With few potential partners left, Maytag could end up with only the option to sell itself to a competitor after these cost efficiencies are developed by its competitors.

What is the minimum evidence that would tell you that you should act immediately? This is a tricky question for the new products design area. If blind spots cause you to wait too long, you can fall behind in introducing the new products. Some clues to timing include large increases in design activities at competitors; expanded scope of new design solutions being sought (suppliers may tip you off to this); more powerful resources available for solving the problems (this could include ventures with partners who have related technologies, adding much more powerful computer and software problem-solving capabilities, and making acquisitions of companies with related expertise such as one in the water treatment area); and actual word of trials being conducted successfully in the laboratory or the field. Stories about speeches made by company executives or disclosed to securities analysts could also tip you off to a new direction that requires an immediate response by your organization.

This drawing is unusually good for helping you see movement and potential in what at first looks like a static situation. This skill is helpful for seeing the way past obstacles to exponential success. Can you see anything black that looks like a swimming fish passing through small spaces between rocks? Depending on where you are in the picture, what obstacles might stall you? How could you overcome those obstacles? Now imagine that your organization is the white material. How can you escape the invasion by the black objects? (Hint: You can change your physical state if you want—perhaps from a solid to a flowing gel.)

Chapter 4
Misused Clichés
The Misconception Stall

His old horse died, his mule went lame,
he lost his cow in a poker game . . .
A cyclone came one summer day,
and blew his house and barn away,
An earthquake followed to make it good
and swallowed the ground where the old house stood.
His auto turned turtle and he up and died
and his widow and children wept and cried.
Still, they thought they were set, that family of eight
But his insurance premiums were out of date.
                                                        —Anonymous

Organizations are hobbled by beliefs that have always rested on faulty
evidence. This chapter helps you to articulate the critical assumptions
you are relying on to run your organization and to check these assump-
tions for their validity. The misconception stall is particularly harmful
because some of your best people realize that the assumptions are faulty,
see actions based on these assumptions as folly, and so lose faith in the
organization and its leadership.

Misconception: The Danger of False Assumptions Abounds

The misconception stall refers to something that people may have believed all their lives or have believed for a long time, even though the

belief is based on faulty evidence. Note that it differs from the disbelief stall that is based on something that is no longer true, but that was at one time.

> *A belief is not true because it is useful.*
> —Henri-Frederic Amiel

One of the most serious causes of organizational errors comes from assuming that something is true that is not, never has been, and never will be true. We assume, for example, that the future can be forecast accurately, or that our competitors will stand still while we make rapid progress. Equally worrisome, we assume that agreement among colleagues means the issues are fully understood. Many believe customers will make their decisions in the same way they always have.

It is important to question long-held beliefs and assumptions. Ask yourself the obvious: Is this *really* true? If you discover that the belief is hogwash, ask why it is accepted as true. Next, find out what would persuade people to change their beliefs. Get that information, and communicate, communicate, and communicate some more.

Titanic Misconception: A Stitch in Time

The fate of the *Titanic* (Exhibit 4-1) illustrates the misconception stall at work overtime. To begin with, it was a monumental misconception to believe that the ship was unsinkable and not to provide sufficient lifeboats to save all passengers in case of an accident. However, the ship in fact was wrecked and sunk because of another misconception, one about weather.

Normally, icebergs in the North Atlantic would have been floating far north of the path the *Titanic* followed on that frigid night in April of 1912. The *Titanic*'s captain had heard a report from another ship that icebergs had moved to a more southerly latitude than normal. If so, the icebergs could pose a threat to the speeding superliner. His fateful misconception was to disregard that report because he believed that icebergs did not travel that far south in that season.

The captain's misconception illustrates the danger of basing key decisions on a single measurement. If he had double-checked with other available sources of information, such as other ships and shore

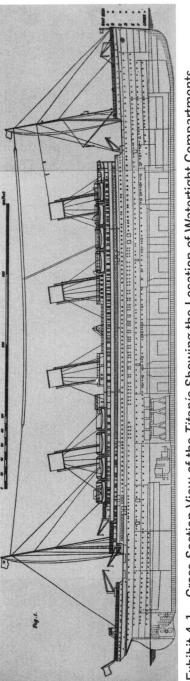

Exhibit 4-1   Cross-Section View of the *Titanic* Showing the Location of Watertight Compartments.

The Mariners' Museum/Corbis. Reproduced with permission.

stations, he might have had a confirmation of reports of icebergs in his vicinity in time to turn farther south or to slow down and avoid disaster.

Once the *Titanic* was in extremis, misconception once again ruled that night. The captain of the *Californian,* a ship large enough and close enough to the *Titanic* to rescue everyone onboard, was stalled by an equally tragic misconception. The watch alerted him to the *Titanic's* distress flares, but he imagined them to be a kind of celebration on the maiden voyage, not a desperate cry for help. All this captain had to do was to wake his radioman and have him ask the *Titanic,* "You're not sinking, are you?" This was, as they say, a no-brainer. Yet this misconception prevented the rescue of most of the *Titanic's* passengers, and 1,503 people lost their lives.

Misconceptions bring truly titanic consequences. Let us consider what could have happened instead.

There needn't have been any casualties at all had the ship slowed down in the iceberg-laden North Atlantic or, better still, had the *Titanic* sailed the longer southern route. The *Titanic* would have arrived to a traditional festive welcome. A horrific chapter in ship history would have been avoided. After the *Titanic* went to the bottom, the pace of transatlantic sailings slowed dramatically. So did the rapid interchange of ideas that went with widespread contact among businessmen, scientists, artists, writers, and composers on both sides of the Atlantic.

Had the *Titanic* arrived safely in New York City, it might have plied the Atlantic for a quarter of a century with her sister ship, the *Olympic.* Later, the luckier *Olympic,* fitted, by the way, with sufficient lifeboats to accommodate its entire complement of passengers, endured a less spectacular collision. It survived a 45-foot hull gash and limped back to port for repairs. Both of these giant ocean liners could easily have outrun German U-boats in World War I just as the Cunard Line's *Queen Mary* did in World War II. Had the *Titanic* and her sister ship been rigged as troop carriers to transport troops to Liverpool from the United States, time and again they could have delivered entire divisions with each passage. World War I might have ended earlier than it did. Even the threat of undelivered armies might have deterred Germany from its deadly offensives at the war's end.

Clearly, the world might have been a different place. But what would have inspired the safety measures that arose out of the *Titanic* disaster? Would some other owner have misconceived the dangers of the North Atlantic and sent a different "unsinkable" ship to the bottom?

Would the rule calling for lifeboats for all passengers, rich and poor alike, have been delayed? When would radiomen on oceangoing vessels have started manning their posts twenty-four hours a day?

Misconception caused the Astors to lose their patriarch. David Sarnoff, the young telegrapher whose nimble fingers kept the world in touch with the *Titanic*'s survivors for seventy-two hours, might have remained an obscure figure. Or he might have followed a slower route to the top spot at RCA, where his team brought us color television. Perhaps an ambitious person in steerage who went down with the *Titanic* would have mimicked Sarnoff's rags-to-riches story as CEO of yet another giant company. Or was there an Einstein on board, a Keats, a Michelangelo?

On the other hand, just as well-run companies turn adversity to later profit, some good came out of the disaster. Harvard's famed Widener Library was financed by the Wideners in memory of a family member lost with the ship. Without the sinking, some scholarship from the library's massive resources might have been lost to humanity. Both good and bad result from decisions following misconceptions. Had the *Titanic* somehow survived the iceberg in the North Atlantic on that fateful night, Great Britain's White Star line might still be that nation's top ship operator. The *Titanic*'s devastated insurers might have remained prosperous.

The misconceptions that sealed the fate of the *Titanic* and its last passengers could have been corrected. The lesson to be learned is that we can change course and avoid icebergs. We don't have to steam at top speed through treacherous waters simply because we misconceive the dangers.

Round Out Your View

The voyages that Christopher Columbus took to the New World ended one of history's greatest misconception stalls. While it was clear to the Vikings from the year 1000 that there was a huge landmass just a few months' voyage away, most European sailors were terrorized by the apparent end of the earth at the horizon. Convinced the world was flat, they thought the horizon led to the abyss and oblivion. Columbus was convinced otherwise even as Copernicus was establishing the modern view of astronomy with a global earth spinning around a global sun.

Columbus was confident there was nothing to fear. He had made a point of studying the early Viking explorations. In fact, in 1477, fifteen years before he set sail for what was to become known as the New World, Columbus arrived in Iceland on a Portuguese ship. He went there to find out more about the northern "islands" beyond the Atlantic. So why did he later sail farther south on his famous trip of 1492? Columbus was not seeking a new continent, only a shorter route to India. In sailing the ocean blue, he broke the 400-year European misconception stall. Had they been less timid, the Europeans might have learned about the existence of the Americas in the eleventh century.

Exam Cram

In a wonderful book, *The Unschooled Mind* (Basic Books 1991), cognitive psychologist Howard Gardner argues that people think at three different levels. Gardner defines the five-year-old's mind as the first level. Think back to your beliefs when you were in kindergarten. When you are a small child, someone feeds, clothes, and takes care of you. Five-year-olds develop a whole set of perceptions that guide their conduct 90 percent of the time. Surprisingly, most of these persist through their entire lives. A few poor souls figure that someone will always play that role for them, and this keeps them from being independently effective in many areas of their lives. Another common example is that almost every confident person believes that he or she is superior in every way as a person, a common five-year-old belief.

    The second level of knowledge occurs when training, usually at the high school and college levels, gives teens and grown-ups a grasp of sophisticated concepts—temporarily. The student memorizes the concepts long enough to pass the examination. But, Gardner argues, relatively few adults reach the third level: retaining the sophisticated learning concepts to apply them successfully in everyday life. They revert to the five-year-old's misconceptions that serve him or her in everyday life, or at least for the most part.

    The person who can apply the principles learned in school in a real-life situation becomes a disciplinary expert. If that person thinking at the third level faces a mechanical problem, he or she will solve the problem through something remembered from physics, algebra, and so on. Gardner reported that a very small percentage of the world can do that in any field. Basically, he says, in everyday life the vast majority of all human beings are operating at the levels of their five-year-old minds.

Think of what could be accomplished if you consciously shed those misconceptions and applied sophisticated, adult reasoning based on expert knowledge to questioning existing assumptions.

I'll Get Right on It

Random Acts

Even if people habitually apply sophisticated lessons, they will still tend to jump to conclusions too often. If service is slow the last two times you go to a given store, you may decide this store offers poor service, so you don't go back. Statistically, two experiences do not constitute a trend. You need many slow days in a row to prove the case. It's possible the storekeeper had to be out of town both days you were in and the clerks took advantage. The best restaurant may be mediocre when the chef is away. If the newspaper's critic eats there on the chef's night off, the review won't be a good one.

The executives of one award-winning multibillion-dollar manufacturer were clearly intelligent and were widely admired for their decisions. Ever curious, these managers wanted to measure the actual quality of their decisions. They knew good decision making has to reflect solid statistical values, and they wondered what top statisticians would think of the way they made their decisions. Therefore, they assigned statisticians to follow them around for six months, watching them in action. It was discovered that almost without exception the executives treated random events as representing what was actually occurring in the business.

For a sense of the serious potential consequences of this behavior, view the matter on a personal level. Say you dress in the dark one day. You leave the house unaware that you are wearing casual socks, one green and one black. You attend a meeting and discover your mistake when you cross your legs and expose the socks. This has never happened to you before and you are mortified. But would you buy a color scanner to check your socks and match up pairs as they come out of the laundry? Of course not. That solution to this transitory event would be absurd. All you need to do is turn on the lights before you get dressed in the morning, as usual.

But the billion-dollar corporation's executives would likely view such a random event as the norm. They might waste time creating a process so that the random event would never occur again. Executives at the billion-dollar corporation did in fact spend too much time on trivia while overlooking far more promising chances for gain. In the end, they discounted the statistical study they had commissioned and corporate profits plunged due, in part, to their misconceptions about random events. The lesson: Focus on the areas where action is really needed.

This example shows how wide the gap can be between the perceptions of management quality and the actual effectiveness—another example of misconceptions. You have probably noticed how many "widely admired" companies quickly fall from grace.

When Borrowed Money Is a Drag

Managers know they must reduce costs in this era of fierce global competition. So they may press for lower material costs and, in the same quest for savings, sometimes cut workers to a reckless degree. However, they often miss their largest profit-improvement opportunity: less expensive ways to pay for the capital they use.

Corporations can have any number of misconceptions about the cheapest way to finance their businesses, but the most common of these is the Capital Asset Pricing Model (CAPM). This theory (by definition an unproved assumption) is used in part to help managers compare the cost of equity capital with the cost of debt. It has been frequently revised since its appearance in the early 1960s. Even so, many companies use CAPM to justify taking on debt in countless instances when equity capital is demonstrably cheaper, using a different mind-set and measurements. On occasion, equity even offers a free ride.

Corporate executives have no problem determining the cost of capital if they borrow from a bank. The bank makes the company pay back whatever sum is borrowed plus the interest that is agreed to in the loan agreement. But the cost of equity capital is less easily derived. Based on the performance of the Standard & Poor's 500 stock index, CAPM suggests debt is usually cheaper. However, the model ignores the fact that some companies' shares lag the market, and it overlooks other equity financing benefits as well. If you sell stock, you will, of course, have more cash on hand. But unless you pay dividends, you don't set yourself up for annual cash costs like the interest payments and principal repayments you have with debt. You can earn more profit on the entire cash infusion until the day you decide to buy the stock back in. And you could decide *not* to buy the stock back for ten years, or twenty years, if ever. Furthermore, if, in fact, your share price dropped, you could buy the stock back for less than what you sold it for. Then you would wind up with the same number of shares you had before the financing and have cash left over. And if you had experienced a gain on the round trip with the stock, you would have done so without paying taxes on that gain!

In employing the CAPM model, theorists begin by hypothesizing that each corporation must compete for equity capital with every other corporation. A key measuring stick used in pursuit of this theory is the Ibbotson Associates studies of the performance of the Standard & Poor's 500 stock index. The studies are for the years from 1926 through 1997. Over the 71-year period, holders of the S&P index shares would have averaged 11 percent gains from market appreciation plus dividends. CAPM theorists insist company stock prices must outdo the S&P with 15 percent to 20 percent annual returns, depending upon a company's risk profile. When managements consider the cost of equity capital, they generally factor in this CAPM assumption, then choose debt.

But CAPM theory ignores the fact that some companies' shares haven't advanced much for years. Ironically enough, investors buy lagging shares every day on the assumption that the situation is about to change. They do so even when there is no evidence whatsoever that a change in market valuation is at hand. Let's look at the cost of equity for a company whose shares tend to lag the market.

Let's factor in the actual performance of the stock in recent years. Isn't it wiser to assume that a given stock will grow the way it has in the past than to use the S&P proxy for the growth of stocks generally as with the Capital Asset Pricing Model?

Let's say the stock of a company that pays no dividend offers a 3 percent net market gain to investors per year. Let's treat that stock as if it were bank debt for a moment. If that low growth rate continues, you might well buy this stock back in the future at a price reflecting the 3 percent growth. Thus 3 percent is the approximate annual cost of equity capital for this concern, not some theoretical cost several times higher, as implied by CAPM. If this company must pay 8 percent to take on debt, net cost after deducting the taxes saved would be about 5 percent.

That's far more than the implied 3 percent cost of equity capital for this company.

For a cyclical company, this use of equity can be a smart strategy. Let's say a cyclical stock periodically moves from $10 up to $20, then drops back to $10. Once this stock rises to $15, you have a pretty safe bet that someday you will be able to buy it back at $10. Thus, this management would be smart to sell some stock at $15 with the likely prospect that in two to ten years, it could likely buy the stock back at a lower price (even $10). Ergo, the gain is a free source of capital.

In fact, Wall Street doesn't like cyclical companies that issue equity. For the Capital Asset Pricing Model suggests to the Street that cyclical companies must pay more for equity capital than virtually any other type of company. Yet when a cyclical's fluctuating stock is managed appropriately, it can have a lower cost of equity capital than a steady grower.

The CAPM can be an elaborate, widely accepted misconception stall when applied in many circumstances. Taken without reflection, it appears valid, but it has faulty underpinnings for comparing the cost of debt and equity. Using CAPM, many weak companies take on excessive debt at too large a cost: They experience unwarranted risk. In addition, carrying excessive debt slows their ability to grow, especially during bad economic times. Thoughtful analysis of a company's own circumstances can better determine the likely cost of equity capital.

When the CEO Speaks, People Act

> *"I crossed a parrot with a tiger."*
> *"So what did you get?"*
> *"I don't know . . .*
> *but when he speaks, I listen."*
>
> —Anonymous

Here's a misconception stall more common than the CAPM stall. Top executive assistants at select companies were asked what single thing the CEO did that could be done better. The aides spoke almost as one in reporting that anything the CEO said was treated as gospel. Underlings scurried to make changes even when the CEO had only asked an innocent question, figuring the response would come at no cost from someone who already had the answer. Imagine the overhead expenses that could have been saved if all the needless changes initiated by such a misconception were stopped.

I'd Rather Do It Myself

We lose money on every sale . . . but we make it up on volume!
—An insolvent retailer

Imagine you are taking a walk and you see a dime. You pick it up, just as a $5 bill flies by. You have focused on the dime. Someone else grabs the $5 bill. The opportunity cost of picking up the dime is $4.90. Profitable ventures entail opportunity costs—the costs of not pursuing an alternative opportunity. In general, the opportunity cost of a business or investment venture is measured against the interest yield of U.S. Treasury debt, the safest financial alternative of all. Thus, a business venture that promises a 3 percent return when Treasuries are paying 5 percent would not be considered worth doing. The opportunity cost is excessive.

Corporations that undertake ventures that would better be left to other businesses usually ignore the opportunity cost. They think that they should do everything for themselves to avoid being at the mercy of suppliers. But they often make this exception: They will use outside suppliers when they can save actual dollars. Management authority Peter Drucker says outsourcing should be used to reduce the number of tasks that management must spend time on. Management should focus on tasks whereby it can add the most value to the firm. Outsourcing cost should be a secondary concern.

Keep in mind the hidden opportunity cost when you don't hire someone else to do the tasks at which they are better at adding value than you.

Cutting Costs Doesn't Increase Profits?

Cost reduction seems like something you should pursue whenever possible; but real, continuing cost reduction is seldom accomplished and profit growth is weak for many. Most big American companies today are focused on reducing costs. With few exceptions, they show no real growth in product volume except through acquisitions. The cost-cutters are not, by and large, generating significant new benefits for society in goods and services. What American corporations need to do more of is to produce new types of more beneficial goods and services that people will want to buy in quantity. To focus primarily on cost reduction is a misconception in most businesses.

Government Monopoly Is Highly Profitable: Not

One of the oldest political debates around concerns who should own the means of production. At one time, the state-owned monopoly was such a dependable source of revenue in so many different environments that it spawned the misconception that the state-owned enterprise is a very good way to run a business. Communism borrowed the idea of state-owned monopoly, but the fall of Communism has added to the proof that state-owned monopoly is a bad idea. Disproven though the theory is, the world still has not gotten rid of state-owned enterprises to the extent that is needed. If you simply cured this one misconception stall, you could dramatically raise the standard of living of an entire country. South American countries such as Chile are showing the way and, for the most part, have been experiencing more rapid economic growth. China is now trying to follow suit.

Here in the United States, we scoff at state-owned monopoly and pride ourselves on not subscribing to it. But when you examine municipal government, you'll find that communities actually do operate "state-owned" enterprises. They usually run the fire department, the trash service, the police, and so forth. So you might think that state-owned monopoly must work just fine after all, even though the experiment in the USSR showed the contrary. But consider this: About a quarter of a century ago, an Arizona community began to outsource municipal services such as the fire department and sanitation to private companies. They were able to operate at lower costs than other towns of similar size, and soon other Arizona towns followed suit. But state-owned municipal enterprise is still the standard in this nation. This viewpoint is a major misconception stall. The sooner municipalities outsource to more effective operators, the better.

"We Use All the Most Up-to-Date Practices": Hardly!

When you have the opportunity to interview a number of people in the same industry, you use benchmarking to determine the best way of performing a particular activity. If you are supposed to make a certain number of widgets in an hour, you need to find out who actually makes the most widgets per hour. People almost always believe they already have the best practice in what they do, without even bothering to look around and find out. Random calls in the industry show that, typically, no one knows of all the best practices in their industry, even though these practices are readily obtainable through a variety of means.

Borrowing money, for example, is a visible activity with strategies on record. Borrowing details can be obtained from public offerings or from disclosures in annual reports. Yet, in fact, companies are typically aware of only 20 to 35 percent of the good ideas for borrowing used in their industry. And they use even fewer.

In other areas of management, performance is even worse.

Stallbusters

This section provides solutions to the misconception stall. You will learn how to identify important misconceptions and identify accurate assumptions for immediate use.

Unmask False Assumptions

A company had assumed that advertising would work only when demand was highest for its seasonal food, yet others promoted similarly seasonal products all year around. After many decades, an advertising test was run in the lean period, and sales promptly took off. Do not let false assumptions trap your organization in a misconception stall. Use your own answers to the following questions to expose the false assumptions keeping you from exponential growth:

What are the things that your organization or company assumes will almost always work? Coca-Cola's introduction of new Coke in the 1980s provides a good example for our consideration of misconceptions. Prior to the development and introduction of new Coke, Pepsi-Cola and Coca-Cola engaged in bruising market-share battles in U.S. supermarkets. The first important shot in these battles came in the 1970s when Pepsi-Cola launched the so-called "Pepsi Challenge." Throughout the country, Pepsi offered consumers a chance to taste Pepsi-Cola and

Coca-Cola in a blind taste test, withholding the identity of which was which product until after one sample was declared the better tasting. Large numbers of Coca-Cola drinkers were surprised to find that they preferred Pepsi-Cola. This attack helped lay the groundwork for New Coke. News reports at the time stated that Pepsi-Cola was preferred by people who wanted a product that was sweeter and had more carbonation. At some point in the protracted battles for consumer sales, Pepsi-Cola claimed victory in part of the campaign by saying that it had higher market share in U.S. supermarkets than Coca-Cola did. This announcement was undoubtedly threatening to the managers of a valuable brand franchise like Coca-Cola.

At some point Coca-Cola became interested in producing a new cola drink that Pepsi drinkers would prefer to Pepsi-Cola. In pursuing this opportunity, Coca-Cola assumed that market research to test the preferences for new products almost always works, particularly in taste-based competition. New Coke was thoroughly tested from this point of view. Coca-Cola was so sure that it had a winner that the company announced the retirement of the old Coca-Cola formula. You would not be able to get the old Coca-Cola anymore. A firestorm of protest arose, and soon Coca-Cola's new product was suffering large market-share losses. A few weeks later, Coca-Cola reversed itself and reintroduced its original formula as "Classic Coke." The furor soon died down, and Coca-Cola regained its market share. New Coke all but disappeared in a short amount of time.

Why was Coca-Cola's market research so wrong? According to industry observers, Coca-Cola actually made a miscalculation in its market research. As part of testing the New Coke, the company never mentioned that it might discontinue the Coca-Cola product that had been sold for decades. Consumers apparently assumed that they would be able to get either one. When they could not get the original formula, they felt they had lost something important. There was a strong sense of emotional loss of a tie to one's childhood and happy memories of the past. After all, Coca-Cola is a brand identity as well as a sweetened cola drink. Market research will almost always be right if what you test is actually what is going to happen in the marketplace. Coca-Cola appears to have skipped a step in this process, and that was what misled them about the reliability of their market research for forecasting what consumers would do.

Perhaps an easier way to understand the example is to imagine your feelings if the Walt Disney Company decided to replace Mickey and Minnie Mouse in all future cartoons and amusement parks with two really cute aardvarks named Sam and Sylvia. Doesn't quite seem the same, does it?

What are the things that your organization or company assumes will seldom or never work? The Coke–Pepsi example applies here, as well. Product comparisons are something that are as old as advertising. If your product is better or cheaper, making the comparison may help some consumers to decide to become regular users. In fact, Pepsi sold at half Coca-Cola's price during most of the 1930s and 1940s. In the cola soft-drink category, both Coca-Cola and Pepsi-Cola had avoided such taste-based comparisons for many years. Pepsi had assumed that price-based comparisons were the answer. Later, the Pepsi price was increased. Instead in the 1960s, Coca-Cola was teaching the world to sing and Pepsi-Cola was talking to a new generation. Using market research correctly, Pepsi-Cola accurately perceived that head-to-head taste comparisons would help its product. Had earlier generations of Pepsi-Cola executives tested this sooner (especially when the price was lower and Coca-Cola was ignoring Pepsi's moves), worldwide market share today might look quite different in the cola soft-drink business.

What are the things that your organization or company assumes will probably happen? Again, Pepsi-Cola provides an interesting example here. For many years, the parent company of Pepsi-Cola diversified into all sorts of other businesses including snack foods, a moving company, sporting goods, and restaurants. Although the company probably never said it, those actions gave the impression that opportunities were better outside of the cola soft-drink business. Perhaps the executives felt that they could never break Coca-Cola's very strong position in fountain accounts (typically restaurants, ballparks, and fast-food stands), and outside of the United States where Coca-Cola has and benefits from a wonderful bottling network that would be very hard to duplicate. Coca-Cola also did some diversifying but did it later than PepsiCo did and left the unrelated businesses sooner. Perhaps Coca-Cola was assuming that it would be hard to find a business with as much success and potential for the future as the soft-drink business.

What are the things that your organization or company assumes will be unlikely to or will never happen? Bottlers have usually been very loyal to one or the other of the two major competing companies. Imagine the sense of surprise in the 1990s when Coca-Cola signed up one of Pepsi-Cola's largest bottlers (ousting Pepsi-Cola) in one South American country. Other than filing a lawsuit, there was little that Pepsi-Cola could do. The bottler wanted to be with Coca-Cola. If Pepsi-Cola had been more vigilant in not assuming that bottlers would be unlikely to defect, perhaps instead it would have captured many Coca-Cola bottlers for itself.

On what beliefs are these assumptions based? We cannot know for sure in the cola soft-drink example, but the pattern here suggests that the false assumptions could have been based on the fact that the bottler loyalty problems had not occurred in the past. Generally, the world offers enough challenges that people in organizations will not feel much need to go out and look for problems that may never arise. That approach can be dangerous, however. Not only may those assumptions veil vulnerabilities that your organization has, the assumptions may also veil your best opportunities to pursue vulnerabilities that competitors have.

Have those beliefs been checked recently? This is a wonderful question because many assume that checking something once is enough, another misconception stall. Circumstances change, and something that was true a generation ago may be totally different today. Consider tastes in fashion. What is desirable in one period can be viewed as totally awful in another. Although we do not know for sure about the soft-drink industry, the actions and inactions make it appear that many areas had not been checked in a while.

Are those beliefs still true? Only a careful and thoughtful piece of market research can tell for sure. One fallout of Coca-Cola's problems with the New Coke is that the company's management is going to have a much harder time changing its cola formula in the future, despite the fact that there is reason to believe that the Classic Coca-Cola formula could be improved upon. What do you do if you are the new CEO? The time has probably come to check these areas again. Perhaps Coca-Cola has already done so in a quiet way and is satisfied with the answers. Perhaps not.

On the other hand, Pepsi-Cola might have a very interesting opportunity to do the two-cola strategy. On the other hand, perhaps not. Testing is the answer.

Identify the False Assumptions That Need to Be Changed Immediately

Some misconceptions require more immediate correction than others. This section helps you set priorities for where to turn your attention first.

Which of the false assumptions that you have exposed have large-potential consequences? So far, each assumption we have tested in the cola soft-drink industry has large-potential consequences. This is because the industry is so large and profitable, and because each company has a nimble competitor constantly seeking to find an edge. In this industry, assumption testing should be virtually endless. In your activities, fewer assumptions may have large-potential consequences. Quantification of the consequences helps.

Which large-potential false assumptions are in areas where your organization's actions can improve or make your situation worse? The answer seems to be in almost all areas for this industry. From product characteristics to new product development to marketing to distribution, and anywhere else the company spends its time and money, nearly all areas of these organizations are affected by large-potential false assumptions. This pervasiveness makes the management challenge of addressing assumptions even more interesting because the company that becomes better at identifying the 2,000 percent solutions to false assumptions is likely to be the long-term market leader in its product category.

When would you need to act to get most of the benefit or avoid most of the harm? Clearly, the answer has to be the sooner the better. Neither side in the cola market can assume that the other one is missing a key area.

What is the minimum evidence that would tell you that you should act immediately? You might think that the only evidence that is needed is likelihood of a positive market response. That could be a little misleading, however. Each company also has to consider how its competitors would respond. If Pepsi-Cola began taking large Coca-Cola bottlers, would Coca-Cola's retaliation by taking more Pepsi-Cola bottlers prove to be decisive? The combination of acceptable market and competitive response is the minimum evidence in this example.

Use Assumptions That Reflect Actual and Likely Conditions

In many cases, no one will ever know what is going to happen. Choosing assumptions that will prepare you better for the uncertainty can be very helpful. If you limit your assumptions only to reflect current, actual conditions, you will be very vulnerable to changed circumstances. With more volatile environments and more alert competitors, variation *is* the norm now.

What assumptions have worked best in the past for companies and organizations that operated in circumstances like yours? If you are Coca-Cola, you should examine category leaders in worldwide branded products with aggressive competitors for valuable assumptions. If you are Pepsi-Cola, you should do the same, focusing on companies that were number two in market share and that became number one with high profitability worldwide.

Gillette could be a valuable model here. Gillette always operated on an assumption in its international shaving business that it should make its products available to as many people as possible at the lowest possible price. Then, as people in that area of the world became more affluent, they could afford to buy more from Gillette. By arriving early, Gillette not only had a better brand position but made it far more costly for a competitor to follow, especially where distribution was very fragmented and difficult. Recently Gillette has moved to standardize its shaving products more around the world. Coca-Cola, by contrast, provides a mind-boggling variety of soft drinks that vary from country to country. Perhaps Gillette's assumption about how to compete globally contains one or more lessons for Coca-Cola.

Which of these assumptions fit your company's or organization's values and style? Modern consumer-goods companies are more similar than different in many ways. Many share executives were trained at the same schools and companies (e.g., Harvard Business School and Procter & Gamble). Each company is subject to similar sorts of regulatory and governmental scrutiny. Distribution channels are often similar. Potentially, any idea could be adapted from any company.

In reality, each organization has very different values and style. Popular press reports suggest that Pepsi-Cola has historically been more likely to be an attacker. Coca-Cola, until the South American bottler switch, was more often a thoughtful defender. Coca-Cola likes to work on its overall image, while Pepsi-Cola is willing to create an image tied more narrowly to a segment of the population (especially when Michael Jackson was featured in the company's advertising). Both companies have historically moved more slowly to improve bottling operations outside of their companies than would have been desirable. This seems to suggest a reluctance to push hard in this area.

Following the death of Roberto Goizueta, Coca-Cola appointed a new CEO. The new man is reported to be much more aggressive. Pepsi-Cola should reconsider its assumptions about Coca-Cola's values and style. Coca-Cola may act differently now.

Which of these assumptions would be received enthusiastically by customers, employees, suppliers, shareholders, and the communities you serve? If either company were to become more aggressive in simultaneously improving product taste, strengthening worldwide bottling operations, and finding ways to knock its competitor off-stride, the response would be overwhelming from these communities, unless financial viability (in the form of survival) were to come into question. Coca-Cola probably does not have that survival risk, but Pepsi-Cola might. Dropping the assumption that each company will go for steady, rapid growth in earnings per share would make quite a dent in the competitive marketplace. Perhaps each company should test its investors' preferences for steady earnings growth versus a few years of depressed results followed by an enormous improvement above the current trend line. That could be the controlling assumption in this marketplace for the long run.

Ugliness can be our first perception of something or someone beautiful, and beauty can be our first perception of someone or something ugly. Ugliness causes us to avert our eyes, while beauty draws our attention. Stallbusting is helped by seeing beauty in more of the situations we encounter. What beautiful images do you see in this picture? (Hint: Imagine that you are snorkeling in a Caribbean lagoon on a sunny day as one place to start.)

Chapter 5

Ugly Ducklings
The Unattractiveness Stall

"Are you Isabel?"
"Are you Rodney?"
"Yes, I'm Rodney!"
"Well, I'm not Isabel!"
—Rodney Dangerfield meets a blind date

Our senses are finely tuned to react positively to what we like and are accustomed to and to react negatively to anything that looks, smells, tastes, feels, or sounds different. The reactions based on these senses can be so strong that we never consciously evaluate the pros and cons of what is being experienced. In an increasingly complex world, organizations run the danger of overlooking great opportunities right under their noses and in front of their eyes because the opportunities do not fit the conventional ideal. By reversing the usual approach, you can reap great rewards by investigating the potential of what repels you and what you reject without adequate consideration.

First Impressions Can Be Deceiving

Most people can identify situations in their lives in which they dismissed an opportunity that someone else capitalized on later. Often, these opportunities were overlooked or rejected because they were perceived as dull, boring, or unpleasant. You may recall the tale of *The Ugly Duckling*. It is the story of a cast-off baby bird that is mistreated because it is unattractive to the young ducklings raised with it. Much to everyone's surprise, the duckling matures to become a beautiful swan. Thus, what we call the unattractiveness stall prevents people from seeing the potential that is often right under their noses because they possess preconceived judgments based on insufficient knowledge.

Taking an example from farming, kernels of corn can become infected with fungi and turn smutty: The kernels grow as large as your thumb to the first joint, are black or grayish white, and are as soft and squishy as an overripe banana. Farmers dread grabbing smutty ears while they are husking corn. Smut is so disgusting it has even given its name to pornography. On the other hand, gourmet cooks will pay a premium for smutty ears of corn. They make smut into gustatory delights in puddings and pies. The discerning chef is busting an unattractiveness stall.

It is worth remembering that if Alexander Fleming had been unwilling to work with the unpleasant green mold that affects stale bread and many other foods, the world might not have the wonder drug, penicillin. It is equally instructive to note that Fleming had so many false starts in his early experiments that his fellow British scientists ridiculed him. But he persevered. Few of his critics earned half the honors Fleming was to garner. He won the Nobel Prize for penicillin. And his former detractors found themselves calling him Sir Alexander after he was knighted by his queen.

But how do you feel about pond scum? Maybe you should look beneath its surface appearance. The nutritional supplement, blue-green algae, is freeze-dried from a particular type of freshwater algae that many would perceive as pond scum. New medical research shows that this natural whole food stimulates the body's immune system to resist disease more than any other food or drug ever tested. Also, mental processes and nervous system functioning substantially improved in the latest medical tests. Many more medical trials are underway, because other health benefits are likely. You also absorb more vitamins and minerals than from any other food you can eat in comparable quantities. Improving your health by eating better can be a 2,000 percent solution and make it easier for you to locate other 2,000 percent solutions.

Doctor Edna Aphek of Tel-Hi Networks, Ltd., in Jerusalem, also thinks people should be trained to consider possible uses for things that are viewed as bad or dirty, like mold and mildew or even unexpected results. She notes that in research projects, unexpected things happen.

Even to a scientist, the unexpected can seem ugly at first glance. You can foster creativity by studying the unattractive for hidden usefulness.

Don't Take My Picture, I'll Break the Camera

The Taj Mahal

All too frequently, management becomes engrossed in creating posh office space. Securities analysts consider it a bad sign when executives build lavish corporate offices that are remote from the operations. Corporate castles waste precious capital. They also waste precious management time. Having feathered their nests, executives avoid the ugly duckling sites that need attention. A serious mistake.

For example, the distribution system is often considered an ugly duckling in the eyes of pampered executives who would rather focus on alluring new products than fret about trucking schedules and inventory control. Yet time spent refining the system of trucking, shipping, and warehouses can be golden. Wal-Mart struck gold by focusing on fast deliveries through warehouses serving constellations of stores. With cross-docking, goods are continuously delivered to Wal-Mart facilities to be repacked and dispatched to stores in forty-eight hours or less, often without ever sitting in inventory. As a result, Wal-Mart can reduce prices and attract more value-seeking customers.

The Ivory Tower

Executives dislike having to deal with customer complaints. In fact, very few top-level executives will talk directly with customers. CEOs like to send complaints to the employee in a position to resolve the matter. Sounds reasonable. But a few CEOs who do talk directly with disgruntled customers say doing so is one of their most valuable ways of staying on top of things.

And since most CEOs avoid customer gripes, is it any wonder that company employees dread bringing their CEOs bad news? No one wants to approach the ivory tower with disturbing information. You will recall that in ancient times, the bearer of bad tidings often paid with his life. So workers often sugarcoat the news or badly conceal it. Stallbusters thrive by reporting bad news along with positive ways of dealing with it.

Stall Erasers

Ugly Is in the Eye of the Beholder

One innovative CEO ran a successful restaurant business. He would start his daily tour in the least attractive location: at the dumpster in the back of each unit. He knew that the content of the trash was a key barometer of the restaurant's health. Decaying raw food suggested that the manager was overordering. Occasionally he actually found carefully wrapped, fresh prime steaks. He knew that game plan all too well. A dishonest employee would stash them there for recovery after dark to be taken home or resold for cash. By facing unpleasant aspects of his business, this CEO obtained useful information that could not be found anywhere else.

Floored

You need a different mind-set to think of packaged materials as two valuable items: the goods and the container they come in. The container is the ugly duckling, something that serves its purpose and is thrown in the trash, right? Whoa! Crafty Henry Ford dealt from a position of strength in his negotiations with the battery producer for his Model-A automobile (Exhibit 5-1). He was the almighty to suppliers dependent on his business for their success. So Ford could dictate tight specifications for the wooden boxes in which the supplier shipped the batteries. After Ford's assembly-line worker carefully removed the screws holding the box together and lowered the battery onto a shelf under the steering wheel, he then fitted the pieces of the battery box over the battery and screwed them down. Ford got floorboards, too!

Once you know what you are looking for, the ugly ducklings offer some of the easiest opportunities to identify and exploit. The crucial task is seeing past the negative to discover the positive. This means forsaking conventional thinking.

Exhibit 5-1   Ford, Model-A.
Corbis-Bettmann. Reproduced with permission.

Stallbusters

Distinguishing between an unattractiveness stall and something that is just plain ugly may not be easy, but looking for the buried treasure can turn up a 2,000 percent solution for you. We are going to take an in-depth look at a company that not only finds its own ugly ducklings and turns them into swans but has also made a successful business of doing this for others. You can do the same. In fact, you should.

Find Ugly Ducklings

The easiest way to find out if your company is experiencing its own unattractiveness stall is to seek out the least pleasant sites in your company.

Where are the places that executives and managers seldom visit? Here's a tip: The ugliest, dirtiest, least appealing parts of any business are the places where goods and services are produced for customers. Such facilities usually include manufacturing plants, distribution centers, customer warehouses, and local service centers. It is the rare executive who will take the time to visit these places to seek ways to improve production or service. Executives and managers are more likely to hold meetings with employees in the cafeteria. Or they speak with workers remotely by teleconference from their office sanctuaries.

An interesting example of finding ugly ducklings can be observed in the Servicemaster Company, which provides a variety of mundane services typically required in unattractive locations, such as janitorial services and plumbing repairs. Chairman C. W. Pollard seeks out unattractive sites and even arranges to spend time while traveling to observe other janitorial services around the world. The company now does over $4 billion in annual revenues in such activities, which proves that looking where others do not for opportunity can be a big growth area.

What can be learned by visiting those unattractive places? Servicemaster executives and salespeople often find that the employees in those locations are poorly trained, do not have the right kind of equipment, and see themselves in dead-end jobs. A visit may also find facilities that are dirty, dangerous, and below standard in a variety of ways because of weak janitorial services.

Reports about such unvisited areas may come as a surprise to the organization's executives. The response may be that janitorial services are already outsourced. But how well are the costs and effectiveness of those services monitored? It is not unusual for a national contract to provide these services from Servicemaster at a fraction of the cost of using local providers, some of whom may be providing kickbacks to the employees who hired them.

Which potential customers are perpetually shunned? For Servicemaster, the answer would be "almost no one." The company is very interested in developing human potential, wherever that may be. In fact, the worse the mess, the bigger the opportunity for Servicemaster to make a difference. For that reason, the company especially likes to work in hospitals and other health care locations where cleanliness can make a large difference in people's lives.

Which kinds of potential employees are never hired? Servicemaster has learned that almost anyone can become an effective employee when properly trained, managed, and supported. By comparison, most companies have a very long list of the kinds of employees who are never hired.

Which suppliers are avoided? Servicemaster makes it a company policy to operate in a manner that matches the highest possible personal ethics and morality. An unethical or unreliable supplier would not do well with Servicemaster. That restriction is probably one that Servicemaster's customers heartily endorse.

What services are avoided? To date, Servicemaster has restricted itself to a few types of services. One reason for this is that until recently, the company was a master limited partnership. As a limited partnership, it was difficult for Servicemaster to raise capital for expansion into new fields and make acquisitions using equity funds (the company did not have a common stock until 1998). With the availability of common stock for acquisitions, stock issues to pay down excessive debt left over from the master limited partnership, Servicemaster seems to be focusing much more now on new types of services where its expertise can pay off.

Turn Your Ugly Ducklings Into Swans

How can you learn more about these areas in an open-minded way? Servicemaster usually does this by having an on-site visit by one of the company's most experienced people in that service area. The company has also developed a series of objective ways to measure the quality of what is going on at the site, whether the work is being done by your company, another vendor, or Servicemaster personnel.

Who already sees these ugly ducklings as swans? Why? Those in Servicemaster who would see the opportunities are those familiar with that activity (whether it be janitorial, plumbing, pest control, or disaster recovery). Servicemaster has probably missed a number of opportunities where the company could learn to perform well. For example, many manufacturing facilities have more maintenance people than factory workers. Maintenance is often a problem area, much like janitorial, plumbing, and pest control.

A sign of this problem is that each division in Servicemaster used to compete for its own accounts, using its own salespeople and data. Recently, the company realized that by combining telemarketing activities, sales could be made for more of the company's services at lower costs. This will also probably expand the awareness of the need to solve other problems faced by plant managers, school managers, and hospital and nursing home administrators.

How could each of these ugly ducklings be one of your best opportunities? As Servicemaster becomes more customer-oriented, the company will inevitably try to add new types of customers. To the extent that these customers (such as malls and suburban office parks) have different needs, we should expect that Servicemaster will begin to realize that diversifying its customer types is a key ingredient to capturing new ways to grow successfully. Any one of these new customer types could cause the company to grow rapidly and profitably in a whole new direction.

Who could help you to better see, hear, and feel these opportunities? Senior management of Servicemaster would do well to spend a substantial portion of its time visiting new types of potential customers, observing what their problems are, what types of solutions are working and which are not, and identifying factors that will allow one company to be more successful in serving these needs than another company.

This approach should be dovetailed into a corporate strategy activity to determine what capabilities the company must have to serve the needs of new types of customers. For example, Servicemaster may have a great opportunity to become a one-stop shop for services that people need at home. The company already provides some lawn care and pest control services. Wouldn't it be nice to have a company you can rely on to do all of the simple maintenance around your house at a reasonable cost, the kind of service that condominium owners usually receive from their condominium management company?

How could you easily and inexpensively test out ideas related to the worth of these areas? Since Servicemaster is a large, successful company, it could decide to make local acquisitions in markets where it wants to test expanded services and expanded service concepts. If the tests fail, the businesses could probably be resold to local entrepreneurs who want to be in a narrow-line service business. If the acquisitions were made near the end of a recession, the businesses might even be sold later at a profit when business conditions improved, should the company decide to exit its local test.

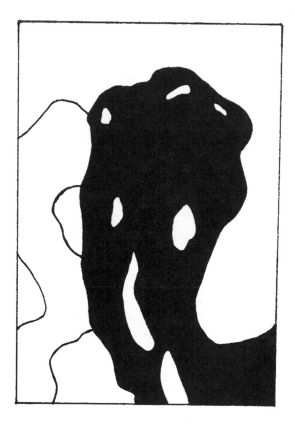

Part of seeing what is happening is also to listen and speak. Many people report that they can hear sounds when they look at Jackson Pollock's drip paintings from the 1950s. What do you hear when you look at this image? Now imagine that there are two people in the image trying to communicate with each other. What are they saying? How could they communicate better?

Chapter 6

Words Fail Me
The Communications Stall

When someone in your organization correctly perceives a high-value opportunity, to capture the benefit that knowledge must be effectively communicated to those who can act. So that you can create truly effective and rapid sharing of critical information and knowledge, this chapter shows you how to overcome the harmful assumption that information or knowledge is perfectly received every time someone in your organization tries to share it.

Film director Cecil B. DeMille spared no expense to part the Red Sea for his epic *The Ten Commandments*. Actors, engineers, horses, and assorted other animals were everywhere. The dust, heat, and noise were ferocious. Finally, everyone was ready to go and DeMille called out, "Roll the cameras." After he finished shooting the scene, DeMille called to a cameraman on a high cliff to check on how that part of the shooting had gone. The cameraman reportedly yelled back, "Ready when you are, C. B.!"

What was the boggle here? What was DeMille's stall? He thought that everyone heard and understood his message whenever he spoke. But in this case, he never checked to see if the camera on the cliff was rolling before starting the scene. The solution: Check first to see if your message is received and understood before going into action. Ask people what they have heard and what they plan to do, and then keep repeating the same message in different ways to reinforce your point.

This story delivers an important lesson: In business, we have to be sure that we all get the message—and at the right time—in order to get the results we want. Too many times messages are either not sent, not received, incorrectly understood, or not acted on in time—as happened with DeMille and his cameraman.

The da Vinci Communications Stall That
Delayed History for Three Centuries

Imagine that you are Leonardo da Vinci's employer back in the fifteenth or sixteenth century. Da Vinci is one of the greatest geniuses of all time, but you have hired him to design your city's fortifications. In his spare time, he is busy designing other things that he does not share with anyone. Da Vinci put drawings of many inventions in his trunk, then turned his attention to the more immediately profitable projects preferred by his employers. In fact, Leonardo was to spend most of his life manually recording his secrets in a novel manner that required a mirror to render the text intelligible. Buried in da Vinci's notes was a remarkably viable design for a bicycle. We did not get actual bicycles on the roads and paths for another three centuries, not until 1839, when a blacksmith introduced pedaled bicycles in Britain.

If only the design of Leonardo's bicycle had been communicated, not stalled, recorded history might have had a faster ride into the future. Increased travel might well have vastly improved commerce and communication. People didn't travel much then. Large numbers no doubt lived their lives without ever seeing the next village. Back then, the Catholic Church was the font of literacy. Catholic monks laboriously recorded Bible text by hand. The priests passed Scripture to the illiterate by word of mouth.

Had they bikes, the monks might have ridden over the footpaths between the parishes with some frequency.

Monks had families and friends among the laity. It is not farfetched to think they might have begun carrying notes between friends and businesses. The demand for literacy could have found its way sooner into the community at large. As growing numbers of people learned to read and write, they would look for easier ways to put ideas in print. The printing press might have become popular sooner to meet the demand. (Also buried in his trunk was a printing press modeled after Gutenberg's that could be operated by one man. Gutenberg's press required two printers to roll the presses.) Progress on the march. As a post office developed, commerce might have bloomed earlier. The powers-that-were might have used cheap labor to build better roads.

Da Vinci fell prey to the communications stall. He normally decided to communicate little about his ideas, and only selectively at that. He may have assumed his employers would only be interested in one or two of his capabilities and stopped communicating about the rest, or he may have feared his ideas would displease the church and lead to excommunication. His employers, in turn, were held back by the misconception stall that Leonardo could only help them in the areas they had already talked about. They never found out about what was in those notebooks.

More typically, communications stalls occur as we try to express ourselves but fail to do so. We hear the words but don't get the message; or we get a message, but it's not the message the sender meant to convey. Remember the childhood game of telephone or whisper down the lane? Kids sit in a circle or a row, and one child whispers a story in the ear of the next one. This is repeated until the story makes the full circuit. The last child tells the story out loud to disbelieving ears because the final version is completely different from the original tale. "The red rooster crowed" might become "The red head drove a wrecked roadster."

Similar mutations occur with facts, expectations, and directives in the business world. As company policy is set forth and circulated throughout the company, by whatever method, the end result is often far from the original intent. This muddying of the message is somewhat understandable when a new policy is passed on by word of mouth, less so when the new program is committed to writing. Regardless, due to the limits of training and the ability to express thoughts clearly, many a written memo (or e-mail) is nearly as likely to be misinterpreted as a verbal policy directive.

Just the Facts, Ma'am

Seeing Is Believing

In the 1980s, there was a U.S. manufacturer that was widely considered to be a top producer of roofing materials. It was prohibitively costly to ship these heavy commodity products very far, so foreign manufacturers were willing to share information with those outside their home market. The division president often visited noncompeting plants in distant locales to get ideas—to see if others in the trade knew something he did not know about manufacturing.

He knew that Japanese companies were good manufacturers, so he flew to the Orient to see how they produced materials similar to his. As it turned out, the Japanese were using the very same equipment he was, but he discovered something amazing. He used thirty people to run each line. His Japanese counterpart used only eight. He returned home elated. He was dazzled by the potential impact on profits and on the company's growth prospects if eight people could do as much as thirty. He was totally open about his plans, communicating them fully to his aides.

But when he told his manufacturing chief the story, the man said, "Baloney!" So the division president went to Japan with the doubter and showed him the lightly manned production lines. The manufacturing chief became equally excited: "You are right!" he said. "You *can* run the line with just eight people." The two came back and told the company's plant managers the story. They said, "No, no, you don't understand what we are doing here. What you say is impossible."

Back to Japan again. This time it was the plant managers who were floored. They said, "You know, you are right! But the guys in the plant won't believe it. Let's create a videotape so the shift supervisors can see that the system works."

The tape was made, and the shift supervisors were corralled and shown the video. "Nonsense," they said. "It can't possibly be. Someone doctored the tape."

The division president said, "We'll go to Japan one more time. But this time, I'm going to ask the Japanese to let us operate their factory for two weeks. We'll man production line jobs and see what happens." Back to Japan. The supervisors worked on the line for two weeks. Then and only then was the division president able to make the change to eight-person lines. In this case, seeing and doing was believing. No amount of *talk* could get the message accepted.

No News Is Not Good News

Some managers are ingenious at conveying a message. Others make no attempt to pass on important ideas and information. There is a difference between failing to communicate effectively and a total lack of communication. Employees do not react well when they receive a poorly conveyed message, but they become far more angry when they feel management does not care enough to even try. When people feel they are being purposely ignored, morale is severely damaged. We all tend to communicate most with the people we like. Thus, when employees perceive that their managers are making little, if any, attempt to communicate, they leap to the understandable conclusion that this is because the managers do not care about them.

Other executives take the high road and wind up at a dead end. These jovial executives are so eager to be liked, they set about to build positive relationships with employees by avoiding conflict. Solving problems is unpleasant and emotionally trying. So they avoid talking about them altogether. Critical problems go unaddressed and the business suffers. In reality, employees react better to effective problem solvers than to bosses who seem to be avoiding conflicts by not addressing them.

Stall Erasers

Overcoming Hostility and Establishing Relationships

The conductor asked, "Where's your ticket?"
I said, "My face is my ticket."
So he punched it.

—Anonymous

Sometimes hostility and competitiveness induce a communications stall. For example, when people negotiate, they tend to be wary and competitive. Professors Roger Fisher and William Ury in *Getting to Yes* (Houghton-Mifflin 1981) find ways to neutralize these negative influences by asking both sides to try to understand what the other person needs to accomplish. When each knows what the other wants, there is more chance of arriving at a solution satisfactory to both, the proverbial win–win solution.

A classic example of competitiveness stalling a team effort occurred at a recent leadership conference. The attendees had been divided into groups and were asked to brainstorm on the same set of difficult questions. The room was full of successful executives accustomed not only to winning but to being the focus of any team effort. Soon everyone was interrupting, shouting, and saying dumb things. One team finally broke the negative barrier by deciding to set ground rules. The most important rule was a decision to "get acquainted." The group members quickly discovered each other's fields of business and specific expertise. Then they turned to the questions. Their initial disagreements dissolved as each expert was allowed to speak in turn. Their ideas and views were then posted on a blackboard. Each executive then felt that his experience was being respected and heard. The team finished quickly and successfully. When time was called, the other teams were still at loggerheads. The lesson here is that you are unlikely to find solutions among high achievers in a group unless you first establish a positive environment for communication.

Establishing a relationship fosters communication even across cultural gaps. A correspondent on National Public Radio argued that the French are not impolite as so many Americans believe but instead are misunderstood. In many cases in fact, Americans come off as rude to the French. All too often, they will walk up to a French person and start speaking in English. If you approach a French person for help, start by saying, "J'ai une problème" (I have a problem). The NPR correspondent said the French love a challenge. This will manifest itself in a polite attempt to solve "une problème." Frigidity will melt as it did in his taped encounters using this approach.

Stallbusters

The most successful managers describe how they can never communicate enough, often enough, or in enough ways. Focus on ways to do this easily, effectively, and efficiently, and you'll soon discover 2,000 percent solutions busting out all over.

Build on Success

Using sources such as the results of employee surveys and individual feedback you have received, select a few examples where communications have worked much better for your organization than usual.

Why do you think that these communications were more success-ful? One company found that it could greatly improve communications by employing a multipart communications strategy. The first part was to focus significant communications around ways that employees could get promotions, raises, and larger bonuses. Employees liked communications that helped them be more successful and were interested in what was said in such communications. The second part was to provide a videocassette recorder in each work location throughout the company so that all employees could receive information and any required training on the spot. Typically, a cassette would be reviewed just before the regular shift started. Then the employees had the chance to use the new information on that shift. The third part was to have a local manager provide immediate feedback on how each employee was doing with the new information. This meant that during the shift after the new information was received, the manager was there to answer questions, demonstrate in person the proper methods, and correct errors as they occurred during the shift.

Another well-known company with a fine reputation for service quality employs a different approach to communicating with employees about what they should be doing. The company starts by selecting employees based on their interest in providing the services the company is selling. Then the company puts the employee through a rigorous training program, starting with two weeks on the company's values and culture. One-third of all new hires drop out or are fired during these two weeks because the fit between employee and company is, in fact, poor. The successful employee is then trained on the job, using a combination of very thorough manuals (often 150 pages long for jobs that competitors train their employees to do in five minutes), for at least six months before the employee is allowed to work unsupervised for even a few minutes. What do you think the average duration of employment is in this operation? You guessed it, only six months. But those who stay do a terrific job of watching out for those who will not stay so that they also do a terrific job. The cost of the extra training is more than covered by the increased sales the company enjoys at premium prices.

What these two examples have in common is that a lot of communicating takes place, the communications are obviously relevant to all involved, and the information is conveyed when and where it will do the most good.

How can those lessons be carried over for other communications? Consider the contrast between the examples and the way many organizations routinely communicate. A standard internal communications approach is to have the CEO make a speech, report on the speech in the employee newsletter, send out a memo, post the memo on the bulletin boards, and then drop the subject. A more advanced communicating organization might also replay a video of the CEO's speech throughout the working areas for a day or two.

Obviously, not all employee communications deserve the amount of attention that the companies mentioned previously use. If the communication is valuable, it is worth communicating in the most effective way. If the communication is not very important, perhaps it should not be made. A large number of items can be covered during the type of question-and-answer sessions that many company leaders hold as they visit various sites in the company. Those questions can also be reviewed for patterns from session to session in order to see where employees want more communication.

Another alternative is to use prerecorded hot lines on various subjects. Those who want to know can then update themselves conveniently. Often the same toll-free communications lines can be used with the same messages for employees, investors, and customers.

If not overused, e-mail can make quite a large difference for routine information. People can indicate what they would like to be kept posted on. Discussion and working groups can be formed for those with interests in certain areas. In fact, some intranets have virtual offices with virtual water coolers where employees can share information with each other, based on mutual needs and interests.

How can the same results be achieved more easily and efficiently in the future? Whatever communication method you use, be sure to measure how well it works so you can see if you need to switch to something more effective next time. A great way to do that is to spot-check what message people have received. If the method is not working as well as you would like, talk to people to find out what went wrong. Then you have a choice between reworking that type of communication to make it better and shifting to another method that works better already with less effort. Whatever your decision is, keep checking on what is working and what is not so that you can run experiments to get better results with less effort.

What was missing from the effectiveness of problematic communications? So far, the discussion has been about getting or not getting the message. Another issue is how motivated employees feel to act on what has been said. Typically, even when a message is received and understood, little action follows. The natural tendency is to go back to what people have been doing unless the message is continually reinforced by a personal commitment that the employee feels. Be sure to consider two other factors that influence motivation: the strength of the emotional appeal of the message and the clarity of telling the employee exactly what you want him or her to do.

Focus on Effectiveness: Results Are Where the Rubber Meets the Road

Who is or was the most effective communicator you have ever heard? Many CEOs will mention either President Reagan or President Clinton. The CEOs observe that each man used simple words in simple sentences to make a few simple points. Compare this approach to the typical communications you send your employees. Many organizations find that their communications have all the clarity, appeal, and immediacy of the latest academic how-to book on some esoteric subject.

Why were they effective? Effectiveness is always to be measured by the person receiving the message. You and another person may draw totally different conclusions about the effectiveness of certain communications. For example, many people who have talked with President Clinton in person report being very impressed by the way he totally focuses on the person he is talking to at that time. The listener feels compelled to pay just as much attention as the speaker is giving.

Students of the subject also point out that each person has different ways he or she likes to receive information, so the best messages are those that communicate in a variety of ways. The more that each person sees, hears, touches, and feels what is going on, the more likely the communication will strike home and create a reaction and subsequent action.

What aspects of that effectiveness can you capture for your organization's communications? Many people would be terrified at the thought of having to be a great communicator like someone whom they personally admire. The idea is not to become a great public speaker;

rather the idea is to capture elements of what works in formats that you can execute well. Training, study, and practice can make a large difference. These questions are intended to facilitate creating understanding to help you decide what training, study, and practice would be most helpful to you and your organization.

Communications Tips

Here is a list of items to consider as key elements for effective communications:

* Reduce the number of messages.
* Simplify the messages.
* Provide powerful experiences along with the messages (like the trip to Japan in the example in this chapter).
* Establish many more regular channels and patterns of communications.
* Get more feedback on how well the message is being understood.
* Increase the frequency of repeating communications.
* Compress the frequency into shorter periods of time.
* Vary the delivery by using different formats.
* Add indications of the area's significance to underscore your message (yelling "Fire" in a crowded theater in the presence of fire and smoke will quickly empty the room).
* Change the behavior of leaders to provide a more consistent message so that the deeds match the words.
* Adjust rewards and other feedback systems to emphasize the message.
* Have more people be messengers (ideally everyone in the organization spends some time communicating—both talking and listening—to everyone else to help reinforce the message).

Chapter 7

Molasses in the Works
The Bureaucratic Stall

"How many bureaucrats does it take to change a lightbulb?"
"We'll get back to you on that."

Work processes that unnecessarily involve many people will cause your organization and its stakeholders to suffer from delays, misunderstandings, high costs, and minimal effectiveness. Organizations need to eliminate the bulk of these work processes and then simplify what remains. A primary advantage of making this change is to free time and resources to attend to more important and valuable tasks.

Like Running a Marathon Wearing Combat Boots: Bureaucracy—Officialism, Red Tape, and Proliferation

Organizations usually see themselves as smoothly coordinated operations, even when they are not. A baseball analogy can help us to understand what effective joint participation looks like. Early in this century, the Chicago Cubs team members Joe Tinkers, Johnny Evers, and Frank Chance were baseball's most celebrated double-play combination. Joe Tinkers would scoop up the ball at shortstop and wing it to Evers at second. Evers would touch second or tag the runner sliding toward him, then snap the ball to Chance at first, who caught it before the hitter could touch the base. The line "DP Tinkers/Evers/Chance" appeared on box scores of the day so often that "Tinkers to Evers to Chance" became part of the American folk idiom.

I Like Company

Most companies start in a Tinkers to Evers to Chance mode. But all too often bureaucracy sets in and the ball gets hung up. Bureaucracy reflects excessive job creation. The stall occurs when more people than are needed are assigned to do the work. Once a bureaucracy is established, job security motivates the bureaucrats to try to propagate the system. It is common sense to use the least number of people needed to perform each activity. High people counts slow things down. By analogy, in a relay race, the more times the baton is passed, the more likely it will be dropped and so thwart a victory.

But there are forces at work that encourage ever larger staffs. Notably, the top executive of a large company is usually paid more than the top guy at a smaller one. This message is not lost on executives elsewhere in the pecking order. The more "report to"s an executive has, the better he or she is paid. So executives overhire.

For several decades, compensation systems have been based on peer-group company comparisons. There is a great deal of checking going on to see what peers of similar-size firms pay their executives. The CEO's board (or the board's trusted aides) checks the range and decides where it wants to fall in that range. Unfortunately, this compensation approach creates a bias toward bigger organizations: layering, if you will. Layering helps kids survive zero weather, but it can freeze an organization solid. It is not uncommon to create more than a dozen layers between the CEO and the lowest-level troops. The batons fall left and right, and 2,000 percent solutions are lost with each drop.

Fiddling With Roman Bureaucracy

Bureaucracies often coexist with wonderful innovation, which helps to offset their weaknesses. Some then confuse the bureaucracy with the cause of the success rather than the parking brake on that success. Consider the Romans, who managed to combine a terrible bureaucracy with road-building skills that we are only learning to match at the end of the twentieth century. Much more attention was focused on the bureaucracy than on the roads that were largely responsible for the military and commercial success that allowed Rome to pay for its inefficient administration.

As Roman legions spread out from Rome defeating all rivals, Rome installed more and more administrators, eventually creating the worst bureaucracy the world had ever seen. Communication ran like molasses, if at all. But at the same time, the Via Domitia, designed and built by the Caesars circa the first century, effectively bore traffic from France—"Gaul"—to Rome. For its time, this was an extraordinary engineering feat. And the Romans, for their part, believed in building roads to last. The roadbed of the Appian Way, for example, was several feet deep. The Romans discovered that a mix of volcanic ash with cement produced a sturdy road-building material that was to last for centuries. This technique was not rediscovered until recently when fly ash from flues was employed the way volcanic ash was in Roman times.

The Via Domitia was a marvel. Residents along its right-of-way watched as civilization passed by in fair weather and foul. Still, this marvel did not cut the time needed to deliver a letter from London to Rome from Christ's birth until railroads arrived in the nineteenth century. Imagine how long it took to get permission to, say, spend money. Assume a response comes back but is unclear. Back by chariot for clarification. How many subadministrators along the way are consulted? Jove only knows. No one would make a move without permission because Roman tyrants were known to chop off the head of any bureaucrat who made a mistake. In time, Rome was not competing well with other civilized peoples operating in parts of the Roman Empire.

While Rome helped invent numbing bureaucracy, bureaucracy lives on both in business and in government. It is well known that the bigger the percentage of gross domestic product (GDP) the government spends, the slower the economy grows and vice versa; that is, the less government takes of the GDP, the faster the economy grows. It is also well known that the economically advanced nations do little to reduce the size of government spending, even though to do so would be valuable for citizens they serve.

Hands Off!

That's *My* Job

At a wholesale drug company in Cleveland years ago, a law student was hired to help two order clerks, Betty and Billie, process sales orders. The orders arrived constantly for most of the day. First, Betty would begin filling in blanks for each order, following a checklist that included stamping a date on the order, putting an "X" in a box to indicate the type of sale—cash or credit—and doing a dozen other checkoff notations. Her chore completed, Betty put the order in Billie's pile. Billie was responsible for another dozen similar checklist steps. Betty was always behind. Billie was swamped. There were thirty-nine checklist items in all. The law student was assigned the remaining fifteen steps by Betty and Billie. No problem. The student laid out orders in rows on his section of the long desk. He sat in a secretary's chair with a wheeled base. To the deep consternation of both Betty and Billie, he would scoot from left to right doing one step at a time sequentially on each order. He finished quickly and would have nothing to do most of the time.

One day, when Betty and Billie were at lunch, the student lined up all the pending new orders on this long table and scooted merrily along, doing each step required of all three employees. He completed batch after batch. Very quickly. By the time Betty and Billie returned from lunch, the law student was sitting there smugly reading the paper. All the orders were up-to-date. There was nothing to do.

Few orders arrived in the normally light hour between 1 and 2 P.M. They were done at the usual deliberate pace by Betty and Billie. Both were sputtering like July 4th sparklers. With no excuse to scoot, the law student waited quietly for a dozen orders to pile up, then scoot he did. He was insufferable. He admits it.

That evening, Betty and Billie, who had worked there for years, complained to management that the law student was handling orders too casually. They had poured over his processed orders and found one series of boxes without an "X" mark. They also griped that he scooted in a distracting, even menacing, manner. Luckily for all, the law student was fired. He found useful work at a law firm.

It is not clear that the drug company missed orders by organizing the order-taking process on a two-person basis. But a better way would have been to have one worker follow through in the entire process, making sure the order form was fulfilled promptly.

Doesn't seem possible? Well, consider how Motorola has revolutionized the world of order fulfillment.

Motorola has what you might call a Tinkers to Tinkers to Tinkers play. Each order moves as fast as a double play and does so without leaving the fielder's glove. Motorola set an objective for filling orders for pagers at a one-hour limit from the time a customer said, "I want to place an order" until the pager was manufactured, processed, and shipped. The trick is that the entire process is handled by one person, working in a totally automated factory. The order person can even arrange for custom manufacturing to a variety of specifications within this highly restrictive time period. In most companies, the order time is protracted. When incoming orders reach the factory, the bureaucratic stall hobbles the process. Sales rarely talks to manufacturing. Manufacturing does not conduct a dialogue with billing, and so on. The ordering department must act first. Then the order goes to the credit department people who must give the customer the green light. There may be individual specifications for the item, which puts engineering to work. Then a bill must be issued. So the billing department gets involved. More than one company has been known to drag this process out for seventy-five days to handle a single order—a ridiculous state of affairs.

If At First You Don't Succeed, Try, Try Again

Left unchecked, bureaucracies can create redundancies that double or triple the workload and still fail. It can happen in the best of organizations. A student working for a college alumni magazine was warned that a mistaken address for an alumnus would bar the possibility of a charitable gift from that person.

So the office created a number of back-up mailing lists. The primary system used metal plates to create mailing labels. The addresses were put on three-inch by five-inch cards, too. There were also handwritten notes appended to a printed alumni book. When the student found conflicts, he was to decide which entry was right, without contacting the alumnus directly; it was considered gauche and self-defeating to make direct contact by this office. Temporary addresses became permanent if the alumnus failed to update. On occasion, the alumnus who did send a notice of return to his or her permanent address was thwarted by the post office that did not get around to sending the temporary address to the magazine until after the permanent address was reinstated. Putting it mildly, the student was never sure which address was right. The new publisher, appalled by the waste of time and money, hired an address service. The service goofed so often that the student was kept busy backing up the new service. The back-up book grew so dog-eared that the binding fell off. Then the student could not use it easily. The student spent one entire school year handwriting the old notes into a new book. The error rate skyrocketed.

Stall Erasers

Standing Room Only

At times, unorthodox measures are needed to get workers to break out of bad habits. It became apparent to a venture capitalist that his two dozen aides were sitting at their desks occupying themselves with administrative chores that didn't add to profits. As C. Northcote Parkinson, distinguished British author, put it, the work expands so as to fill the time allotted for its completion. The venture capitalist's solution: Buy stand-up desks. Almost no one uses a stand-up desk today. And as the venture capitalist had suspected, not one of his dozen or so venture capital aides was willing psychologically or able physically to stand behind a desk all day. They all headed for the field and rounded up prospects, a simple stratagem that brought business.

I Love the Sound of My Own Voice

In a celebrated recovery that helped put Sears back on track, the company fought bureaucracy with novel practices. Ironically, Sears Chairman Arthur Martinez hired a three-star general to break the bureaucracy stall at what once had been the world's largest retailer. Now it might seem ironic to hire someone who had spent his career working for the U.S. government to break through an entrenched bureaucracy, but in Lieutenant General William G. Pagonis, Martinez and Sears had the right man for the job. As the chief of logistics for the U.S. military effort in the Persian Gulf War, Pagonis ran an impressive operation and managed the procurement, supply, and maintenance of equipment and the movement, evacuation, and hospitalization of personnel.

Pagonis proved that the army way of planning, implementing, and coordinating details was the right medicine for a business mired in the mud. He halved the time it took to ship apparel from suppliers to Sears' stores. Following military style, he punished suppliers that missed deadlines by imposing fines. Sears' profits soared. Martinez gives much of the credit to Pagonis.

Another improvement focused on cutting back the time executives spent in committee meetings. In a simple expedient (reminiscent of those stand-up desks), he removed the chairs from meeting rooms so those in attendance would get to the point quickly or shut up entirely. Pagonis was convinced that the chairs inspired verbosity. His meetings rarely exceeded fifteen minutes. At these meetings, those with something to say would speak up. The rest did not. In the past, managers felt that they had to speak to earn their keep. Now they knew better and stopped wasting valuable time.

In breaking bureaucratic stalls at Sears, Martinez was actually emulating the founder of the company, however inadvertently. Biographers recall that Richard Warren Sears did key jobs himself so that bureaucracy could not develop. He was a walking filing cabinet: Sears ran his company out of bulging pockets that were filled with reminders to himself. After a peripatetic day at the helm, he would labor on into the night, sixteen hours out of the twenty-four, writing copy and otherwise molding and building the business he called the Cheapest Supply House on Earth. His one-man band sounds a little like the one-man ordering system at Motorola. It is rarely a mistake to concentrate activities in one person or, at most, in a few people.

Stallbusters

Bureaucracies are serving a purpose; otherwise they would simply be eliminated. Usually they proliferate as a result of processes that are ineffective or inefficient. In this section, you will learn how to deal with opportunities to improve.

Spot Checking

Every organization has more bureaucracy than it needs. You need a starting point to reduce it. A high percentage of bureaucracy involves having checkers checking on checkers, which is usually done in the laudatory name of effectively controlling the organization. The trouble is that much of this checking is unnecessary. Spot checking often works almost as well and is a lot less expensive.

How do you determine how many "spots" to check? Find an outsider who knows how to do statistical analysis. It might be a professor at a local college, or even a high school math teacher. Have the person look at all of the areas where you check everything and suggest a way that you could just sample-check a minimum number of instances.

As an example of this statistical issue, you will find that a random sample of a few hundred to a thousand or two will often provide useful answers even when hundreds of thousands or even millions of instances are being considered. Have you ever paid attention to the sample sizes (how many people are interviewed) for national elections? Rarely will the number of people interviewed exceed 2,000. Yet the answers will often turn out to be remarkably correct when the final voting returns are in.

Airlines rely on this factor to save a lot of money in calculating how much each air carrier owes each other air carrier when passengers have flown on different airlines using the same ticket. Long ago, the airlines found that they could honestly settle with each other by looking at only a tiny fraction of all these transactions.

Even the Internal Revenue Service only audits a tiny fraction (usually around 1 to 2 percent) of all the tax returns it receives. By carefully selecting to audit where errors and fraud are most likely to occur, the IRS is able to be effective without reviewing everyone.

Improving Processes by Streamlining

For many products and services, it takes weeks or months to process orders even when the goods and services are already available. The problem is that the customer's eventual satisfaction has to wait for dozens of people to make one tiny input. The order in process will be sitting with nothing happening for almost all of that time.

How can you streamline fragmented processes? Locate all of your activities that are highly fragmented across the organization (such as order processing—which will include everything from credit checking to issuing invoices to planning production). Read articles about how others have redesigned these processes to simplify them, speed them up, and reduce the number of people involved. Go visit some of those companies. Get help from someone with process redesign skill or outsource the function to a specialist.

A classic example of this problem comes with ordering a custom item from a company that has little interest in having a large business of producing custom items. You may have to call the order-processing people dozens of times before anyone will call you back. If you are not available when the call comes, you get to start all over again. Once you talk to a human being, there is a lot of information you have to give. Chances are you will provide incomplete or incorrect information. Undoubtedly, this will generate more calls at some point. If the process takes long enough, the materials being used will change, and you will have to respecify your needs before you can have the order filled. At that point, the person who is supposed to take the next step may be fired, get a new job, or go away on vacation. Your paperwork may totally disappear—an enormous cost to you and your company.

Another wonderful example of this problem comes when "no one is in charge." Say your organization's telephones develop a glitch. Who will fix it? Will it be the local Baby Bell? The company that made your telephones? The company that made your organization's telephone switch? The company that wired your offices? Your long-distance carrier? A contractor hired by the building you are in? Most people have had the experience of having to hire all of these people to visit at least once before the problem can be diagnosed, so that the proper person can fix the source of the problem. Ma Bell, we miss you.

Having considered the problems, let's consider a star. Many people report wonderful experiences placing orders with L.L. Bean. Questions are short, relevant, and delivered in a friendly way. Based on past purchases and your interests, your order taker may suggest other items that you will decide to buy—both because you need them and because the price is right. Your order will soon arrive, without errors. The company employs a sophisticated combination of computers, management processes, and training to give these good results. Large numbers of companies travel to Maine to observe for themselves how L.L. Bean does this. Perhaps you will, too.

What more can you do to identify problem areas and effect solutions? Physically follow your products or services from when the customer is first contacted to when it eventually uses what you have provided. Find all of the delays in providing for the customer. Measure how much those delays cost you and the customer. As before, read articles about how others have redesigned these processes to simplify them and reduce the number of people involved. Go visit some of those companies. Get help from someone with process redesign skill or out-source parts of the functions to a specialist.

Today, the global standard for elapsed time in most advanced busi-nesses is very short, from a few hours to a few days, depending on how complicated your customer's needs are and the process involved to sat-isfy those needs. In industries where parts suppliers provide the goods to their manufacturing customers "just in time" (just before the part is used), the suppliers usually determine what and how much to ship to the customer rather than waiting for an order. This form of automatic replenishment is probably going to become a standard for many indus-tries in the twenty-first century.

Go for Massive Continuous Improvement

Many people are quickly satisfied when they make an initial improve-ment. That initial change can be misleading because if your perform-ance was awful to begin with, the improved performance may be merely less awful, rather than good. So you must continually improve in these important areas as rapidly as you can. Every time you look at the rede-fined process, you will find more opportunities to improve. To monitor your ongoing process, ask yourself the following questions:

What should you be measuring? Create continuing measures of how effective and efficient you are in those important areas identified above. Effectiveness relates to factors such as customer satisfaction, total time elapsed to perform the total process, avoiding harm to cus-tomers, and ease of use. Compare your experiences with service provid-ers that annoy you and those that delight you to understand possible measures of effectiveness to use in your own business or organization. Efficiency relates to the cost of delivering the service and the number of errors you make that do not affect the customer but have to be reme-died anyway.

How can you measure these areas? Monitor and report how you are doing in these areas using sampling techniques. The frequency of these reports should be quite high because you want to pick up new problems quickly. Some computer systems have internal measures that do this automatically for those who work in the process.

How often should improvement goals be set? Set new improvement goals at least as often as annually. If you set improvement goals more frequently and reward people accordingly, results can improve even faster. Some organizations have found it valuable to do this as often as once a month. However, a drawback of too much frequency is that it may focus too much attention on improving what you are doing now, and too little on changing the nature of the benefits you provide to improve things for customers. So it is possible that you get better and better at doing the wrong things. Generally, you will want to spend some time being sure that you are doing the right things first, before worrying about doing them better. This is a source of error that you will constantly have to monitor. Bureaucracies love to create inertia in places where it can be harmful.

Chapter 8

Mañana

The Procrastination Stall

Whenever I feel like exercising,
I lie down and the feeling invariably goes away.
　　　　—The late Robert Hutchins, famed educator
　　　　who was president of the University of Chicago

When the danger of action is greater than the danger of inaction, orga-
nizations are wise to take the time to assess the situation before acting.
Unfortunately, the reverse is often true. This chapter shows you how to
determine where immediate action is wise and how to organize to obtain
the benefits of needed rapid action.

Warning! Watch Out for Dangerous Delay and Risky Inaction

The procrastinator (Exhibit 8-1) believes that if he or she does nothing
and waits long enough, any bad situation will resolve itself. Or if it does
not resolve itself, it will simply go away. Many even insist that procrastination is a form of work, explaining that they are letting their ideas
percolate. With that point of view, they feel no guilt about any delay.
The fact is, almost any direct action is better than no action. Usually,
nothing much is lost in trying, and when you keep trying, you keep
learning, especially from your mistakes.

Exhibit 8-1 Procrastination Cartoon.
Michael Witte © 1997. Reprinted with permission of *Discover Magazine.*

Thomas Edison made numerous unsuccessful attempts to invent the lightbulb. After each failure, his cheery reaction was that, on the contrary, he'd discovered lots of things that didn't work. The natural tendency in such circumstances is to procrastinate until a better solution magically appears, but Edison didn't know the meaning of procrastination. He kept on experimenting until he succeeded.

When fear is an element, that fear can create a procrastination stall that may lead us to disaster. In the 1930s, an American helium-filled airship was swept aloft by a sudden wind. It is told that the rope crew was carried away. Most let go right away and got off with sprains. Others held on until they lost their grip. Each time a man let go, the dirigible leapt higher. Those who hesitated longest fell to their deaths from hundreds of feet in the air.

Don't Think Too Long About That

Fear always springs from ignorance.
—Ralph Waldo Emerson

Fear and Trembling in the Executive Washroom

Fear rules many business leaders and their fear comes in different guises. One of America's most admired CEOs only made acquisitions of privately held family-owned companies headquartered in small towns. This company had a very good success rate with acquisitions of all sizes and could have grown faster by buying other types of companies as well. But the CEO would procrastinate when presented with the idea of buying a good public concern. Colleagues said the CEO had an excessive fear of negative publicity. He feared that he might look foolish in the type of public scrutiny that follows an offer for a widely held public company. Hold onto that thought for a moment, and see if it could apply to you or your organization. It may be that the potential for embarrassment affects some of your decisions and behavior. Psychologists tell us that fear of public ridicule and of public speaking are among the most common and intense human fears of all.

Another CEO operated the executive suite like a merry-go-round. He always had three or four people competing for every position. He fired the top person in each function or subsidiary operation every time a budget was missed for which the person was responsible. Unit heads frequently lost their jobs, especially during recessions. It turned out that the CEO had a great fear of being fired himself. By being tough on his people, he felt the board would be more dependent on him. As you can imagine, there was not much teamwork or sharing of information in this company. No one wanted to rock the boat. Procrastination became a way of life. Each business unit lost market share almost every year, and profit margins were weak and becoming weaker. Whenever the company sold a business, that business quickly became more profitable under either the same management or new management operating with less fear.

Similarly, when major layoffs occur, many of the survivors feel worse than those who are laid off. They will do anything to please if they cannot easily find other jobs, including simply maintaining the status quo. A worker in one company watched as seventy-three people were fired from her department. Only she and four others remained. When the ax finally fell on her, she was almost grateful. The terrible strain was finally over. She said that she had done nothing novel or even new and had not improved her skills during the eight years that she survived. Procrastination became her major weapon as she temporized to put off the inevitable. (Incidentally, her former company still performs poorly and has since been acquired, leading to still more layoffs.)

A different type of fear dogs those who aspire to be CEOs. Companies often pick two to five contenders and stage a two- to three-year "beauty" contest to see who should be the next leader. During that time, luck plays a role. Put yourself in that position. If your unit does well and no one else's does, you get to be the big boss. As you can imagine, almost no one in that position is going to try anything that might not work perfectly during the beauty contest. Key programs are detoured or put off because of the risks of failure. Imagine the subliminal message each of the workers is getting! Fear stalks the hallways while delay sucks black ink from the bottom line.

It is far easier to stand back and let others be innovative. But that's the way to ruin, not to progress. One CEO took avoidance to an extreme. At a strategy session with the CEO's senior management, an executive shared a list of all the issues that the company had known about for five years but that had never been resolved. The CEO complimented the executive on his work and then picked up all copies of the document listing the problems and destroyed them. He said, "This information is too important to get out." But we know that the first step to solving a problem is to get it out in the open where it can no longer be ignored.

But What If . . . ?

Anxious business executives often connect their fear to everything that happens, not just those things that they should fear. For example, a company that had a lot of failures with advanced-technology products began delaying debuts and finally decided to pursue only low-technology products. Ironically, many of these advanced-technology areas in which the company had tried products later proved very successful—for other companies. The company had simply developed its products a little ahead of the customer demand. But they had exited the field before they could reap the rewards of their advanced technology. They had programmed themselves to fail. The product technology stepdown made things worse. The company's low-technology products were also unsuccessful.

Talk It to Death

I will never put off until tomorrow that which I can forget about forever.
—Anonymous

Some corporations create monuments to procrastination. They bury their problems in committees or hire outside consultants. These actions give the appearance of doing something worthwhile to resolve the problems. All too often, there is no actual plan, just a vague commitment to consider a plan. People within the organization know that something is wrong, but they get the impression that the identified problem need not be fixed right away. Employees relax, figuring it will not be disastrous if the problem is not actually addressed for six months or a year.

Consultants frequently abet the corporate delays by setting up a game of musical chairs. They convince corporate leadership that the problems need new approaches. So they rework the organization chart. Everyone gets a new job. This is action, but it is not useful action. It is the "who's on first?" version of a procrastination stall, which is only good for delaying the time needed to solve a problem that threatens serious consequences. The board is happy because the CEO is doing something. And the CEO, just a few years this side of retirement, manages to avoid making difficult decisions that may cause him corporate pain.

A Diversionary Tactic

For a time, AT&T institutionalized procrastination. Instead of more seriously addressing important problems in the long-distance market, AT&T's Bob Allen diverted investor attention from the core problem when he made a spectacular acquisition.

In doing so, he bought a company AT&T could not run, NCR (National Cash Register). Chairman Allen also hired a potential successor to placate the board of directors who nervously worried about Allen's procrastination. In retrospect, it seems possible that Allen had no intention of stepping aside. Allen fired his chosen successor peremptorily. But don't waste tears on the would-be Allen successor. The man won a corporate lottery. After just nine months in the wings, he was awarded $26 million in severance compensation. But that's peanuts. Allen's apparent procrastination-stall attempt to diversify when he should have focused more on the core business cost the company a king's ransom. The NCR debacle, its purchase at high cost and later sale at a lower price, cost AT&T more than $5 billion, not to mention that the takeover cost thousands of dedicated NCR workers their jobs.

Stall Erasers

Behold the turtle. He makes progress only when he sticks his neck out.
—James Bryant Conant, American educator

Practice, Practice, Practice: Success Through Simulation

Some businesses try to determine why employees fear certain activities in hopes of discovering a method for overcoming the fear. Computer-based simulations help decision makers understand how to manage their businesses in turbulent times, deal with business and moral conflicts of interest, and make acquisitions at a reasonable price when the pressure is on.

Those with irrational fears and those who work in situations where fear can be paralyzing are asked to do simulation planning exercises. When nothing is actually at stake, they learn to perform the feared activities without incident. For example, utility employees are put in a simulated nuclear plant and faced with a potential meltdown if they don't act rationally. They've already been trained to deal with crisis without fear. They become better performers in fact, like the pilot in a flight simulator who can practice difficult maneuvers on the ground.

These days, even pilots of oceangoing oil tankers attend simulation schools, much as airline pilots have for decades. Every possible emergency is thrown at the oceangoing pilots. Later, when at sea and a real problem occurs, it is second nature for the pilot to do the right thing. The *Titanic*'s crew could have used this training.

Companies of every sort can do the same thing for their people by thrusting them into real-life situations in which errors are tolerated as learning experiences for workers and for the company. When simulations are based on issues your business actually faces, comfort and effectiveness grow. It is also helpful to talk to people at other companies who are good at overcoming feared activities. These outsiders can dispel concerns that are founded in dread but not in actual experience.

Listen, the Answers Doth Bark!

Wise corporate leaders keep track of issues as they arise to be sure that something is being done about them beyond simply creating a plan to do the plan. Effective cost-cutting programs have found that tracking suggestions from the date they are offered until they are dealt with—and with progress reviews along the way—is very helpful. A few intrepid companies go so far as to allow all their suggestions to be implemented automatically after a few weeks, if no one objects in the meantime. What is needed is a bias for action, with follow-up to understand how the measures are working.

Do It Yourself

Bringing in outside consultants can aggravate the procrastination stall in several ways. Not only does it give leaders an excuse to stall, it focuses the responsibility for action on outsiders. The CEO can blame the consultants for risky or unpopular decisions. This tactic is an unsatisfactory example to set for the company. It is better to be forthright and decisive: Handle the decision in-house and take the heat if any develops.

A Foolish Consistency Can Risk All

> *It's true, I'm a monogamist, but the first time I married,*
> *I was monoging with the wrong person.*
> —Anonymous

Avon was once one of Wall Street's Nifty Fifty stocks because it had churned out 15 percent earnings gains year after year and similar stock market gains for its shareholders. Its thousands of door-to-door salespeople could work for the company as long as they liked. No threat of downsizing here. But, as more and more housewives joined the nation's full-time outside-the-home workforce, the growth of this business that once made prosperous entrepreneurs of thousands of women faded like lipstick applied before morning coffee. When Hicks Waldron was named CEO at Avon, the Avon Lady was ringing the doorbell way more than the cash register. Avon was becoming a loser, not even earning its dividend. Still, Waldron promised publicly, "I'll never cut the dividend!" Whoops. It was soon clear that Waldron was out on a limb, a tiny one at the top of the tree at that.

He could have dug in his heels and used a procrastination stall, thus wasting assets, or he could change his mind about the dividends and deal with reality. Waldron decided to play it smart. He looked for and found an innovative way to solve the problem. He and his investment advisers offered the widows and orphans (Wall Street shorthand for investors who live on dividend and interest income) a share-for-share tax-free swap for a new class of stock. The new shares paid dividends at the old rate and were set up to do so for three years. Shareholders seeking appreciation held the old common shares on which Avon cut the dividend. The income shares sacrificed some of the common stock's appreciation potential, but during a three-year hiatus, income holders had time to sell the special shares in an orderly fashion and reinvest elsewhere for income. The income shares then became the reduced-dividend common after the three years ended. By not letting himself be paralyzed by the fear of looking foolish, Waldron avoided a procrastination stall and found a 2,000 percent solution.

Stallbusters

In this chapter, you have learned a lot about how inaction can be worse than action in many situations. The next section will help you identify such circumstances in your own organization and create an appropriate bias for action.

Action First

Unfortunately, there is often little incentive for procrastinators to change. Contrast this with the circumstances of the oil rig worker on the burning platform towering over the North Sea. He's been warned that to jump is to die. Neither can he procrastinate without dying. He jumps. Incredibly, he survives the plunge.

Creating a bias toward action, where inaction is more dangerous than any decision, is something that most organizations fail to do. Most organizations operate on the assumption that all action needs to be considered first. An interesting example in the late 1990s of a company that went from being biased toward inaction to being biased toward action is IBM. During the years when it appeared that IBM could do no wrong, the company fragmented authority and required dozens of people to coordinate with each other. Decisions were always delayed, and so were the results of the decisions. IBM found itself a weak follower in more and more circumstances. The new CEO, Lou Gerstner, changed things by personal example and by sharing values that emphasized taking personal, timely, appropriate actions. Those who persisted in the old ways soon found themselves looking for work elsewhere.

If you think about how your organization works, you should be able to identify areas where action can precede in-depth analysis. Answering the following questions will help you identify those areas:

When should the customer be considered right and receive immediate recognition and resolution? Let us consider a high-technology product with a high degree of technical content, such as a high-speed communications switch for sending data over telephone networks. You are now the customer, and you cannot send your data from point A to point B. As a result, your operations are all shut down until the problem is fixed.

Clearly, you as the customer cannot solve the problem without the manufacturer, even if the problem is at your end. The manufacturer's knowledge is essential to your success. Advanced suppliers of such switches have responded to this circumstance by providing service people located at the customer's equipment site. When a potential problem is seen, the equipment automatically contacts the equipment supplier's on-site service person. In an ideal situation, the solution is found and the problem corrected before the customer even experiences a problem.

In some critical applications, such systems have built-in redundancy so that the operation is routed around whatever is malfunctioning. If that sounds far out to you, long-distance telephone companies have had the capability for years to automatically route your calls around busy switches and circuits to reach the number you dialed.

Beyond this example, the customer should also get assistance immediately whenever delay will be harmful to the customer or to the valuable relationship that you want to maintain with the customer. Recently, a financial planner told a story about how his clients call him to bail their children out of jail, to help them rent summer homes, and a thousand other tasks apparently unrelated to financial planning. The planner does these things willingly because each additional service helps cement the relationship and deepens the bonds of trust and mutual support. He is confident that he will get the business when more financial planning is needed by this or the next generation in that family. Of course, common sense should dictate the reasonable limits of taking such actions.

On the other hand, there are times when the customer is obligated to pay for what is needed, for example, when the customer needs something beyond the bounds of the relationship or the business obligations. If a customer wants you to repair his or her car, and you are selling small amounts of pads and paper, you should certainly assist the customer to get help but expect the customer to pay the mechanic. In some rare circumstances, even that repair may be something you want to pay for. Some retail stores are so helped by having a reputation of taking goods back without question that there are stories circulating about women's clothing stores providing credit for tires that were returned—even though the stores did not sell tires. Don't let eventual payment solely determine the timeliness of your response.

What threats to safety require immediate action? Certainly, safety always requires prompt attention. Sorting out who pays can be dealt with later. A national electric supply distributor has an interesting strategy. A task force at corporate headquarters monitors reports of possible killer storms. At some point *before* the storm hits, the company dispatches to the area an appropriately large army of trucks filled with portable generators and other electrical goods normally in short supply during emergencies. The concept is that the company's distribution centers are likely to be put out of business by the storm. Each truck is designed to set up business in a parking lot. Products are sold at normal prices, and on-site credit is granted without question.

As a result, thousands of businesses and organizations have been able to get back on their feet faster, providing services essential to the community's health and safety, due to this company's remarkable service. The company reports that a large number of these customers become committed to it for life. "A friend in need is a friend indeed" is one of the values that this company practices to its own credit and benefit. If your organization has procrastinated about having essential supplies, remember that like emergency generators for hospitals, they can be lifesaving.

What similar opportunities does your organization have to be of service in dangerous circumstances?

What competitive actions require immediate responses through use of best judgment? The answer to this question varies a lot from business to business, but when a customer is being wooed by a competitor, the customer will normally expect that you will be able to provide a rapid response in light of their importance to you and relationship with you. Nothing can be more harmful than to get caught up in delays relating to your people not wanting to address the issue of a possible customer defection. On the other hand, if the competitor or the customer is merely faking interest in customer switching, then you are being taken advantage of. Policies can help a lot in a situation like this. The person hearing about the problem can have the authority to make certain concessions without further checking with headquarters as long as the proof of the competitor's action meets certain requirements (such as seeing a copy of a proposal on the competitor's stationery).

When two people in different parts of the organization do not agree, when should one of them automatically prevail, when should an automatic rule prevail, and when would a coin flip suffice for the decision? Of course, ultimately you will have to decide for yourself which is which, but some examples may help. In the first part of the example, the two areas might be sales and manufacturing. Since neither area is in charge of the other, there is a turf issue here that can result in a procrastination stall if people avoid dealing with the issue. Who should automatically prevail when . . . That is a question worth a meeting by the two heads of the functions. To ensure the quality of the results, you might want to have someone participate in that meeting who understands the financial consequences of the decision so that an informed choice can be made. Perhaps sales should prevail when a large, profitable customer is involved. Perhaps manufacturing should prevail when manufacturing capacity is strained and quality may suffer.

An automatic rule could be that whoever shows the most economic benefit to the company from their proposal should prevail. A financial person could be an arbiter.

A coin flip is probably fine in situations where the issue is not very important either for the short term or for its precedent-making value, such as whether to paint a blue or a yellow stripe on the product. But such a dispute can have real costs in product delays if it is not resolved promptly.

What problems should receive immediate attention because they almost always get worse if ignored? An excellent example of this sort of problem would be a new pharmaceutical product with unwanted side effects. Sometimes these side effects only show up after a new pharmaceutical has been approved for a certain use by the Food and Drug Administration. Let us say the product is supposed to help glaucoma, but more people using the product are having strokes than should occur among the patient population.

The reasons for quick action should be obvious. If the pharmaceutical is contributing to strokes, it is easier to change who gets the product or how it is used than to rehabilitate people who have had strokes. In some cases, the people die and the loss is both permanent and unable to be offset completely to the patient's family. Second, the problem is likely to get worse as patients take the product for a longer period of time. Third, there may be other side effects that the company has missed. The stroke problem is a wake-up call to go back and review all of the data to see what else is going on.

It's OK to Take a Chance on Action

Many delays occur because employees are afraid that the consequences of mistakes will fall heavily on them or their careers. Downsizing and other cost-cutting phenomena have made this problem worse. To overcome the bias to play it safe, everyone needs to be clear about when they can and should act. Some hotel chains give a desk clerk authority to spend up to a few hundred dollars to resolve an issue that a guest brings to the clerk's attention. If the guest then compliments the employee to management, the clerk can receive an award for the action.

How can people be encouraged to overcome procrastination? For the circumstances where you have decided that immediate action is appropriate and desirable, spell out who has authority to do what and be sure that punishment and negative feedback are banished for those who follow the spirit of the policy. Also provide an opportunity for positive recognition. Work with those who will have the authority in order to address their issues. Make them feel comfortable with the authority, and be sure they have the tools to get the job done.

A good example of where this situation is important can relate to the use of complicated financial products that hedge against certain kinds of risk: economic (such as commodity prices rising too far) or financial (causing interest rates to be fixed at a certain level, rather than rising when general rates increase). Often these financial products work well in a narrow range of circumstances but can be a disaster for the company outside of that narrow band. The celebrated lawsuit of Procter & Gamble against Bankers Trust is believed to have involved some financial instruments of this type. As soon as someone in the company realizes that the financial instrument is dangerous, quick action is needed. Delay can expand a loss of millions into tens of millions. Since no one can forecast the future, you have no way of knowing if conditions will get better or worse, but you are probably better off not taking the risk. On the one hand, you take a sure loss, some of which may be recouped by continuing. On the other hand, you face a real risk of an enormous loss disproportionate to the potential loss reduction. Reward your people for quick action in these situations.

A Deadline for Action

Simply because inaction is not instantly harmful does not mean that you can dillydally. You can estimate how much your decision can be expected to improve by various types and degrees of further analysis and compare that possible benefit to the cost of delay. Then set a deadline for a decision and action that is shorter than the time a delay for analysis and decision making will use up. After all, we want to get some gain from our thinking. A good rule of thumb is to get the most improvement compared to the cost of delay. This viewpoint will bias you toward action, even when delaying. You may also find that you have made a mistake and an immediate decision will be more valuable.

Imagine that you suddenly find yourself being sued by the federal government for all kinds of issues. The relevant attorneys offer a settlement that avoids large litigation costs and distraction. Your instinct may be to grab the deal. However, that can be risky if you do not understand the future costs of the settlement. Also, you may be able to negotiate a better settlement. Although you will probably settle the case, you would be wise to spend a little time first to understand your choices before taking the settlement. You may be able to propose something to the attorneys that is viewed as more favorable to them and that actually costs you less in future flexibility. Consider questions such as the following to help you frame how long you should delay:

Worst case, what can a delay cost because of the amount of time needed to analyze the subject to different degrees and thoroughness to reach a decision?

What is the minimum amount of time realistically needed to make a significantly better and more valuable decision?

One of the best ways to make exponential organizational progress is to create a current or wind of change that pushes thinking and actions into new, coordinated directions toward solutions. In this image, see how the objects flow smoothly around the elongated circle in the center to make progress toward the upper right-hand corner. Imagine that you are already using the new thinking process described in this part of *The 2,000 Percent Solution* to create that progress by flowing around your organization's obstacles. What opportunities or advantages for your organization does this image suggest?

Part Two
A Stallbuster's Guide in Eight Steps

In this second part, you will learn the universal process of uncovering and capturing maximum opportunity by asking new questions. You will learn more about the last three perspectives discussed in the Foreword, which will provide the most value to your organization.

This part of the book offers the most effective means for overcoming your most intransigent and costly stalls, from measurement to best practice to people and incentives, including actual hands-on solutions. No one idea presented here will solve problems all by itself. You need to assimilate and use all eight steps, one by one, as they build on one another.

Step One is to understand the importance of measuring performance—"Measuring Caverns Measureless to Man."

Step Two is to choose a particularly important process within an organization or a company. Once you have chosen this focus, determine what it is about this process that you want to measure so as to make more rapid and significant progress—"Too Many Trees."

Step Three is to identify the future best practice in that area and measure it—"Where Many Cooks Improve the Broth."

Step Four is to find ways to implement beyond the future best practice—"All Aboard for Best-Practice City."

Step Five is to identify the theoretical best-way-to-do-something practice—"Perfection as Only You Can Imagine It."

Step Six is to pursue approaching the theoretical best practice as soon as possible—"On the Trail of the Holy Grail."

Step Seven is to be sure the people and incentives for achieving these results best match the task—"The Square-Peg-in-the-Square-Hole Opportunity."

Step Eight is to keep repeating the first seven steps because you will improve each time and refine your skill with this new stall-busting set of habits—"Mustard Repeats!"

Chapter 9
Measuring Caverns Measureless to Man

Step One: Understand the Importance of Measuring Performance

I'm at least six feet tall . . . would you believe five feet eight?
—Anonymous

All of the errors involved in stalls described in Part One can be overcome by having measurements in place that your organization understands, pays attention to, and knows how to respond to. This chapter explains how to create a universal understanding of how to use measurements to eliminate stalls and to point the way to faster progress.

The main reason most of us overlook opportunities to improve is that we have no relevant measures in place to help identify the opportunities. Without measurement, would-be stallbusters are mostly up the creek without a canoe. Read on to see if you recognize yourself or your organization and to learn the importance of measuring performance as part of a 2,000 percent solution for fostering more growth.

Don't Tell Me, I Examined It Myself!

The story of the three blind men asked to describe an elephant suggests how hard it is to find the right measurement for a given situation. The first blind man felt the leg and said the elephant was like a tree. The second felt the trunk and said the elephant was like a snake. The third felt the tail and said the elephant was like a worm. Many conclude from the story that using many perceptions and measurements is not as good as one solid overview. In fact, the tale points to the need for many more measurements. If each blind person had gone all around the elephant, each would have done better in trying to understand what an elephant was. If a sighted person had been around, that person could have described the elephant for the three blind men in order to provide an overview. Understanding would have grown. Unfortunately, organizations often operate like the individual blind man, using one incomplete measure to provide an overview. For example, it may be that the quality problems in the U.S. automobile industry during the 1970s related in part to the marked tendency to pay too much attention to one measure—cost—and not enough to measuring how poor quality was affecting profits by driving customers to foreign builders of higher-quality cars.

Like U.S. auto builders, most people view the measuring process too narrowly. A young corporate planner once went to a seminar given by famed corporate strategist Peter Drucker. The young man knew that everyone in his company admired Peter Drucker. He thought Drucker would agree about the importance of his own pet measurement. Then he could beat everybody over the head with Drucker's answer and get his own way. The young man asked Drucker to pick the best single measure of corporate performance. Drucker paused. Then, with irritation in his deep, gruff voice, he said "My dear sir, you obviously know nothing. There is no single measure of corporate performance that is any good. Use them all and try to develop new ones and each will teach you something you need to know."

Drucker's point is that measurements are highly subjective and also highly imperfect. Would-be stallbusters are going to need lots of measures. Unless you get carried away, the more measurements you do, the better. For each time you measure, you create the potential to learn something new. You will know that you have gone too far when new insights and opportunities worth far more than the cost of measuring fail to be exposed by the newest measures.

I'd Rather Not Know That!

Drucker's name and his approach to measurements came up at a recent management meeting. One CEO had been an officer in the Air Force in the 1950s. He told the others that Peter Drucker had presented a seminar on personal improvement for his Air Force group years earlier. Drucker told each man to measure in great detail how he spent his time for one week. This CEO said he had done just that. He then explained that this encounter was a life-changing experience. He has never had to measure his time since because the exercise revealed all his bad habits. It told him how much of his time was productive and how much was not. The CEO also knew what his good and bad habits were so that he could be on guard in the future.

But this CEO's example is rarely followed. Few write down how their job time is being spent. Few care to measure their own output. And employers who try to get cooperation in such measurements may face resistance, particularly when young people are involved. Workers can feel it is somehow unfair to do this or feel they are being picked on, even when they are allowed to come up with their own measurements.

Try this experiment yourself and you will see what we mean: Measure how much time you spend on the phone, how much doing routine tasks, and how much you accomplish overall. You will see that measurements can help redirect your efforts into more productive activities.

Be sure to take action based on what you have learned. Otherwise, your new measurements could merely contribute to a bureaucratic stall.

A Perpetual Measuring Machine

Even asking people to think about using more measurements to identify stalls causes concern that this will create confusion or won't be worth the effort. Here's a story that shows it is worthwhile. On first impression, you may think that the measuring was overdone, but clearly that isn't so.

Some consultants and executives from other companies visiting the top division of a major firm stopped by the finance and data processing units. The visitors looked in each person's work area and saw cubicles brimming with daily personal performance measurements. The measurements covered the walls. In most cases, the employee had personally created several dozen measurements directly related to results from his or her job and how the worker set about performing tasks (where results were difficult to measure). The concept was that by making the measures of performance visible, workers would themselves be encouraged to focus on improving personal output. Workers could also see whether they were increasing their output as well as how they were doing relative to other workers. The measures let everyone measure each other's performances.

If a worker had a problem in a given area, the other workers quickly became aware of it, and those who were doing better in that same area would often stop by and make suggestions that could help. Since much compensation rested on department performance, there was an incentive for workers to help each other. Did everyone perform well initially? In some cases they did, but in others they did not. When they did not, it was soon apparent, and coaching and self-measurement helped them make rapid progress.

These workers also derived a sense of the relevance of their measurements because each experienced improvement. By seeing each other's measurements, the workers also got more ideas to improve their own performance. These workers made enormous strides. Personal productivity gains of 25 percent a year were not uncommon. (Compare this percentage with the standard benchmark for such gains. Those who study productivity will tell you that if a worker can manage 2 to 3 percent gains in a single year in an office environment, he or she is doing exceptionally well.) Furthermore, corporate productivity in these functions grew by a similar amount because of the measures.

Some corporations are unwilling to consider that they can do better, and they commonly settle for 2 to 3 percent annual productivity gains when this level is clearly not the limit. Limited expectations are telegraphed to workers, and thus lower productivity follows predictably.

Let's look at another example of how expectation measures can affect performance. Consider a student who, many years ago, worked for two different managers at the Fuller Brush Company. Fuller recruited its managers from the ranks of its successful door-to-door brush salespeople. Like the salespeople, the managers were given considerable latitude. The bosses could run their areas as they saw fit, so long as they did a reasonably good job of meeting Fuller's modest sales targets.

It is worth noting that neither sales manager the student worked for was college trained. And actually the one who got the better results was functionally illiterate, barely able to read and write, though he had a lively mind, and, as his wife said, "could talk the hind leg off a billy goat." This man developed the better intuitive measure of a salesperson's ability to produce results if he or she was willing to work hard.

Both managers had districts in industrial towns peopled by blue-collar men whose wives stayed home. The student first worked for the less effective manager in Martin's Ferry, Ohio, a steel mill community next to the Ohio River near Wheeling, West Virginia. The manager told the student he could make $75 a week by giving away thirty of Fuller's familiar vegetable brushes a day as a small gift to gain entry. Then he would have a chance to sell as much of the Fuller line as he could. Each successful sales encounter using this technique led to the sale of two to three items, and the student did make $75 a week.

The student later spent a summer in Pontiac, Michigan, a car-building town, and again sold Fuller Brush. The savvy manager in this area told the student instead, "I don't want you to knock off until you have sold $100 worth of Fuller each day." This manager had already inspired two other salesmen to reach national prominence at Fuller, including the company's top salesman who carried three product cases. With the contents of the three cases spread out, they made a home look like a retail store. So the young salesman, inspired by what the manager said and by the example of the older men, did not always sell $100 worth of Fuller a day, but he almost always did and, as a result, earned $200 a week, more than double what he earned before. This was big money in preinflation times.

Where tangible results are less clear, measurement can still help. Many experts will argue that you cannot measure the output of many kinds of white-collar work such as financial analysis. But one company *did* find that it was helpful to measure the time spent on various tasks, such as time *doing* financial analysis, as opposed to the time needed to put the data together *for* the financial analysis. By measuring time allocations, people became more aware when they were spending time on low-output activities, such as assembling the data for the financial analysis, that could be done by others whose time was less costly, in wages, to the company. Behavior rapidly changed as a result, leading to much more delegation of simpler tasks.

End Results vs. Causes

As you can imagine, the best measures start with causes rather than outcomes. However, the smart way to look at measurements is to assume that you are probably only measuring outcomes as opposed to causes. For example, a passing automobile is highly polished. But is this because it is just out of the new car showroom or because the owner is a car buff, figuratively and literally? We really do not know without more information. The quality you are observing, in this case a highly polished car, is the result of *unknowns*. Experts tell us that we will have to ask "why" a number of times—try five to ten times—before we will reach causes.

Financial measures that most companies rely on to assess performance mostly describe outcomes. Earnings per share measures what a company earned in the last period, whether a quarter or a year. It tells you where you have been. It is a result of things that you did earlier, some of them good and some not good. What you need to do is to begin to replace end-results measures with measures of the causes that create the end results. For example, if your customers think what you are doing is great for them, then presumably they will be loyal and buy more things from you. That can mean your company will post higher earnings per share or have more equity when the next period ends. As you understand more about the causes, you increase your understanding of what actually brings you the good or bad end results.

If your sales go up, what were the things that changed before your sales went up that might have helped? Consider factors such as more distribution, better quality, price reductions, new products, and changed promotions. If profit margins got wider, what elements in the picture improved first? Consider factors such as price increases, cost reductions, economies-of-scale effects, and new ways of operating. The more systematic you are in tracking these measurements, the better.

At this point, if you are fortunate enough to know statistics, you have a wonderful additional tool. But even if you do not have a knowledge of statistics, you can draw graphs to find performance-measure trend lines that seem to move together among factors that could be connected. If two or more do match, these may be linked by cause and effect. But be careful. To understand the trend lines better, the next step is to get a person trained in statistics to help you with the statistical analysis.

People usually learn enough in statistics to figure that if you run two sets of data through a computer and the computer indicates some kind of a match, it may mean something. Some forget the statistical rule that there must be a logical reason for the match, a cause and an effect. So it is important to get verification of a connection by talking to those who understand the situation to see if logical cause-and-effect conclusions can be drawn about the paired data.

Another approach to determining cause and effect is that you can also run experiments, observe reactions, and make judgments about probable causes and results. What will happen over time is that, hopefully, you can eliminate or reduce your focus on measures that are probably not the causes of the end results you are looking for. You will be on the verge of busting a stall caused by looking in the wrong direction. And you will be on the track of moving to a superfast-growth 2,000 percent solution.

When Almost Perfect Isn't Good Enough

After the Japanese skunked U.S. manufacturers on quality issues, some American firms may have overreacted. They created new management systems focused excessively on quality improvement programs to the exclusion of sufficiently developing other important processes. Manufacturers measured the number of defects per million parts. Motorola's Six Sigma system was among the most notable quality processes. Under it, Motorola strove for no more than three defective parts per million. The Malcolm Baldrige Award went to Motorola for some of this work in 1988.

However, the quality program often became all consuming, which led to other problems. Executives for companies that use such measures may tell you they seldom make mistakes anymore—almost no defects. But you may also find that they do not grow as fast as other companies do, and, even more important, that their profits lag as well. How can this be? Isn't product quality the key to customer satisfaction? Well, yes, product quality is important to customers. But it is not the only thing. They will undoubtedly have to add a number of other measures before they take into account all of the potential causes of customer satisfaction and dissatisfaction. Examples include how swiftly goods are delivered and how well they operate and are serviced once they are in the customers' hands. Mighty Motorola had a profit stumble in the late 1990s that some in the press have attributed in part to delays in developing new-generation digital pagers and cellular telephones. Motorola had relied on analog designs too long, even if those analog products were almost perfect according to the measured number of defects. In response, Motorola notes that profit problems in 1997 and 1998 primarily relate instead to a weak Asian economy, a recession in the semiconductor industry, and a recession in the paging industry.

Solving Yesterday's Problem

> *The moving finger writes; and having writ, moves on . . .*
> —Edward FitzGerald, *The Rubáiyát of Omar Khayyám*

One of the key lessons in business is that excellence is a moving target. When you satisfy the customer in one area, you need to determine other wellsprings of customer dissatisfaction. It's like Maslow's needs hierarchy: We have physiological needs first. We need to breathe. We also need food. And we need water. When those needs are satisfied, we look for safety and the avoidance of danger. And so forth in ascending hierarchies of need. Customers have similar needs hierarchies. Which comes first? When you first offer an innovative new product, the customer just wants to be on the list of those who will, in fact, get the new product. The question at that point is whether the customer can get the item at all. But once that need is satisfied, the customer's need shifts. The customer is likely to focus on the product's dependability. Or she may seek a competing product that does more work at a similar price. Xerox provides a classic case. Before Xerography, Eastman Kodak offered copiers that used photosensitive paper and liquid hypo solutions. The operator played darkroom developer. The user of the copier dipped the paper into a developer solution. The Kodak system was not only expensive, but the damp copy was messy.

No wonder everyone welcomed the dry copies introduced with Xerography from the Xerox Corporation. Xerox was on top of the world with its invention for years.

But in time, as its patent exclusivity ended, Xerox faced tough competition from Japan, and its dominant share of market began to erode. Finally, however, Xerox staged a strong offensive with simpler, cheaper models of copiers. In fact, Xerox won the Baldrige Award for one of these new copier machines a decade ago. The machine was created because Xerox management believed the company's primary problem concerned the way their machines were designed. They concluded, quite correctly, that their copiers were, by and large, too expensive to make and sell, too unreliable, and too costly to repair. But having devoted its full attention to these important issues, Xerox did not initially consider whether the level of service the sales force was providing its customers was affecting company performance.

Since the sales department wasn't yet being measured for quality of service, the new machines, outstanding though they were, did not produce all of the rise in market share Xerox had expected. Part of the problem was that the sales force was poorly motivated to call on smaller accounts, the area where Japanese competitors were strongest. The salespeople were indifferent to accounts that would not buy many expensive machines and wouldn't call on customers if they didn't feel like it. One unserved customer knew an officer of the company. He was forced to call the officer to arrange for a simple sales call to have an opportunity to spend over $20,000.

Eventually this issue was addressed and Xerox snapped back. Xerox now, in the late 1990s, can be considered a progressive company. While most companies measure elements that *used* to be important for the customers, by learning that customer concerns change over time, Xerox now correctly focuses on the customers' current issues. Continuing, multidimensional measures keep Xerox agile in focusing attention on the most productive areas.

Measure Yourself in Your Customers' Eyes . . .
Then Look to Other Stakeholders

One consumer products firm measured fifty elements in the order process so that orders would be correctly processed and correctly delivered. The company was error-free 99 percent of the time on *each element* of the order. It had been quite smug, but, in fact, one order out of every five went out improperly. Several times a year, each individual customer experienced an error. Doesn't seem possible? Well, do the math. The company overlooked the fact that a 1 percent or less mistake rate for each element of a fifty-element order led to botched-up orders 20 percent of the time. The 1 percent or less error rate is compounded. The company went from being complacent to realizing it was really annoying the heck out of its customers. It had made no effort to create measures relevant to the customers.

Every company needs to address each constituency it serves to avoid stalls: the customers, the suppliers, the employees, the shareholders, even the towns and countries in which it operates. Measurements of effectiveness should include how employees' ability to perform is affected by the company's actions and policies. The company needs input from suppliers to learn how to work more effectively with them. The company needs to measure how its decisions impact the people in the community. With all these constituents plugged in, the ability to focus on potential progress and make effective decisions soars.

The Mismeasure of Man

Companies that pioneer a new product or technology are often overconfident at the beginning concerning their production efficiency. The reason is that their productivity per worker rises rapidly. What they may fail to appreciate is how very much productivity should soar. If your productivity rose by 15 percent this year, but you had the potential for 50 percent gains, you may have actually lost ground against current and future competitors. Always ask yourself if what you are measuring can tell you what you really need to know. It is a fact that, historically, measures have been adopted and fervently pursued that made no sense at all.

Stephen Jay Gould, in his book *The Mismeasure of Man* (W. W. Norton 1981), talks of the time when pseudoscientists measured skulls to determine intelligence levels. They assumed that the bigger the skull, the brighter the person. We now know this assumption was clearly incorrect. A different pseudoscience, phrenology, was in vogue at the turn of the nineteenth century. Researchers had no reliable measure of intelligence, but the phrenologists believed that certain mental faculties and character traits were determined by the configuration of the skull. In the Middle Ages, thinkers lavished time on how many angels can dance on the head of a pin. It seems we human beings have always had a penchant for coming up with nonsensical or, certainly, noncausal measures.

Rose-Colored Glasses

One of the best early studies of productivity was conducted at Western Electric's Hawthorne Works in Chicago, Illinois (see Elton Mayo's *The Human Problems of an Industrial Civilization* [Macmillan 1933]). It was done by a careful researcher, Professor Elton Mayo of the Harvard Business School. Mayo was attempting to determine ways to improve productivity in factories. This work grew in part out of his preliminary studies of the impact of illumination on productivity in 1924. He followed up this research with his Hawthorne Effect Studies from 1927 through 1932.

This research exercise by Mayo shows how easy it is to get offtrack when measuring the causes of productivity. It turned out that following changes in factory illumination, productivity grew. (A substantial number of other elements of the work-related environment we won't touch on also seemed to help.) At first, it seemed that added light increased productivity. But the productivity gains were not lasting. Other seeming improvements to the work environment were added one at a time and evaluated. Each time, productivity rose and stayed up for a period of time. Then it would fade out. Perplexed, Mayo and his colleagues restored lighting conditions to the original level. Productivity promptly rose, then faded again. Mayo soon learned that merely varying the lighting brought immediate but temporary productivity gains.

Mayo and his people decided lighting levels were irrelevant to productivity gains. Style of management and how change itself was handled led to the improvement. Later experimenters trying to measure productivity gains realized they had to normalize measurements for the Hawthorne "placebo effect" of improved performance after making any change before concluding that productivity gains arising out of specific changes were lasting ones. At Hawthorne, employees and their managers responded to the latest superficial change but soon reverted to form. Variety was merely "the flavor of the month," as it were. Before long, no one paid as much attention to illumination or similar ostensible change.

Even so, many executives draw false conclusions about the widely reported Hawthorne experiments, noticing only that if they put in new programs, they initially get better results. There were even efforts to institutionalize the Hawthorne effect, literally change for the sake of change. The problem with this idea is that the small improvements that might result from these types of change are often not worth the resources they would consume.

Causal Measurement in Days Gone By: Rocket Into the Space Age

Anyone searching for reliable measures of cause and effect can learn from some of our clever ancestors. Isolating one key relationship that could easily be tracked often made all the difference. Napoleon reportedly measured his soldiers' tooth decay and surmised that certain regions of France produced stronger teeth than others. He preferred to recruit from areas of France where the populace had strong teeth. It was one of several attributes Napoleon believed would make a man a better soldier. Until Napoleon made the mistake of invading Russia, his armies dominated Europe.

In feudal times, pride was a factor in farming success. Freeholders, unlike the serfs, were by definition landowners, though their plots were mostly quite small. Since they were freemen and not part of the feudal lord's estate, they took pride in the fact that they could grow what they pleased. They often planted badly. Crops were relatively poor. By contrast, the estate managers, who were working for the lord of the manor, not only measured the seed they planted, they also measured how much grain it yielded. They were able to isolate better seed and optimum quantities of seed per planting. Theirs was a more systematic approach. It brought superior results. The soil the managers farmed brought far bigger harvests than the freeholders' land.

The wheat goes on. Here's an example of crop measurements from the space age. Farmers today use satellite technology to determine which parts of their vast acreages need which fertilizers and in what quantities. The farmer fertilizes appropriately based on what the crops actually need. Growing conditions are different, depending on the amounts of sun each plot gets and depending on the different slopes and altitudes at which the land lies. Measurements, in this case, are related to causes. The measures based on satellite data have raised productivity markedly. This increased productivity saves time and resources and is good for the environment. Farmers also earn more.

Obviously, farmers are dedicated to growing bigger crops. If the farmer sells more grain, he earns more money. The farmer using satellite technology is the modern-day equivalent of the feudal estate manager. As these farming examples suggest, the more things you measure, the more you can learn and the better you can do.

Nevertheless, organizations sometimes grow so accustomed to a single measure that they may not realize the measure's limitations. Farm tractors cost a lot more now than they did in the 1930s, but they also do a lot more. If we measure by the rising cost of tractors relative to the thirties, a time when tractors were much simpler, we come to a discouraging conclusion. But measure by constant dollar cost of the tractor per acre plowed, and the results look great for the modern version.

Feedback Nourishes Learning

Although most people use measurements to improve their performance and that of their organizations, some people will draw incorrect conclusions from those measurements, especially if the initial feedback is negative. Instead of continuing to try to improve, they are defeated and give up. Instead, what you want to do is use measurements to isolate what is holding you back, change that factor, and get ready to enjoy exponential success.

Michael Dell of Dell Computer Corporation has racked up sales of well over $10 billion a year—breathlessly—with impressive help from mail-order and telephone sales of Dell's superb personal computers. By being the innovator in direct sales over the telephone, Dell has had an advantage in understanding what personal computer users really want. Through this access, measurement of customer desires has driven a strategy years ahead of competitors in a highly competitive market so that Dell has emerged as the worldwide leader in personal computers in late 1998. But Andrew Grove, chairman of Intel, Dell, Bill Gates, and every other player fear the impact of that imponderable juggernaut, the Internet. For his part, Michael Dell is working to turn the Internet into a major part of the company's business. Dell and his team are spending a substantial amount of time figuring how to use the Internet to keep Dell Computer ahead of its telephone and mail-order rivals. Many believe malls will shrink in time as the Internet becomes the primary shopping center. That is not the only hazard in the high-tech world. Inventory can become obsolete overnight and cost the manufacturer millions of dollars, even threaten survival. Compaq, formerly the world's largest personal computer builder, is restructuring to build business computers only as they are ordered. Dell used this approach long before Compaq thought to copy the idea. As for IBM, its resellers are customizing individual machines for their customers.

Stallbusters

Becoming an effective stallbuster is greatly helped by becoming more productive in the most important things you do now. That will free up time to work on more productive areas and give you the personal experience to be an effective coach to others in your organization. Then, using the personal improvement measurements that you have succeeded with, you can help your organization transform itself.

Use Measurements to Improve Your Own Effectiveness

You need to apply the 2,000 percent solution of utilizing measurement in your own life before you can hope to do the same for an entire organization. Write down how you spend all of your time for a week. As you jot down what you are doing, put an assessment next to the time period stating how effective and productive you think the time spent was. At the end of the week, summarize where you were effective and where you were not. Ask yourself the following questions:

How could I avoid having to do the least productive tasks at all in the future and get better results? Let us assume that you find you are checking up a lot on the work done by people who work with you. Are you doing this because you feel more comfortable doing this, because you find many errors, or because a procedure requires that you do this? If the problem is that there are a lot of errors, how can the errors be reduced so that you do not have to do this error checking? For example, can the work be done in a way where it will be automatically checked by a computer program before it arrives at your desk? Or, are the mistakes due to inadequate training or equipment? In either case, sit down with the people who are making the errors to find out how the errors can be eliminated while reducing the work involved. Better yet, first ask if the task needs to be done at all. If the answer is yes, can the task be simplified in ways that will make it easier to do in an accurate way? Then you should consider how the remaining work can be automated using standard software solutions. George Reiswig, former CFO at Perdue Farms, has reported great success with this approach.

How else could I have gotten these tasks done to get better results in less time? In the meantime, perhaps you could have grouped all the checking together and done it at one time so you were more efficient. Or, alternatively, if the mistakes tend to be repeated ones, you could have checked the work in the beginning stages and corrected the errors then so that some repetitions could have been avoided.

How could I delegate these tasks to others for better results? Who is better at error checking than you are? Who is better at finding ways to avoid errors in the first place than you are?

How could I automate these tasks and achieve my purpose? If you are taking the information and simply putting it into another report, how could the report be generated automatically by the receipt of the information? What error-checking questions could be in the software?

Why was I ineffective when that occurred? What are the lessons? Why was I effective when that occurred? What are the lessons?

Time-Wasters

* Repetitive activities (such as executives handling customer concerns) that could be eliminated with advance planning and guidelines
* Activities that you are forced to do because you have never trained anyone else to do them (such as preparing data for financial analysis)
* Activities where someone else is much better equipped to do the task (performing statistical tasks if you are not a statistician)
* Activities you are pursuing without the information you need (as Xerox was doing before sales quality was measured and increased)
* Activities you are pursuing that should involve someone else who is not normally present (such as planning what inventory to build without talking to the people in sales and manufacturing)
* Activities that are mistimed (done before or after the most effective and appropriate time to do them, such as training people in new activities that will not start for months)
* Activities that occupy your time but that are caused by something else that could have been prevented through better planning (a good example is scrambling to make quarter-end budgets—since customers wait to order at quarter end because your company offers the lowest prices and best terms then— because the organization is always in budget trouble)

After you select the areas in which you want to improve, you need to begin regularly measuring what you do in these areas so that you can see how you are doing at improving. The following questions will help focus your improvements:

How much time am I spending on these activities? As a rule of thumb, you should be trying to eliminate the least productive 25 percent of how you spend your time. As you repeat the process, you will actually be eliminating different activities each time. For most of us, less than a third of how we spend our time delivers almost all of our business effectiveness. The ratio may be even more skewed in your personal life.

How am I spending the time I free up from this activity? It is terribly important that you swap the newly available time for a more productive activity, or you are fated to have to remove this new activity as well from your weekly schedule. Be sure to examine your activities overall to find important areas where you are spending either no time or too little time. A good example is time spent on furthering your own knowledge and education so that you can be more effective in your future work.

What are the benefits from the shift in time application? The answer to this question is the acid test of the new time allocation. It will help you avoid the potential waste in shifting time that was discussed in conjunction with the previous question.

What is the benefit to me from the activities I am measuring? This is a critical question. Only if you feel that you are benefiting from the changes will you find this process to be worthwhile enough to spend time on it. For example, a good personal benefit can be to reduce the number of times you have to stay late unexpectedly to work in the office. Having your workload more under control, more predictable, and potentially more portable are all benefits that can result from measuring your activities.

What is the benefit to others from the activities that I am measuring? Be sure to include your family and friends in your answer, as well as those you work with. You may be surprised to see how much low-value activities are stealing time from those you care about.

Use Measurements to Improve the Effectiveness of Others

After you have finished your personal measurement exercises, you will be prepared to be a helpful coach to others. You need to have walked the talk before talking the walk to others will do any good.

How can you get other people interested in measurements? Describe your own experiences with personal measurement to a few
people you work with who are interested in improving personal effectiveness. Be sure to explain how large the benefits have been for you
compared to the effort required so that a reasonable expectation will be
established to pique curiosity. Many people find that this can be an
important life-changing experience. You may even develop deeper, lasting friendships with those coworkers.

A great way to open a discussion of measurement exercises is to
explain how you felt when you were first asked to do them and what
your concerns were, and then candidly describe what happened during
and after you did the exercises. Ideally, the exercises have helped you
so much that people who know you have already noticed a difference.
Perhaps they have even asked you what caused you to make so many
changes. If that happens, you have a great opportunity to tell them
about your experience and encourage them to follow your example.

How can you help other people through the measurement process?
Encourage the individuals to follow the same process you used. Remind
them of the idea from time to time, and update your experience for
them. If you notice that they seem to be having trouble getting started,
ask them what problems they are encountering. Then ask how you can
help. Some people may simply need a "buddy" to help them. In that
case, you could simply suggest that they drop by daily and work on the
exercise with you for a while until they get the hang of it.

Applaud those who do pursue the process, and encourage them to
share the results with you. Give them lots of praise that you genuinely
feel. In praising them, be sure to praise the goodwill being shown by
trying, the effort they are expending, and the things they are doing well.
If something is not to your liking, be sure *not* to criticize in that area.
Instead, you can ask them questions they can answer themselves that
might lead to improvements in that area. A good way to do this is to say,
"That's an interesting idea you have there for saving time. I often find
that the more ideas I come up with to save time, the more likely I am
to find a really big time-saver. How many ideas can you think of?"

How can the measurement message be spread even further? At
whatever point colleagues have found this exercise to be valuable, begin
to encourage them to pick some colleagues to coach, as well. Share with

them your experiences in doing this type of measurement work with colleagues. If each person takes the time to help just a few others, these benefits can quickly be transferred to many people. If everyone made it a practice to follow this process over the course of a month, and then began to share it with one other person each month thereafter, the number of people who would be helped would grow rapidly because the number of people involved would double monthly:

Month	People Helped
1	1
2	2
3	4
4	8
5	16
6	32
7	64
8	128
9	256
10	512
11	1,024
12	2,048
13	4,096
14	8,192
15	16,384
16	32,768
17	65,536
18	131,072
19	262,144
20	524,288
21	1,048,576

Think how good it would feel to help that many people make large, important changes in their lives as a result of starting your measurement activity. And it would take less than two years to accomplish!

Chapter 10
Too Many Trees
Step Two: Decide What to Measure

Measurement does the most good when focused on and used for the most important management processes in your organization and when designed to help you to succeed with your most important opportunities. This chapter shows you how to decide where to apply measurements, what to measure, and how to use the measurements to achieve exponential success.

Having created an environment where the value of measurements is appreciated, your next step is to address how measurements can help your organization to improve the most. The best way to do this is to focus on a particularly important process within your organization or company, especially if you suspect there is a large opportunity to improve. Then you should determine what it is about this process you want to measure so as to make more rapid progress. If you are a laggard in developing successful new products in an industry where that skill is critical, the new product development process could be a fine place to start. If your service costs are high and service costs are a very important factor in profitability, you could choose your service process instead. Using the experience you gain in the process, you can later extend this approach to other important processes.

Tend to Your Organization's Large, Low-Hanging Fruit

Companies that achieve exponential growth are far better than others at measuring the processes they use where major positive benefits can be created easily. For the most success in this effort, you should be sure to consider emerging areas of opportunity that are likely to be created now and in the future. Since few organizations can accomplish more than a few changes at a time, be aware that employees tend to focus on areas with the most immediate *personal* benefit, such as salary increases or better working conditions. This focus can negatively affect the bottom line relative to areas with larger, long-term potential, such as better service for customers. In general, many high-potential payoff areas for your organization are being ignored now unless they are strongly linked to pay and promotions.

There are thousands of processes that a company can measure. But again the tendency is to measure a process that is psychologically or emotionally satisfying and that is not truly important to success. Thus, precious capital is more likely to be spent on a larger parking lot for employees than on a process adding directly to profits, like reduced costs. Lots of mistakes are made in deciding which ideas are the best ones to go ahead with. In that an organization can only absorb a limited amount of change in a given period, change implementation capacity must be treated as a scarce resource. Thus, each change contemplated must be seen in terms of its relative overall importance.

CEOs must be careful to focus on things that actually change behaviors in ways meaningful to company prospects. It is a fundamental error to zero in on areas solely because they enjoy the greatest internal support. Remember: Every worker's first priority is likely to be a pay raise. The wise CEO will crank in wish-list items of all the other constituencies—the customers, the suppliers, even the community. Certainly the shareholders. The firm then benefits through improved profitability. Ideas offering such benefits include, for example, new products and services, better pricing, and reduced costs—all fruitful areas for change.

A basic tool in managing change is listening. Paraphrasing the real estate agent who stresses location, the successful executive knows that she must listen, listen, listen, As indicated, she must heed every relevant group, not just customers and company shareholders. She must hear employees and company suppliers, as well as the fifth constituency: people in the communities where the company has operations. To be effective, managers must talk to a representative sample of each group at a minimum, and, if possible, each manager should broaden the samples to best discover important areas of dissatisfaction and sources of delight.

Change Is a Moving Target

The process of making changes is an evolving one. Circumstances change over time. At one time U.S. auto quality was so poor that people sought out cars that didn't break down. The result was that many Americans bought Japanese cars. But when car quality improved in American plants, quality vis à vis Japan was more or less neutralized as an issue. American car builders then shifted their focus to improving dealership repair service, which then became a major element in their success. But soon, as the newer, better cars became an increasingly large part of the vehicle population, the repair business part of the dealership issue became less important. Cars did not break down as they had in the past.

At that point—and once again—styling became important. The Lexus lost ground because it did not look much different from Japanese cars that were far less expensive. Lexus rivals made much of this, too. Detroit dodged that bullet.

Next, there was a major shift in demand. Americans wanted sports utility vehicles and minivans. We fostered the truck/minivan craze. Japan did not at first respond.

You will fail if you keep measuring the same thing. As each shortcoming is overcome, customer cravings will move on to something else. The able executive will constantly shift what is measured, how important that measure is, and what actions are taken to reflect the current and likely future environment.

Finding the Suggestion-Box Winners

We find a startling success story relative to Step Two at one of the world's leading companies in the humdrum consumer products business, an industry not known for progressive ideas. The company had finished last in all the usually tabulated measures of success for investors—profit margins, profit growth, and return on investment. Management was appalled. It decided to put forth a company-wide effort to discover ways to become number one in these measures. Rewards were offered for the best ideas from employees. Being a large company, tens of thousands of ideas poured in. Judges were chosen who could appreciate and understand each idea from a technical point of view and know if it was a good one. The review team consisted of executives from every functional area: manufacturing, distribution, marketing, sales, research and development, purchasing, finance, and human resources. The reviewers were senior-level managers in positions to implement the ideas they selected.

The reviewers were able to identify the good ideas right off the bat. There was absolutely no confusion on this point, no mystery about it at all. The good ideas had two characteristics: (1) They had enormous, immediate, and long-term benefits, and (2) they were easy to implement right away. Despite this awareness, the executives felt that it was important to consider all the suggestions, so they also pursued scores of ideas that they were convinced were of little, if any, merit. In fact, so many ideas were being worked on that the small number of really good ideas were not pursued as aggressively as they should have been. Once top management discovered the unfocused approach was hurting the good ideas, they added a special management process. Fifteen executives were assigned to the overall improvement process to make sure the top twenty ideas got proper attention. As it turned out, 1 percent of the ideas brought 95 percent of the eventual improvement. By pursuing those few good ideas, they got exceptional results. Had they worked on all of the ideas at once, they would have gotten almost nowhere. As a result of this focused effort, three years later the concern was in the number one position in the key financial measurements of the industry.

Less Is More

A similar lack of focus hurt a major retailing company in the late 1970s. This retailer's sales had been in retreat for years and the business was barely breaking even. In an attempt to turn around the flagging operation, management implemented 100 improvement projects, all of them scheduled to be finished in one year. But, unfortunately, a year later every single project had failed. Then management focused on improving the retail operation and selected the few areas where the biggest improvement could be made. They worked on four areas, none of which, by the way, were on the original list of 100 improvement projects. They learned that they had missed the highest payoff opportunities before. Soon, they were earning high profits.

Have a Nice Day

When there are multiple problems all screaming to be addressed, how do you focus effectively? One of the world's largest retailers faced customer gripes on every important shopping issue. The service was said to be poor, there were too few clerks to serve the trade, the merchandise was not well chosen, and the prices were considered high. As we have already seen in considering what are causes and what are effects, one of the major issues in problem solving is to know in which order to address the obstacles, not an easy matter when virtually every key element in the business is out of whack. What's more, the nature of all of the other problems will shift each time a single problem is successfully addressed. At each resolution point, it is important to reexamine the issues to be addressed.

The retailer in question experimented differently (changing prices, goods offered, staffing levels, training, compensation, and store layout) in its stores throughout the world. It then measured which stores did well and which ones did not. The idea was to identify the conditions that seemed to be most associated with good results in the successful outlets. It was found, for example, that if shoppers were happier, the store earned higher profits. That part might seem obvious. Less obvious, perhaps, is that what first made customers happier was happier employees. What worked best for increasing the happiness of employee and customer alike was to allow the employees to spend the time needed to provide good service. Previously, store employees were kept busy simply checking out the customers. Many customers needed help in selecting items as well.

The retailer studied staffing levels in the successful stores and how the workers spent their time there. To re-create the successful conditions in each store, help was hired as needed, and the efforts of employees who were unhappy, ineffectual, or misusing their time were redirected. Once the retailer knew employee happiness was the key to happy customers, the company created a wall chart for the clerks in all stores. Each employee was told to come by and note what actions or factors improved their attitudes. Within weeks everyone understood the relationship of how more staffing could create happier employees and customers, and, thus, better results for the shareholders.

In such an improvement plan based on measurements, employees have to understand the effects of one part of the system on the rest so that they can work on the right elements. The measurements need to be in a very simple form and fully disclosed so that people can gauge the impact of the measurements. This type of system creates a valid understanding of what needs to be done. One reason infants learn to walk is because they see everybody else walking. They persist even though they keep falling down. They have to observe so they know that what they must work on is putting one foot before the other.

We say we need higher profits. But we do not usually get that by firing lots of people. We get that by getting everyone focused on the right areas to improve. After discovering that customer happiness was related to employee happiness, the retailer found new ways to improve profits. For one thing, it changed the performance measure, setting higher goals on the amount of goods people bought when they came to the store. Shoppers said they would shop and buy more if the outlets offered women's clothing in greater variety. Management obliged. The result was more purchases per customer and per store. Profits, which were already rising, went up even further. This retail company has now done several rounds of such analysis. The company went from having its worst year in history to its best year ever in profits. But attitude was key. The company might not have sold more women's clothing if unhappy clerks gave poor service.

The Elevator Stall Can Cool Your Scrambled Eggs

It is not easy to give better service if a company is unaware of why service is falling down. Consider what happened at a major hotel chain. This sophisticated chain had aggressive initiatives for solving problems. It sought customer comments through guest complaint cards and by using direct interviews. Management learned that guests were dissatisfied with the hotel's room service. It took too long to get breakfast to the room even if the guest left a breakfast order on the door handle the night before. The chain gave this complaint top priority. It added more people to deliver room service. It even added to the hotel kitchen staff. But the situation got worse, not better. They examined the process further. They checked inventories to be sure they weren't running out of eggs or other breakfast food items. They counted the number of deliveries made by each waiter, noting the elapsed time from the moment an order reached the kitchen to the minute that the order was delivered to the guest's room. Wait! They were on to something here. Deliveries took far too much time. The hotel management then asked the room-service waiters to talk about all the things they were doing and what problems they faced in the process. With this systematic process, the hotel chain discovered the bottleneck in short order. It turned out room-service waiters had to wait for up to eight minutes for elevators to arrive at the kitchen or the guestroom floor.

Further checking revealed that housekeeping was delivering sheets and towels during high-pressure times on the elevators, e.g., the breakfast rush and when guests were leaving. Since housekeeping had to unload large amounts of linen to each floor, individual housekeepers kept elevators stopped while the linen was unloaded. Once the elevator stall was identified as the problem, housekeeping delivery schedules were changed. Room-service complaints dropped to near zero.

As so often happens in organizations, a key issue, in this case a turf battle well-known to maid and waiter, had not been communicated to management. In process measuring, we often find that factors thought to be completely unrelated to the core issue turn out to be the critical ones.

Shareholders: The Ultimate Customers

Investors can make or break many company programs through their support or lack thereof. Oddly enough, the financial people may stand in the way of honest efforts to please the shareholders. One company that did very poorly in terms of share price decided it had to change direction. It was suggested that the company measure the attitudes of shareholders and potential investors. But the company CFO said it would be a waste of the shareholders' money to try to find out what they wanted to do with the company. Yet the CFO insisted his purpose was to make the shareholders happy by *not* spending the money. The thought of listening to shareholders was a novel idea for him. The company eventually did solicit shareholder views, after the CFO was dismissed. The benefit of listening to them was many hundreds of times what it cost to obtain their input. The same company found itself with limited information in many areas of critical importance to its success because of this approach to saving money.

Consider another example of misdirected emphasis. CFOs and controllers love to benchmark their own operations. Large organizations are willing accomplices. They can tell you down to a fraction of a penny per invoice how the financial operations are doing compared to rivals at other firms. Trouble is, efficient financial operations usually cost less than a penny on a dollar of sales. Take that to zero and you will not change much in the corporation's overall results. Put one-tenth of that effort into the right parts of a key process, and you will make real head-way. Do that five times over in key processes, and you are wooing the 2,000 percent solution for the entire organization.

Different Strokes for Different Folks

Once you have isolated a good process to measure and where in the process to look, you must decide *what* to measure about it. Many errors can occur at this point in the decision making.

Many of the communications stalls that you now know about can return to haunt you if several different people are responsible for the same set of measures. They will think they are measuring the same performance or conditions, but often are not. To cite an odd case for emphasis, on the same day in the northern and southern hemispheres, one location's normal temperature will be a lot warmer than the other's. Fail to adjust for that factor, even if you measure on the same day with everything else the same, and the result will confuse you. A retailer needs to offer the right goods for that day in that location.

Stay with the weather example for a bit and let it snow for a while. The amount and type of snow has a big impact on gas utilities because snow can be a building insulator. It is said, by the way, that the Eskimos have several words for snow. Nolan Doesken has a dozen ways to measure snow, and for good reason. Doesken is the assistant climatologist for the state of Colorado. He says his studies of state records show that some National Weather Service stations will measure as much as 50 percent more annual snowfall than the nearby volunteer stations. One reason (and there are many others): The National Weather Service measures every six hours, whereas some volunteers measure just once a day, enough time for the snow to compact under its own weight and throw the measurements off. As natural gas delivery to homes is deregulated so that competition grows, gas providers need to measure market potential and price elasticity accurately. Better measuring can help, especially if everyone measures the same way.

Similarly, the water content of snow in Colorado is always lower than many people assume, thus skewing an important factor in gas consumption as well as in water supply calculations, in avalanche warnings, and in information concerning the potential for floods.

The Riches Are There If You Only Look Up

Perspective often plays a key role in measuring. The personal outlook of the decision maker can cast a long shadow on a measurement's validity. The treasurer of a well-known but temporarily strapped public company was feverishly seeking to raise cash. His search was focused on the value of items on the company's balance sheet. As he sat in his office worrying, he was staring at a painting, one of several dozen owned by the company, that had been done by a famous American artist. The paintings were worth millions of dollars. But because the paintings had an accounting value of a few hundred dollars each, and he did not know art, he could not factor in the true value of the paintings for his hard-pressed corporation until a visitor pointed it out.

The Footloose Cannon

In days of yore, the inadequacy of measuring sticks was clear to everyone, but no mere mortal was prepared to do anything about it. In England, the foot was *the* foot—the length of the reigning king's foot. (In France, the similar standard measure was *le pied du roi*.) When a carpenter said, "Long live the King," he meant it—fervidly. Imagine the chaos that would follow if a half-grown size 8 prince took over from a dying size 11½ king!

Even earlier, before the king's foot became the standard unit of measure, a foot was the length of just anyone's foot. When an English king ordered a six-foot bed for his wife, the bed-builder used his own foot as a rough measure and cut the bed accordingly. The queen jumped in and gave her head a thump. It seems the bed-builder's foot did not quite measure up to his king's, and legend has it the poor guy lost his head over the issue.

Other measures were skewed in similar ways by personal differences. A fathom used to be defined as the length of a man's outstretched arm as he hauled in a line. A depth-seeking sailor would drop a weight tied to a line to the bottom of the ocean, then count how many times he pulled the line through one outstretched hand to the one that was reeling it in. Imagine the problem this presented for sailors seeking the depth of the water in normal times, let alone emergencies. ("No shorties, please, we have enough trouble in this gale just trying to keep afloat without landing on the rocks.") Finally, six feet was settled on as a proper fathom. This was after the foot became twelve inches.

Without standard measures and ways of measuring in advance, you, too, will have similar problems.

Stallbusters

This section will help you find your biggest and best opportunities to benefit from measurements by locating your most important processes, their most critical factors, and what to measure.

Identify Your Most Important Processes

How can you identify the processes most important to your organization? The simplest way is to begin by estimating how long your organization could survive without them. Then, you can also consider how long the organization would prosper if they were done poorly. For another perspective, speculate on how long you will last if you perform the process less well than competitors.

If you have a good understanding of the potential benefits from these processes if you did them better, you can ask a parallel set of questions about the missed opportunities that exist in each process.

If you did the process as well as you can imagine it, what would be the size of the benefit compared to how well you are doing today?

If you did the process as well as you can imagine it, what other opportunities would that open up?

What would those opportunities be worth?

If these ideas for identifying your most important processes do not help, you can pick from among the frequently important process areas given in the following list. These processes often receive limited measurements in organizations, and their importance may not yet be fully understood. A benefit of reviewing this list is to see if there are processes you should be focusing on that you wouldn't normally think about.

Begin by reading the list and writing down any initial thoughts you have about the potential importance of these areas in your own organization. Then go back to the preceding questions that look at the importance of process areas. See if you can quickly eliminate some areas and highlight others for more consideration. If you find that you do not know enough to evaluate the importance of a particular area, plan to discuss the subject with someone in your organization who does. In fact, one alternative is to have a group review of this list to narrow your attention to one area for initial focus.

Samples of Potentially Important Processes to Measure

* Tracking of why large institutional investors do not buy your organization's stock
* Developing new products and services that provide customers with major benefits over competitors' offerings
* Focusing marketing based on total cost to serve each major customer versus what the competitors' costs are for the same account
* Shifting your mix of customers, products, and services to reduce costs versus competitors
* Identifying and implementing your most important cost-reduction opportunities
* Identifying and implementing effective programs in your organization's largest opportunity areas
* Reducing cost of capital in ways other than by reducing borrowing and refinancing for lower interest rates
* Tracking the effectiveness of compensation and recognition for reinforcing the behavior that you want employees to exhibit
* Obtaining win–win ideas for mutual benefit from suppliers and the communities you serve

Break Down Your Process Into as Many Subprocesses as Possible

The simpler the aspect of the process that you seek, the easier it will be to find, measure, and learn from it. Also, you can assign the further analysis of subprocesses to different groups of people who are already more familiar with these areas.

How do you go about dissecting a process into its subprocesses? If you are not sure how to do this, hire someone with experience in process analysis to help you. A local professor will often suffice for the purpose and will not usually be terribly expensive.

Find the Critical Factors of the Most Important Process

Once you have selected an important process to focus on, you need to narrow your attention further to reveal the most important parts of the process. The following questions will help you do this:

Who can help you determine the critical factors in the process you are focusing on? Begin by asking everyone affected by the process what is most important to them in what the process does or should do. Ask these people not only "what" other areas they think are important, but also "why" they consider those areas of this important process to be important.

What can you measure that may cause or influence the process's important aspects? As an example, imagine that you are measuring your process to shift your mix of customers, products, and services to reduce costs versus competitors. Since this process relies heavily on measurements in many different areas in order to be effective, focus first on aspects influencing measurements, such as the availability of the information to do the measurements, the accuracy and timeliness of that information, and the availability of the measurements to those who should be using them.

A process like this also relies very heavily for its effectiveness on how people in the organization are motivated by working on the process. You will want to see how well aligned the personal objectives of each person are to achieving this process, how directly compensation reinforces the process, what effect promotion practices have on the process, and the comfort level with the time allocated to the process.

This process is also very dependent on how well everyone in the organization understands it. How well trained are people? What is the error rate in key areas? When and where are mistakes most likely to occur? What opportunities are most frequently missed?

In addition, you naturally want to consider the overall effectiveness of the process. How closely does your mix of customers, products, and services match the profile that would give you the lowest cost you can imagine versus competitors? Where you are far off from the optimal level, and what are the causes?

You will have your own ideas about influential aspects that can be measured, but you should remember that at this point, the more questions you ask, the better. Just don't make the evaluation too cumbersome. If you have engineering training, you may have the skills to draw a process flowchart that will identify all the steps in the process as one way to spot areas to measure. If you do not have this training, you can learn more through the type of training that is frequently provided by consultants during reengineering projects. If your company has participated in any reengineering projects, chances are that someone who worked on such a project can provide you with the necessary information or training you need to prepare a flowchart.

How can you check your conclusions about the critical factors of important processes using statistical analysis of the relationships you are looking at? Most people find that the relationships are more complicated and different from what they initially understood them to be. Consider our retailer with stores throughout the world as an example of how this analysis can be done.

Start by Measuring Everything You Can Think Of (That Seems Worth the Cost) Concerning the Process Output and Its Causes—And Then Narrow Your Focus

You may be wondering why this topic is in the Stallbusters section. It's here because the main point of this chapter is the importance of narrowing your focus on what to measure. Therefore, you need some way to reduce to a manageable number all of the many measurements that could be used in the process in order to begin tracking your organization's effectiveness efficiently. Beginning to eliminate some measurements while paying more attention to others is an essential part of this second step in the eight-step process you are learning.

What you need to do is create data that can be used to statistically identify and connect causes and effects. For example, product-quality measures may tell you that your products have no defects. That observation about product quality is probably accurate if you also find you are outperforming your competitors in market share, profit margin, and customer satisfaction growth. If these things are not occurring, something is wrong with your measures. You will need to add more measures until you find out why you are not growing in these critical areas. (Recall that, as previously stated, the best sources of measures are those defined by the people who are affected the most by your processes.)

You can also save a lot of time now (if you like) by thinking ahead to something we do not cover until the next chapter. In that next step, you will be using the measures you selected to compare your organization to other organizations. To make this step easier and faster, find out now, while you are picking your measures, what measures are most available for comparisons outside of your organization, and be sure that you include these on your list.

Be careful in deciding not to do a measurement because of expense. Not all expensive measures are a bad investment. It all depends on the size of the potential benefit relative to the cost. Spending a few hundred dollars for a cheap measure that will not help you is a waste of money, while spending several million dollars for something that will make you many billions could be a real bargain, as long as you have enough money to do so.

A company that used this second step in the eight-step process found that a single measure (which cost more than all of the other measures combined) provided almost all of the insights into how to improve an essential process. Had the company stopped looking because of the expense, the firm's business would probably be less than half its current size and operate at less than a quarter of its current profit level.

Chapter 11

Where Many Cooks Improve the Broth

Step Three: Identify the Future Best Practice and Measure It

This chapter begins to explore the fourth of six perspectives outlined in the Foreword to this book: a call to set objectives and plans beyond the best of what someone will soon implement as tomorrow's best practice. This chapter will show you how to identify what the world's future best practice will be.

After focusing on one important process for your organization and deciding how to measure that process, your next challenge is to identify what the best-in-the-world performance of that process will probably look like (in or out of your industry) for the next several years. We call that performance the "future best practice."

Chances are that your organization does not yet really know how to find out about the elements of best practices that, when combined for the first time, will drive you well ahead of the competition. Much of what is written about so-called benchmarking (of which more is coming up) will not be of much use to you. This chapter will give you shortcuts to identifying future best practices and the lessons of many years of experience in this area.

It is never smart to assume you know the right answer before you pursue best-practice methods. Nevertheless, when savvy people innovate, they tend to smugly pursue creating in their own way without looking further. They easily forget that industry is filled with bright peo-

To identify what the best practice in the future will be, you need to have those who will be using the information look outside your organization to others, who are setting the pace for best performance in your important process areas. Assembling ideas from different trends in subprocesses for best practices from a variety of the best-performing organizations will allow you to establish a new process that will outperform any other organization in the future. For some, this drawing will portray such a search process. Do you see any pairs of eyes?

ple. Some will have worked with processes similar to theirs. Introspective factory managers cannot realistically hope to match best practice in every manufacturing process, yet many bet that they can.

For one thing, it's a sure bet that you won't find all the best practices inside your organization. You should be aware that for each critical task within your organization, there is almost always someone on the outside who does that task better than you or anyone else. In fact, the key to the future best practice probably lies in another industry. We can learn from those who are the best at a given task. This is why, for example, we take lessons from the golf pro. But remember, no individual or company is likely to achieve the future best practice in more than a few areas. Just so, the golf pro who is the best at putting may not drive the longest ball. Therefore, your task is to look deep and wide, to access many industries and organizations, to find and pursue the future best practice in the tasks that are important to you. This is the trail to becoming the very best you and your organization can be, and it is the road to the 2,000 percent solution.

Not Just Copycatting, But Innovating

Just what is the future best practice, anyway? Best-practice thinking evolved to the form we are discussing out of simple benchmarking. A benchmark is defined as a standard of excellence against which rival products are measured. Crafty industrialists are notorious for buying a competitor's successful product and dismantling it. The engineers check out the design to see how it works. They note good aspects and bad, ways the item could be improved, and estimate how much it would cost to make. If the design team can do a better job, they produce their own version. This kind of dissection and copycatting goes on all the time. The auto builders do it. The microchip companies do it, too. It explains why the military gets excited when the latest version of the enemy's best fighter plane is captured intact.

But the future-best-practice approach goes far beyond learning from the competition. You are seeking the best means over the next several years of achieving excellence in a particular process. Forget slavish copies. You have to go further. Here's why.

First, tomorrow's best practice is already being developed somewhere else. By the time you match what is currently out there and get to market, you will be behind someone else. Like a marksman aiming at a moving target, you must aim ahead of where the best-practice target is now to find where the future best practice will be.

Second, you need a clear-cut edge beyond the future best practice to make serious inroads in a marketplace. The bigger the advantage over your competitors, the better. This target means aiming where you hope no one in your industry, or any other, is even trying to get as yet. Obviously, copycat techniques will not be enough to get you far out in front of the pack.

Third, you need to move beyond copycat techniques because people outside of your own industry may know more about everything you do than does your entire industry, and their viewpoint is advantageous in several ways. People outside your industry have the added benefit of being easy to access. They have less reason to hold back information. There are rarely legal problems with sharing. Also, they feel repaid if you give them ideas about how they can improve their own performance. So the price is usually right.

No Assuming Allowed

When we begin to act on our assumptions about what will happen, other things can go wrong. Consider assumptions about how others will behave. Let us look at safety on the road as an example. Many years ago, a young man discovered the danger of making assumptions while driving. He had stopped to make a left turn on a lightly traveled secondary road. He assumed that if a car approached from behind, the driver would swing the wheel to the right and drive around him. You would think a ton of metal at rest on a highway would have registered in the approaching driver's mind, but she was so preoccupied that she hadn't noticed the car in her way. The young man's car was hit by this vehicle, which was going almost forty miles an hour, and was totaled. Luckily, he wasn't killed or badly injured. Research indicates that on occasion drivers become so preoccupied or distracted that they overlook the obvious. Perhaps the distracted driver was humiliated by the boss a few minutes earlier. Or her husband may have walked out, leaving her penniless and with children to feed. Or perhaps she had just flunked out of college. All of this can happen to sober drivers. DWIs add a wild card to the equation.

Assumptions about color recognition also played a part in this accident. Some colors clearly do not register as well as others. The young man's jolly green giant of a car was low on the color-recognition scale. He vowed never to have this experience again. When he discovered yellow was the most conspicuous color, the color most likely to be noticed, he ordered a car that looked like a four-wheeled banana and drove it for years. Just the same, he kept an eye on the rearview mirror when turning left. In the same vein, fire companies bought trucks from the one-time market leader and now-defunct American LaFrance in red only. Fifty years ago, the prevailing wisdom was that red was the most conspicuous color, but, in fact, it is not as arresting as yellow. So Mack and its rivals in the fire-truck business feature yellow now.

Best practice on the highway also calls for a series of defensive measures, especially if you ride a motorcycle. Motorcyclists rode with their headlights on years before it was required by law. When a driver looks in the rearview mirror, the driver expects to see another car. Since the driver doesn't expect to see a motorcycle, it may not register. But a biker's lighted headlight coming up from behind is attention-getting. Similarly, Sweden, Finland, and parts of Canada call for the use of headlights on all vehicles during the day so that drivers will be sure to notice each other. Drivers should not assume that their vehicles will be seen simply because they are there.

Some seasoned drivers who skid off the road will swerve into the nearest tree. At the Indianapolis 500 one year, the pace-car driver steered smack into the only barrier in sight, a referee's observation tower. This is an inexplicable but common phenomenon and not just on the highway. On a golf course, a bride stood behind a tree while her new husband drove a golf ball off the tee. He sliced it and hit the bride's leg. He later learned that the golf course groundskeeper and his fellow workers tried to hide off to the side, but balls hit them with uncanny regularity. In the quest for best practice, never discount an answer as unlikely. Test it first.

These days, best practice in driving calls for lower speed and the use of air bags and seat belts. After air bags were introduced, drivers and riders felt secure. Many stopped buckling their seat belts. This reflects the assumption, not based on best-practice results, that air bags do it all. But testing shows that air bags work best for those who also use seat belts. Therefore, seat belts are a current best-practice element in safe driving.

So we see that assumptions about future best practice are dangerous. In future-best-practice research, it is essential that you avoid preconceived ideas, however logical. Do all your homework, including questioning assumptions.

The Quest for the Best

It is easy to say that best practice is found in scores of factors, but the practical question is, where do you start your quest? If you are a manager, start within your own corporation, particularly if yours is a large one. If you were a shaving cream manufacturer, you would probably have several facilities worldwide. You should visit them all. You will find some do better work than others. So you will learn a lot internally, but without locating the future best practice. When you make these visits, you should quiz your people as to whom they know in other industries who have related practices that are worth studying. Give serious concern to what you have to be a lot better at in your process. Have you a quality problem? A cost problem? Both? You may find answers in a repository near at hand.

Go to the library, and don't forget to use that biggest of all libraries, the Internet. Check for articles in which other people have worked on similar problems. It's no mystery: Those who work on future best practice like to brag about the good job they did. There's another major resource you can tap for free. After Malcolm Baldrige, the popular Secretary of Commerce in the Reagan administration, died tragically in a rodeo accident, the Baldrige Award was set up to honor him and business quality. The winners of the Award must release information concerning their accomplishments. Write-ups about the winners are fine public sources of information on best practices. Simply call the companies.

There are also a number of databases devoted to best practices, most of which charge fees. Some of the leading accounting firms keep data on industries they serve. By referring to these data, you can find out who is doing what. Frank Zarb's Houston firm, The American Productivity and Quality Center finds databases that keep track of best practices. Profnet at http://www.profnet.com lists professors and other experts who are available to reporters and other researchers.

So don't hesitate to go to academia for additional best-practice information. Professors at universities who are experts in their fields can be a bountiful source of information. The most knowledgeable professors are often brought in to companies as consultants. Some of these academics have observed hundreds of situations close at hand and probably still monitor some. They may be restricted by confidentiality agreements, but they can nevertheless tell you where to seek out future-best-practice ideas.

But, even if they give you a dozen leads, you can be sure that you won't find all the best practices. When you visit those leads you got in academia, ask them to point you to other best-practice ideas they know about. To get the future-best-practice ideas you need, you may have to work with scores of other companies and organizations. You may find only one element of the best practice at each of dozens of companies. Not even every part of a given task will be done best by just one firm. Many different companies may each do one aspect of the process you are exploring better than any other. What this means is that if you can put these many perspectives together, you will have a better practice than has ever before been realized. Thus, you are not just matching a rival or a single organization when you develop a best practice by finding pieces of the process in various places. You are moving well beyond the former best practice because you are putting together a new best practice comprised of many individual parts never assembled together before.

Finally, do not limit your quest to the United States and Canada. Very often the best practice, or at least elements of best practice, will be found abroad.

Ever Onward

Do not forget that achieving the future best practice is a continuing effort. When you develop a best practice, someone else will soon learn about it. Whether or not the word gets out, someone else will, in short order, figure out a newer, better process. It is routine for innovators to believe that once they have the current best practice, they are set for twenty years. In fact, you need to repeat the future-best-practice process search every year or two. In some industries, particularly high-tech ones like microchips, the future-best-practice quest has to be continual.

Make your pursuit of best practice nonstop for a very obvious reason: Being good at this work can be a core competence that provides a very large and increasing competitive advantage. For example, the sooner you know what future best practice needs to be done next, the more time you have to develop and enjoy a new advantage. While pursuing future best practice, be circumspect about what you have been doing, lest you awaken a sleeping rival. Be sure you do not confuse your efforts with what others call best-practice research. They usually measure just a few comparative aspects, often small ones that won't be best practices by the time they are implemented.

If you do your work on future best practice well and thoroughly, you will be able to identify:

* Several current best practices from outside your industry that your competitors are not yet using
* The current best practices in your industry being used by competitors
* Where both sets of current best practices will probably evolve as processes and in performance levels over the next five years
* A way to assemble many of those current and future best practices together in a new way that far exceeds the likely effectiveness of any existing organization in this area over the next ten years

Most benchmarking people ignore all these lessons. But if you follow the path we have set out for you, you will be well on your way to exponential success.

My Fleet's Bigger Than Your Fleet

Perhaps no greater folly ever occurred in pursuit of best practice than that exercised by King Philip II of Spain when he assembled the mighty Spanish Armada in 1588. The Armada was to sail to England, invade, and seize the throne for Philip from the upstart Queen Elizabeth who was challenging Spanish hegemony at sea and in the colonies. Since Spain was far wealthier than England, this seemed like a simple task. All King Philip had to do was to round up a superior force and create a massive Armada to transport it, and a British disaster would fall naturally into place.

But King Philip and his advisers assumed that he would be fighting a foe with ships and forces just like his and in ocean conditions like those experienced in Spanish waters. He picked the Spanish ship model as the best practice. His ships were massive. But they were also slow, and some were manned by inexperienced seamen. Some lacked guns and skilled gunners; others lacked ammunition. To top it all, King Philip named an unseasoned duke to lead the Armada. As the Spanish approached from the south, the British got to the windward of the Armada, forcing it into the English Channel, which can be very rough even in good weather. The British, with their smaller, more maneuverable ships and skilled sailors, had a marked advantage. They bested the Armada in three minor sorties even though they were outnumbered by two to one at all times, and many of Britain's ships were merely converted merchant vessels. The Armada soon fled north and dropped anchor off Calais. The British sent fire ships (vessels filled with gunpowder and set on fire) toward the Armada. The Spanish, in a panic, cut their anchor cables. Heading north, the Armada rounded the tip of the British Isles and sailed into monstrous winds off Ireland. Many ships foundered and washed up onto English and Irish shores. Half the Armada was lost and the rest limped back to Spain. What the Spanish thought was a best practice couldn't have been worse. Beware the excess confidence that comes with wealth and power. You may stop measuring and stop weighing practices to determine which are best. You may lose everything.

Shaving the Stubble off a Bad Practice

And you thought putting the toothpaste back in the tube was hard.
—Anonymous

Let's dream up a company that plans to make shaving cream and has decided to learn from future-best-practice research. As a starting point in looking for the future best practice, it would be great if the company could go to a competitor and look into the plant to see how the cream is made. But Gillette, the top shaving cream producer, will naturally bar the door.

However, Gillette can't keep you from picking up its shaving cream at the pharmacy. You should buy all of the brands and see how the product you are making compares to them. Even though you can't get in your rivals' factories, that doesn't mean you can't test the shaving cream itself for potentially key data.

But doing that is only the beginning of your odyssey. The shaving cream industry is large and powerful. It is intimidating. But it doesn't have a lock on the best ways to do every part of every process. Here's your problem. You want to put a large amount of product in a very small container. Hmm! The chemical industry is good at this. Chemical companies compress gases in hardened steel vessels, so that industry deals with higher pressures and greater densities than you will ever use with shaving cream. What's more, chemical concerns provide safety packaging. You need that, too. Chemists also know more about chemicals than the shaving cream industry does. You can also buy stable mix technology from the chemistry industry. You are not a threat to them.

It may seem odd to turn to another industry to solve a problem. It is not widely known, but problems of crucial importance to a company or even an industry are often solved with technology that has existed for years in a different industry. To wit, the food industry has scrambled to reduce bacterial contamination after a series of food poisoning debacles. Having no homegrown solution, the industry turned to chemistry. It turns out, in fact, that DuPont had worked through parallel product integrity and purity issues years earlier. Subsequently and serendipitously, DuPont met representatives of the food industry. To the benefit of both sides, the problem was addressed and solved through best-practice product integrity methods.

Be aware that your way of thinking about a problem, your mindset, may stall you. In shaving cream, uniformity of product may be an important product quality. But actually, freshness is the primary concern. If chemicals degrade, the product won't function properly. This is a preservation issue. When you talk to the chemical company, stress that you want the first and the last shave from the can to be identical. Then the chemical company will seek out chemicals with appropriate, compatible shelf lives. If, however, you tell them you have a uniformity or mixture concern, but don't mention the issue of degrading, you might get only half the answer you need.

There is much more to do. You have to contain the cream. You must check out the can companies. Ask about their most innovative products. They will welcome you because you are a potential customer. They want to help. With luck, they may need a client to launch a novel new can that happens to work well for you. Your next stop may be at the factories of manufacturers that make enclosures for the can top. Again, you are their potential customer. They are also eager to help you succeed.

If you are wise, you will also consult industrial sources apart from chemistry, people with hands-on experience in the special problems of creating aerosol cans.

You should do this work personally, asking many questions. You often won't be allowed to make actual measurements about the processes once you are in the plant of the support company. Even if you could measure the processes you like, you'd need your own equipment so that your measures would be comparable to theirs. But get details on every measure you can think of when doing your research.

When it comes to marketing shaving cream, Gillette certainly won't help you. But others will. What you are trying to do is to market consumer products to men. There are related problems in selling men, say, cologne and briar pipes. You can go to such nonrival sellers for future-best-practice information. There are also marketing consultants who can help you find the best practice in the field.

If you learn your lessons well, your shaving cream will produce much better shaves, be less expensive to manufacture, stay fresher longer, be perceived as the best by consumers, and command a premium price while you gain market share relative to your competitors. Ideally, competitors will not be able to duplicate your achievement for many years. You will probably use a combination of trade secrets, patents, exclusive licenses of technology, and sole source–supplier relationships to accomplish this result.

King of the Hill

Don't argue with him, he's a millionaire!

—Anonymous

It is natural to assume that the high-performing companies—the GEs, the Xeroxes, and the Microsofts—use only the current best practices, but that is usually not the case. The older the company and the bigger it is, the fewer future best practices it is likely to develop. Oddly enough, marginal companies tend to be better sources for future-best-practice information, the kind of information that can bring you 2,000 percent solutions, because low-end companies have serious cash-flow pressures. To survive, they have to focus on efficiency in all of their endeavors. They have fewer ingrained procedures. They are not in a manufacturing rut. They start with a fresh slate. Ergo, they tend to get better solutions. Microsoft was a teeny company when it got the contract to develop the operating system for the IBM PC. Founder Bill Gates quickly scanned the competition and found a program he could build on for only $100,000. Over twenty years, this program has added many billions of dollars in value to Microsoft and to Gates himself.

I'm Smarter Than Henry Ford

> *You can have any color you want, so long as it's black.*
> —Henry Ford to buyers of his best-selling Model T automobile

When you meet with others to study future best practice, be sure to ask "why" the actions that are taken are an advantage; otherwise you may misinterpret the answer.

This quote from Henry Ford provides a good example of how we can misinterpret the basis of a practice. Ford is often viewed as having been insensitive to customers. Maybe. But he was actually reflecting the difficulties of putting a good paint job on a car in those days. Use any color but black, and the results were poor unless you paid a fortune for the work. A parallel situation occurs when American executives visit Japanese factories. Everyone notices that everything is highly compact, but visitors draw the wrong inferences. Knowing that land is very expensive in Japan, Americans figure they now know the reason for the compactness. Japanese executives will patiently explain (if you ask them) that the main reason for compactness is to ensure good communications among workers. The farther apart people are, the worse the quality of the products they make. So even in Japanese plants in the United States, the factory floor will usually be quite compact.

Stallbusters

This section will provide you with questions, perspectives, and directions for how to locate pertinent future-best-practice information, capture the key insights from that information, and identify how to move ahead of the rest of the world in the most favorable way to you.

Look in All the Obvious Places for Future-Best-Practice Information

You may not be familiar with data sources for future-best-practice information. Many of these sources are similar to those used by organizations to do legal, ethical competitor intelligence gathering.

Where can you find future-best-practice information? Many seminars and books are available on this subject to help you. There are also service firms that will do the research for you. People who have written about these subjects in the past may also be helpful to you in locating sources that are publicly available. A good place to start is to call publication editors whose subjects cover the processes and subprocesses that interest you.

What databases exist that already measure the processes you are interested in?

What companies have been written up for excellence in these areas?

Who do experts say are the best they have ever seen?

Who do the best in the field pay attention to?

Look in the Not-so-Obvious Places for Future-Best-Practice Information

Experienced stallbusters know that looking in uncustomary places often turns up the best information, but that it can also be the most work.

How do you identify an unusual source of information? Pick a meaningful sample of companies that could have processes like yours (from anywhere around the world and in different industries). Call each of them and ask several different people in the organization what they do and how well they think they do it.

Go visit any that sound interesting to check them out.

What is the best way to get information from another organization? When you visit a company with a current best practice, do not start with the CEO or his or her top aide in seeking data on best practice. Go to the firing line. For finance, see the top financial person, the CFO. If your best-practice issue is quality control, see the person who manages quality. Each specialist will have measurements in place and know who is most knowledgeable concerning that area in the organization. Talk with the people involved with the specific best-practice issue so you will understand what they think about the problem. They may give you a better way to think about what you are trying to do.

We learn best by doing things. If you are seeking best-practice information about a product, ask for a chance to help turn out the product "hands on" or to work in a company lab. If at all possible, put your own measuring rods in place and measure personally. If you don't see the actual facilities that turn out the product and don't see how the item is manufactured, you can't draw sound conclusions.

Be Prepared to Do Your Own Measuring

How can you quickly determine if there is an advance here over what you have already learned elsewhere? Canny stallbusters will have already tested the answers that were received in the telephone conversations by asking clarifying questions. One such key question is: What can be seen and measured by doing a personal visit? If the answer is "not much," then you can probably do without the visit, *unless you get access to more key people this way.* Invariably, there will be one or a few items of information that can quickly validate the efficacy of the process you are investigating. For example, if you are looking for a computer help-desk activity that is remarkably efficient and effective, you should be able to visit and find one person sitting there with nothing to do. That follows because most problems have already been resolved in the past by the help desk. You could not see the help desk and its level of activity unless you visited.

The company may also keep records that can help you understand what is going on. If the help desk claims to resolve problems quickly and permanently, there may be computer records to back up this claim. See if the company will let you review this information during your visit.

Who should do the measuring? Have people do the measuring who will be using what they learn, once you are fairly sure you are on to something. This is important because these people will know what measurements to make in order to create valid comparisons, and no one will believe that the practice is any better unless these people report they found it so. For example, people who work on or with computer help desks will know that employees in companies may not be calling the computer help desk for other reasons. If the help desk is very ineffective, people may find it a waste of time to call. Or, it may be easier to call the manufacturer or software provider help lines for specific questions. On the other hand, the computer users may all be computer scientists who do not need any help. The computer help-desk measurers will undoubtedly do a user survey of some sort to test these kinds of measurement issues.

Estimate How Quickly the Future Best Practice Will Change in the Future

What kind of information do you need to make such an estimate? Here, you will probably have to rely on historical data, in part, to find out how fast progress has been occurring. Be sure also to ask your information sources about how fast they expect improvements in the future. Check with suppliers and experts to see what they say as well. Assume that these estimates are unduly optimistic, unless they are much faster than what has occurred historically.

See if you can establish why the improvements are occurring. In the early days of semiconductors, people assumed that particular subprocess improvements would always cause all of the improvements. Actually, new improvements came from unexpected areas. The real limit to improvement speed lay in the goals that the organizations set for improvements.

Ask what could change to make much larger and faster improvements possible. Ask about this subprocess when talking to people in parallel areas. For example, talk to customer market research people concerning what they think about shareholder market research. You will be able to tell from their giggles that most of what is touted now as best practices in shareholder market research was obsolete in customer market research practice by 1970.

If the area looks very important, get expert help to sort through all of this.

Be prepared to search high and wide, especially outside your own industry, for most of the key lessons. Use your own measurements on the processes you study that you will use in your own company later. Do not rely on the current-best-practice model's measures.

When you're through researching the future best practice, you will have moved ahead of everyone else in your universe in understanding, and by a wide margin. But do not become overconfident; you will need to start the process again no later than within one or two years.

Chapter 12

All Aboard for Best-Practice City

Step Four: Implement Beyond the Future Best Practice

This chapter completes a call to set objectives and plans to achieve well beyond the best of what someone will soon implement as tomorrow's best practice. It shows you how to set objectives way beyond tomorrow's best practice and implement this new target in a timely and cost-effective way.

Once it has been identified, go as far ahead of the future best practice as you can and bring everyone in your organization up to the required new level of that practice in the critical areas. Successfully leapfrogging the future best practice calls for using your best change leaders to unify the effort. But everyone must be involved in order to implement beyond the future best practice in your organization. Leaders must be steadfast in the belief that implementing beyond the future best practices for your organization is a 2,000 percent solution for success. They must train everyone else so that achieving beyond the future best practices becomes part of the corporate culture. Capture the benefits of the combined activities that exceed future best practices as rapidly as possible for yourself or for your organization. Study without eventual implementation is ornamentation, without benefit. Knowing the future best practice, however, may not be enough to teach you how to implement beyond it.

Those you assign to implement the new path must closely examine what your future-best-practice model organizations do in the various subprocesses. They should become equally comfortable with what the future level of best practice will be in those model organizations. You must train the implementers so they can adapt what your company does now to your new models of exceeding future best practice. Potential helpers in this process are high performers in your company, those who work with the processes in a hands-on way in the model companies, professors and consultants with expertise in these areas and with relevant experience at the model companies, and training experts. We discuss this point in more detail in Chapters 14 and 15, so be sure to look for this information when you implement these projects to exceed future best practice.

Triage for Maximum Effect

Organizations can succeed in making only a limited number of large changes at one time. Narrow your focus to a few areas of highest promise so that you do not water down your potential for results. Some aspects of change will be difficult because you have limited or scarce resources. Each change in a manufacturing process, for example, may require the time and attention of the same people, including the most capable manufacturing manager. These people also have to complete their regular, ongoing tasks. Budget to pay for the costs of the change can also be a limited resource. Further, testing the new process may require diverting some plant machinery to this use that is needed to make existing products.

Another limitation is the difficulty of the task itself. People can learn how to do back flips, but they will be kept pretty busy learning how. Many new beyond-the-future best practices present the same degree of challenge. The concept of what is needed may be quite clear, but the details of successful implementation can be excruciatingly unforgiving of even tiny errors. You will also find that some tasks match up poorly relative to the skills and experience of your people and those you can hire to assist you. Yet another problem can come in the communication challenges of coordinating a process across several different functions (such as marketing, manufacturing, finance, and human resources). Such coordination may be critical and will also be time-consuming.

This part of the process will surprise you: Just as the triage doctor or nurse prioritizes patients for treatment on a battlefield or in an emergency room, you need to first segment those aspects of exceeding future best practice into ones that:

1. Can be implemented almost immediately with little effort.
2. Can be implemented within two years with effort and attention.
3. Can be implemented over more than two years.

In your triage agenda, you can probably do most things that fall into the first category easily, quickly, and with little help unless they stymie a high-priority item from the second category of activities. The challenge comes in selecting from the second and, especially, the third categories. You probably cannot make more than three or four changes at the same time that affect exactly the same people. Their ability to absorb change will be your limiting factor, rather than good ideas, time, or money. Create the best balance of near- and intermediate-term benefits, with the least strain on the people and the resources of your organization. Use outside resources as aggressively as you can and still get timely, cost-effective results. Organizations tend to become stalled if some of the benefits of change do not arrive quickly.

A famous research project tested the ability of salespeople to concentrate by giving them the task of throwing wadded paper balls into a wastebasket. With the wastebasket too close, the salespeople lost interest because the task was too easy. With the wastebasket too far away, the salespeople lost interest because they succeeded so seldom. However, by putting the wastebasket where about one toss in three succeeded, the salespeople enjoyed themselves and wanted to keep playing. In many ways, organizations act like the salespeople in this example. Make a goal or task too difficult or distant, and interest soon disappears. Also, take into account which of the tasks your people will pursue with joy and which with foot-dragging. Joy works better.

Give high priority to the items that will give you the most benefit over the next two years and beyond, while creating a balance so that some significant benefits will be realized every six months or so. Establish your future-best-practice priority for an action with initial benefits in six months if benefits from a project of greater value will not kick in for years. If you do not keep the change momentum going, you will never get to the deferred benefits you hope will occur. You also want to establish an environment of constant, major improvement as your organization's standard way of doing business.

We're Almost Done—In

Future-best-practice ideas with long time horizons often carry the seeds of their own destruction. This circumstance has proven to be a real hazard for many organizations that invest in computer systems that take more than two years to complete. In such cases, the winners are usually the consulting firms that produce these systems while the loser may be the organization that paid for the new system. A recent study of companies that used computer systems to successfully develop best practices shows that the benefits from the new systems were always partially activated in the first six months. The total project may have taken more than two years, but early benefits were being enjoyed in the meantime.

Let us return to the shaving cream company example from Chapter 11 to show how this process of controlling timing and benefits works. We find that the product's freshness can be improved right away by making some chemical changes in the product and by using better mixing equipment. We also find that shaving quality can be improved a little by using new types of lubricants, captured in a physically altered form. Implementing this change takes longer because some custom equipment needs to be designed and built. Eighteen months will be required. Other shaving quality enhancements will have to wait until a new type of shaving can is developed, which can take more than three years. The aroma can be greatly improved with another chemical processing method that will take two years to develop. The physical appearance of the shaving cream can be upgraded in three months. The most important improvements in shaving quality will follow developing a genetically engineered beard softener that will probably take four years. A number of other opportunities exist.

We can begin to establish priorities by constructing a table of projects, size of benefits, costs, scarce resources, and time involved, as shown in Exhibit 12-1. Based on the triage approach, improvements in "freshness," "appearance," and "other" probably belong in category 1; that is, they can be implemented almost immediately with little effort. Changes pertaining to the "shaving can" and "beard softener" are clearly in category 3; that is, they will be implemented over more than two years. "Lubricant" and "aroma" improvements belong in category

Exhibit 12-1 Shaving Cream Example Triage Table.

Project Area	Size of Benefits	Costs	Scarce Resources	Time Duration
Freshness	Small	Tiny	Manufacturing people	Weeks
Lubricant	Moderate	Moderate	Manufacturing people	18 months
Shaving can	Large	Moderate	External partner	3 years
Aroma	Moderate	Small	None	2 years
Appearance	Small	Tiny	None	3 months
Beard softener	Enormous	Very large	Cost	4 + years
Other	Small	Very small	Few	Weeks/months

2; that is, they can be implemented within two years with effort and attention.

As you can see, when to start category 2 and 3 projects becomes an issue because the beard softener project is expensive and will take a long time. You might delay the start for a year until profits grow from freshness, appearance, and other improvements. Because making changes in both freshness and lubricants is a strain on manufacturing people, you may decide to delay the start of work on the lubricants until freshness is done. Some might choose the opposite order by considering lubricants that are more valuable than freshness.

The table lays out conflicts and optimization potential. Good judgment has to take it from there.

Since we will consider adding in other tasks later on in the eight-step process, you may want to wait to see what all the alternatives are. You may find that some of the beyond-future-best-practice opportunities identified here are of a lower potential than the opportunities that unfold in Chapters 13 and 14. If developing the theoretical best practice that we discuss in Chapter 13 will take you longer than a few weeks, you may want to plunge ahead with the beyond-future-best-practice improvements anyway. In this case, our recommendation to you is that you reserve some change capacity (such as budget, time of key people, and analytical resources) beginning around the time that you will have some new projects to add. This may mean that you will choose to mine category 1 from the triage list more heavily than category 2.

Outsourcing for Outstanding Possibilities

The best way to determine how long it will take your company to implement the desired combinations of practices is to see how long it took the organizations where you found elements of the beyond future best practices to implement them. You will need to consider whether you will be a faster or slower learner and integrator than they were. You can cut off a lot of time and effort if you can hire the company you studied or some of its current or former employees (or someone else very capable) to outsource that part of the beyond-future-best-practice process you are pursuing that the other organization is expert in providing. The fact that you have found a great subprocess does not mean that it makes sense for you to become an expert in that area. You should decide if you want to outsource when you begin to find ways to exceed the future best practice, and you will find it efficient to know that you have the option to outsource through a contact you made during your studies.

Go Where the Benefits Are Greatest

At Thermopylae in 480 B.C., the Spartans fought a remarkable battle against the greatly superior Persian forces under Xerxes who were attempting to invade the Spartan homeland. In an open battle, the Greeks, with only 400 men, could only hope to last a short while against the 180,000-man Persian army. They needed circumstances in which they could turn the tables so that their small force could, in effect, outnumber the invaders. The narrow pass at Thermopylae provided this unique opportunity. It was the only way into Greece from the north, and it could be defended with a relative handful of men because only a few invaders could enter the 50-foot-wide pass at a time.

The Spartans lasted until a treacherous Greek guided a Persian detachment over the mountains to overpower them from the rear. Nevertheless the Spartans, under Leonidas, were famous for their defense of the pass, which is a fine example of future best practice in military strategy in its day.

Similarly, the United Nations' forces in the Gulf War did not confront the Iraqis head-on, which would have been to the advantage of the well-entrenched Iraqis. Instead, the U.N., seeking the greatest benefit, used a best-practice concept like the Persians used in attacking from the less well defended rear. The U.N. knew that if its forces could sweep laterally across the desert to thinly defended turf behind the Iraqi lines, they would not face the most effective force of the Iraqi army and could earn a relatively easy victory.

In any effort to exceed the future best practice, go where the benefits are greatest by concentrating your resources where they will face the least resistance and be most effective.

Stallbusters

In this section, you will learn how to anticipate problems you may have with implementing beyond the future best practice, how to adjust for those potential problems, and how to create the highest likelihood of achieving a 2,000 percent solution.

Capture Your Track Record for Implementing Beyond Future Best Practices

Organizations vary widely in their ability to exceed future best practices by assembling best practices in new combinations from the various sub-processes. You need to understand your existing capacity to do this before choosing and organizing what you will implement. A common error is to overestimate the effectiveness of your organization in implementing ground-breaking new directions for your industry. First ask yourself:

What significant attempts has your organization made to improve over the last five years? You will use what you learn to help you accurately describe the cost, time duration, and scarce resources involved in each potential project to exceed future best practices. Answer the following questions about those attempts:

Which attempts achieved their purpose on budget and on schedule?

Which attempts did not?

What were the apparent causes of the two types of results based on discussions with those who were involved?

How many successful implementations were key individuals able to work on at once?

Finally, ask yourself:

What could you do in the future to improve your organization's track record? Be sure to consider better planning, adding missing resources, better training, and so forth.

Develop Your Plans for the Potential Beyond-Future-Best-Practice Projects to Pursue

The ideas for which projects you want to consider will come from the various research efforts you put into determining what the best practices will be in the future for the various subprocesses. To begin to develop those plans, ask yourself:

Which projects are reasonable to consider doing because the cost/benefit ratio is favorable, the total cost is not outlandish compared to your organization's resources, and there is a reasonable chance of success? You should then rely on the normal project-development process you use to develop the potential project plans, unless project development is the process that you are improving. Be sure the output of these project plans can be summarized in the manner shown by the shaving cream example in this chapter.

Compare Your Plan to Past Results

Which of these potential changes look like your successes of the past, and which seem like your past misses and messes? Be sure to adjust the project descriptions for the table used with the shaving cream project to reflect this perspective. If something is too risky, you should probably drop it unless you can redefine the project to be pursued in some much lower risk way that will still provide the right level of timely benefits.

Do the opportunities to use your strengths in implementing beyond-future-best-practice changes provide you with enough benefit to exceed the future best practice? For many the answer will be no, and that should be clearly understood during the subsequent management efforts.

If not, what are the simplest, most effective ways to enhance your organization's ability to provide or absorb more valuable improvements? Many who have been reluctant to do the necessary outsourcing of projects to exceed future best practice and normal internal activities will now see a logic in supplementing the internal resources where that outsourcing can be most easily done in order to accomplish more as a total organization.

What is the risk of failing to succeed? In some cases, it is only lost money. In other cases, you may actually be worse off than if you had never started or you will also have missed other opportunities because scarce resources were involved. When survival is at stake, organizations surprise themselves with what they can do. If you stay within your current ability to change comfortably, will you be healthy and viable? If you can answer "yes," the solutions you have identified are probably okay to meet your needs. If not, you need to communicate the danger and get the support that survival instincts normally inspire. Good luck!

Looking Ahead

Remember to keep some time available to look at the opportunities that you will develop from considering Chapter 13. Ideally, you should pick projects needed to surpass future best practice to mesh with the projects that will come out of your work from Chapters 13 and 14. How to do that is described in Chapter 14. Completing your thinking about surpassing the future best practice is an essential element of integrating your implementation with what may be even better opportunities that you are about to uncover through using the remaining chapters. However, while you prepare for the considerable improvements attainable via the next two steps of the process, you must strive to capture the benefits of what you have just learned.

Chapter 13

Perfection as Only You Can Imagine It

Step Five: Identify the Theoretical Best Practice

This chapter introduces the fifth of the six perspectives outlined in the Foreword: a call to go for the maximum result that can be achieved with reasonable risk and resources, far beyond merely exceeding tomorrow's best practices. This chapter shows you how to identify what can realistically be achieved as a maximum result.

It is axiomatic: Tomorrow's best practice is bound to be better than today's. And the day after tomorrow's best practice will be better than ever. It is helpful, therefore, to use the concept of theoretical best practice to try to see where we are eventually headed so we can get there sooner—an insight both new and revolutionary for most organizations.

The theoretical best practice is simply the most effective process that can possibly be accomplished by anyone. It will usually exceed the future best practice by a wide margin. In corporate communications, for example, a theoretical best practice would mean having everyone hear and act on a message in appropriate ways within a few seconds. We know that is possible because those seeing a fire, smelling smoke, and hearing a fire alarm in a building will respond appropriately in that amount of time. You must understand that your organization's actual performance today represents a tiny fraction of what is possible. The theoretical-best-practice concept can help you set more appropriate goals to take advantage of this.

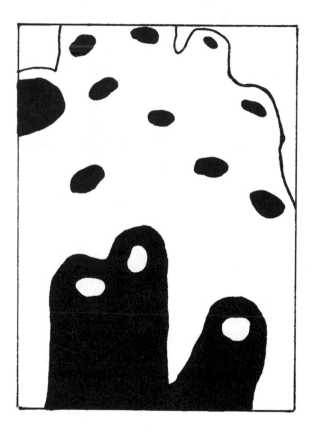

The theoretical best practice (the most effective practice that can possibly be accomplished by anyone) will usually exceed the future best practice by a wide margin. The theoretical best practice will often be quite different as a solution from the future best practice, as well. This image symbolizes that difference with the dark shape in the foreground being the future best practice and the white object in the background being the theoretical best practice. The inverted shades within the images are there to remind you that the theoretical best practice may require doing some things in ways opposite to what the future best practice may require in order to achieve the best possible results.

We will begin by saying that it is a lot easier (and more instructive) to identify the theoretical best practice than to identify the future best practice. With future best practice, you have to take many precise measurements in many places. This measuring is not easy if, for example, you set out to determine the distance between the Earth and a faraway star. But with theoretical best practice, you can usefully extrapolate by relying on the many dimensions of your imagination and your own personal experience. You should be able to imagine ways of doing something better than has been done by you or anyone else before.

Theoretical best practice has to be a big stretch. So the purpose of this step is to set an optimum, but realistic, goal. Set your sights far enough beyond tomorrow's normal best result so that you don't settle for small improvements when you can have much larger ones. Goal setting using theoretical best practice may be the most important lesson in this book. It is *the* key to the most effective way to 2,000 percent solutions.

How High Is Up?

Managers often complain that they do not know how tough to make corporate goals. Imagine that output from your operations has been rising at 5 percent per year in units while revenues per employee have grown at 3 percent per year. Many will be tempted to set this historical performance as a target. However, if you now learn that you have been losing lots of market share because competitors have been growing at 12 percent a year in units, you may feel differently. You may want a higher target. If you also learn that launching a planned new service this year will expand your total volume by more than 20 percent this year, the target may grow further. Then if you find out that you have just signed a major customer who will double your volume, the goal will probably rise again. Add more information that tells you that you have not been calling on the twenty largest potential customers, and another quantum goal increase occurs.

Like the salespeople tossing wadded paper into wastebaskets mentioned in Chapter 12, most leaders strive for goals that are 30 to 50 percent likely to be reached. The setting of goals that have to be stretched for can expand performance by creating more realistic interest in employees. Usually, managers set goals that are too easily reached, but sometimes the goals are simply unattainable. Either way, easy or hard, the leaders get lots of complaints about the goals. There is considerable negotiating by affected persons who want the goals at lower levels. Solving this problem effectively can bring major success. Utilizing theoretical best practice provides a major improvement in goal setting by identifying both a higher standard and one that is achievable and credible to employees. You get more stretch with the same degree of psychological comfort.

This story about the creation of a large fortune is instructive concerning how theoretical best practice can be useful for guiding action. Early in the twentieth century, no one knew how to get at the oil and gas under a body of water, whether the water was in a lake, a bayou, or the ocean. One wildcatter had the foresight to realize that someday it *would* be possible to drill inexpensively in shallow water. He looked for fields where there were successful oil or gas wells surrounding bodies of water and bought the rights to drill under the water, even though no one yet knew how to drill there. He was confident there was oil or gas there and he was mostly right. For pennies per acre, he ultimately added tens of millions of dollars to his family estate. Here was a man who understood the reason for determining the theoretical best practice.

The actual best practice of his day didn't permit drilling for petroleum in shallow water. The technology of the day did allow the building of structures in shallow water (he had seen piers and bridges jutting from the ocean floor and lake beds) and building watertight pipelines. If these capabilities were combined, he reasoned, you could drill and transport petroleum products from wells situated underwater. He estimated that this approach would cost four times the usual cost. To offset his added cost, he then looked for wells on dry land that produced much more than four times what normal wells produced. This is exactly the thought process needed to identify the theoretical best practice. This kind of abstract thinking applied to your potential can put lots of money in your organization's pocket, and in yours, too.

Bill Gates Shows You the Money

Bill Gates, founder and largest shareholder of Microsoft, may be providing another such example today. He believes that electronic images will be cheap to provide and of high quality in five years or so. Gates, widely reputed to be the richest man in the world, has focused on the theoretical-best-practice opportunity presented by personally buying the electronic rights to every piece of art that he can acquire, even when he does not own the artwork itself. These rights were purchased when there was little electronic communication via the Internet and other media, and detail portrayed was poor. So the rights were purchased cheaply. The situation is changing already. When we use the Internet in the future to order electronic copies from Gates's archives, we will be making him even richer.

Meantime, Microsoft's ubiquitous software is another way we all make him richer. You will recall the operating system he first sold to IBM was so primitive that would-be rivals turned up their noses at it. Gates focused on theoretical best practice and won by anticipating that a large market would develop for personal computers and that most software would be for the IBM PC standard. His thought process involved extrapolating Moore's Law (that integrated circuits double in effectiveness at the same cost every eighteen months) and banking on customers' preference for IBM.

Warren Buffett Pumps Up the Money

Warren Buffett, chairman of Berkshire Hathaway, has added new meaning to the term "getting full credit." Buffett is a great student of finding good stock value. From his studies, he learned that human psychology can create much added stock price value. The theoretical best practice in this arena is to have your company's stock sell at a premium to its current value based on historical and current performance because of anticipated successes you will have in the future. Also, the better your current performance, the higher the potential anticipation of future performance is likely to be. You can build a pyramid of wealth on other people's hopes, if you inspire them enough. Con men who offer investment pyramid schemes (like Ponzi) have known this for years. While Buffett is no con man, he knows how humans think. He has one of the best investing track records ever. The money he manages grows very rapidly. He goes his terrific track record one better: He lets the world know what he has bought, after he has bought it. Because his reputation is so stellar, others buy the same stocks, pushing the prices up higher than they would otherwise go. Because he is smart, they make him look even smarter. He also tells his story in his annual report. That creates a mystique about his work. One result the price of Berkshire

Hathaway stock goes up faster than the value of the portfolio. Buffett approaches theoretical best practice in share gains.

Encountered on an elevator at New York's Plaza Hotel, Buffett was as nice as his reputation. He provided directions to lost souls on the elevator as though he were a helpful hotel employee rather than one of the world's richest and smartest people. There was not a bodyguard or groupie in sight. Unless you knew it was he, you might have thought that you had just met the hotel manager. Now, that is a very satisfying theoretical best practice—lots of money, fame, and privacy as well.

No Hits, No Runs, No Errors

> *He throwed that out there like a strawberry at a battleship.*
> —Red Jones, for years Cleveland Indians Commentator

Baseball is a good metaphor in seeking an understanding of what a theoretical best practice is. In baseball the defending team has nine players on the field at all times. Many skills are involved: teamwork, throwing, running, catching. But the focus is on the pitcher, who can make or break a game. It is not unlike a self-directed work team with one person being critical to the team's efforts due to a special skill such as, say, statistics.

So baseball pitchers can give us further insight into theoretical best practice. For a pitcher, theoretical best practice is winning every game he pitches. But there is another part to theoretical best practice here: For the team to win, the pitcher's team also has to have good hitters. The pitcher can't win the game if his team scores no runs. Also, the pitcher who performs at theoretical-best-practice levels is influenced by the fielding work of the team. If the other team makes fewer errors and scores lots of unearned runs, the pitcher also won't win. Thus, a high level of fielding competence is needed, too.

Now to the pitching itself. We realize that the more stuff the pitcher has, the more likely it is that he will win. Ideally, he should have a fastball, a sinker, a slider, a curveball, and a knuckleball. The more pitches he has, the more chances he has to catch the hitter unprepared. Great pitchers have at least two great pitches. Sandy Koufax had both a great fastball and curveball. Most pitchers have a change-up. Koufax had a change-up, too. No great careers have resulted from a single pitch.

So our theoretical-best-practice pitcher has to have several pitches and they have to be very well executed. His fastball has to be fast enough that the batter can't make very good contact with it. The curveball has to curve enough that the batter can't easily reach it. The knuckleball has to be so slow and has to drop so much that it eludes the best batters. To determine what theoretical best practice is as far as the various pitches are concerned, some work is required. Measurement of physical potential is used by engineers to help us determine what the theoretical best practice is in many cases. For pitching, we'd have to have a mechanical device with the ability to throw the fastball and the other pitches in various, precise ways. We'd have it throw the pitches in random order to all kinds of batters in the major leagues to find out how often the other side can hit our robot pitcher and how often. We would have to figure how many times to throw the fastball and the other pitches and in what ways. We'd have to note that the opposing batters will occasionally hit some home runs. Our team might now average hitting one home run and scoring three runs per ball game.

To determine how good our offense has to be, we have to look at what our theoretical-best-practice pitcher can hope to accomplish. In our example, let's assume that the average runs per game by the opposing team is one. However, there will be a statistical variance. If the batters hit a home run every fifty-seven times at bat, the home runs will occasionally cluster. You could have three home runs in one nine-inning game. Usually there will only be one home run. In any case, the home team batters would always have to score a minimum of four runs to ensure that our pitcher always won.

It would take a theoretical level of four runs or more per game for our team to win every game. Usually the opposing team will score one run and we will score four, assuming the same pitcher remains on the mound for nine innings. We would also have to factor into the analysis the effect on the game of some of our relief pitchers who don't pitch quite as well. We might need five or six top relief pitchers to win every game. Errors in fielding would also have to be considered.

Locating the theoretical best practice is the key to setting the right objectives for your organization. Done properly, you will greatly expand your employees' and colleagues' sense of what can be accomplished, while you instill confidence that the large gains are reasonably likely to occur. This will, in turn, help motivate everyone in your organization to enthusiastically pursue these new "stretchier" goals. Your organization's performance will soar as a result, creating the exponential success of a great 2,000 percent solution.

Getting From Point A to Point B

Theoretical best practice helps on a personal level, too. An avid Boston Celtics fan was planning his route to the Celtics stadium. He began by asking everyone he knew how long it took them to get to the games and what route they took. Not one had a good route or a time-saving set of directions. Due to widespread construction in Boston, traffic was atrocious. Finally, the fan realized that he should test every possibility, a kind of theoretical-best-practice approach.

He scouted all of the routes that led directly to the Fleet Center where the Celtics games are played. He did a similar study of all the routes that led to the Fleet Center access routes. He then calculated the time it took to do all of the different combinations of routes. He settled on one that was quite illogical as the crow flies. But the series of route changes when used together took a third less time than any alternative because the normal approach was to try to reduce distance, not elapsed time.

Mastering the Masters

> *Tiger, Tiger, burning bright*
> *In the forests of the night,*
> *What immortal hand or eye*
> *Could frame thy fearful symmetry?*
> —William Blake, *The Tiger*

One of the best ways to understand how effective an individual or organization can be is to use the example of a phenomenal athlete who amazes people with his success. Ask those who competed in the 1997 Masters Tournament in Augusta, Georgia. They will tell you this much: Tiger did not land in the woods (Exhibit 13-1).

Learn from Tiger's awesome work in that classic, which he won with the lowest score in Masters' history and at the youngest age ever. The twenty-one-year-old actually exceeded what everyone believed to be the theoretical best practice in one area. During an entire week at the Augusta National Course, one of the hardest in the world for put-

Exhibit 13-1   Tiger Woods Winning at the 1997 Masters Tournament in Augusta, Georgia.
John Iacono. Reproduced with permission of *Sports Illustrated.*

ting, he made every single putt of ten feet or less. Experts on the topic would have told you this accomplishment was impossible. Top pros usually make half their putts from six feet. Dave Pelz, an engineer, did some widely publicized mechanical tests and discovered that if you place a golf ball on the green and perfectly line up and roll the ball from twelve feet out, it will drop into the cup only half the time. So much for precision. Yet it happened. If you study his following year's performance in the Masters, the full scale of this accomplishment becomes clearer: Tiger might also have won in 1998 had he putted as well as he did in 1997.

Tiger Woods's sport is dominated by men taught by professionals. Initially, Tiger did not learn from a pro. Taught by his father, a nonpro, this wunderkind doesn't take a full backswing from the ball as other top golfers do. He has perfected an unorthodox drive in which he hunkers down with a short, wicked swing and generally hits the ball farther and more accurately than anyone else who hits it a long way. Tiger Woods can hit the ball longer distances than the powerful John Daly. The conventional wisdom holds that if you try to hit the ball as hard as Tiger Woods hits the ball, you lose accuracy, as Daly often did. But at the Masters in 1997, Tiger Woods basically landed his hard hit drives on the fairways every time. So much for a sport dominated by trained professionals with lesser skills than Tiger's.

Obviously, Tiger Woods played terrific golf in winning the 1997 Masters. Best practice here is to note the actual best score ever posted at Augusta under the same playing conditions. Tiger Woods went way beyond, breaking the existing record. Theoretical best practice goes beyond what Tiger Woods was able to accomplish, too. Theoretical best practice will tell us what would happen if every shot were as perfect, which duffer and champion alike know is simply not possible.

One way to approach theoretical best practice is to figure out what is the most the human body can do—how hard a human can swing the club and hit the ball, and how accurately that human can hit the ball toward the target. Tiger's best swing will show high accuracy. It's possible for him to hit well repeatedly, just as a top concert pianist can play a piece of difficult classical music repeatedly without error. But golf is not a precision instrument. Some golf factors are uncontrollable.

Theoretical Best Practice: Every Golfer's Dream

Theoretical best practice in golf calls for hitting the ball well enough to birdie each par-three hole. (A birdie is one under par.) This accomplishment calls for hitting each tee shot so perfectly that the ball lands close enough to the hole—say no more than three feet from the pin—so that every putt is likely to drop. Golf courses typically have four par-three holes. So our analysis calls for three-foot putts every time and three scores of two and one score of three (theoretically missing one three-foot putt and one birdie as well). Due to roll, you will likely miss a three-foot putt one time in four.

The course will also have four par-fives, and we know from the performance of people who do long-drive competitions that it is possible for people to hit the ball with some accuracy for distances of 300 yards. What those facts mean in theoretical best practice is that after the second shot, the ball should be on the green and three feet from the pin again. Theoretically, you would sink three of the four putts. So you would score three eagles (which is two under par) and another birdie.

The rest of the eighteen holes (ten of them) are par fours. Theoretically, you have to assume that your accuracy at 300 yards will now give you three-foot accuracy from the pin on the second shot. You'll land close to the green or on it with the first shot so that a chip, a putt, or a pitch will get you near the pin. This means that after the second shot you'll be three feet away from the cup. Assume you make 70 percent of these short putts so that seven out of ten holes will be birdies. You'll also have three pars. For each eighteen-hole round, your score will be seventeen under par. Tiger was eighteen under par in total for the four rounds in the Masters. Theoretical best practice would be four times seventeen or sixty-eight under par.

Basically, theoretical best practice works backwards: We start with what is perfection given the natural limits of human beings. We then begin to consider what we have to do to reach perfection. Tiger Woods averaged 323 yards off the tee at the Masters and would have had to learn to hit more accurately to achieve theoretical best practice. He did get a lot of birdies. What made him succeed was that he played the par-fives exceedingly well. He played par golf on the par-three holes. He had bigger gaps from theoretical best practice on the par-fours than on anything else. Using this comparison, he could analyze the gaps in his game on each hole and focus on his bigger gaps on par-fours.

This discussion is only to show you about theoretical best practice. We do not intend to knock a man who is arguably as fine a player to ever swing a golf club. Tiger is young. He will no doubt continue to improve, perhaps dramatically so. Neither he nor anyone else short of a robot can reach theoretical best practice for an entire round of golf. He has, however, come closer than anyone else. Way to go, Tiger!

The Unsound Sound Barrier

In a Smithsonian Air and Space Museum audiotape, famed test pilot Chuck Yeager recalls the missions of test pilots who tried and failed to exceed the speed of sound. The planes would shake so much that they would tear apart. There were lots of crashes, and lives were lost. Theoretical best practice for an airplane was, therefore, believed to be flying at or just below the speed of sound back in the 1940s. But then the planes were redesigned. Yeager, who was lucky enough not to attack the sound barrier with the poorly designed planes, says the advanced plane he flew was buffeted a lot. But as soon as he passed through the speed of sound, the air became smooth.

Those who have flown on the Concorde do so with the knowledge that this once-hazardous crossing of the sound barrier is quite safe. There is a Mach meter in the front of the cabin. Passengers who know about the sound barrier tense up as the Concorde approaches Mach 1 (the speed of sound). But nothing happens. Pioneers had set a theoretical-best-practice limit that was too low. Had Chuck Yeager and his unlucky peers observed the Mach 1 barrier, there would have been no space program.

Theoretical Best Practice in Historical Perspective

Modern people see themselves at the end of a continuous evolution of talent and knowledge. We do, in fact, stand on the shoulders of those who went before us. Perhaps we should examine history more carefully. Sports history suggests that the pursuit of theoretical best practice in sports has been limited due to a lack of historical perspective. For decades, runners thought it was not humanly possible to run a four-minute mile. Finally, in 1954, Roger Bannister ran the mile in under four minutes, specifically in three minutes, fifty-nine and four-tenths seconds. The record fell again quickly after that. Now no miler worth his salt is content to do less. Runners are still shaving seconds.

Long jumpers are setting new records almost every year. Or so it would seem. But archeologists have gone back to study the beginning of sport in ancient Greece. In the excavations, they have found the long-jump pit the Greeks used 2,000 years ago. The long-jump pit suggests that athletes may have jumped twice as far as long jumpers today. However, the archeologists also dug up pieces of pottery that depict athletes doing long jumps with weights in their hands. They would swing their weighted arms forward at takeoff and then let go of the weight, so went much farther. Is that an illegal assist? Perhaps. In 1937 Cornelius Warmerdam won fame in breaking the impenetrable fourteen-foot barrier in pole vaulting and eventually jumped fourteen feet, seven and five-eighths inches, with a stiff pole. Today the record is over nineteen feet. But the pole is flexible, not stiff.

Rapid improvement is often called a mutation. There are cases in which a superior athlete like Tiger Woods does the impossible and thus overwhelms the competition, causing them to stop pursuing the best practice. In the face of rapid progress, people will assume that no further work needs to be done. But theoretical best practice should raise the hurdle constantly to an ever higher level. Artificially low targets are and have been the bogeyman of progress. Until we know what can be achieved, we will not attempt that which is possible.

Stallbusters

Since you probably never thought about theoretical best practices before reading this chapter, one of the best things we can do for you is give you some thinking practice on the subject. Experiencing this way of thinking will help you exponentially improve your organization's effectiveness by applying this new thinking to your biggest opportunity areas. Your objectives should be to capture this skill as a permanent part of your organizational and personal perspective and to share these exercises with others to expand the use of this valuable, new habit.

Examples of Personal Theoretical Best Practices

What examples can you think of relating to theoretical best practice in individuals? List at least five activities where human beings perform thousands of actions in a row without making a single error. (Breathing is a good example.) Note how this success occurs. Subconscious mental processes guide breathing. The purpose of this exercise is to help you realize that errors can be eliminated in the theoretical best practice.

List at least five examples of communications being received and understood correctly every time. (Schoolchildren leave the classroom when the dismissal bell rings, and thousands know it is New Year's when the ball drops in Times Square.) Note why this success occurs. Repetition of the messages and personal significance play a big role in both.

Now that you are getting the idea, list at least five things different from what you've already listed that your parents did correctly every time (they earned or found enough money to feed you or grew the food you ate so that you could grow up). Note why they were successful (they placed a high priority on feeding you).

Now, give yourself some credit and find at least five other things that you do correctly every time (you consume enough liquids to keep from becoming dehydrated). Note why you are successful (your body tells you that you are thirsty, and you treat this need as a priority).

Hopefully, by now you realize that human beings are routinely capable of flawless performance in many ways. That makes creating greater results in many other areas much easier to consider.

Examples of Organizational Theoretical Best Practices

What examples can you think of relating to theoretical best practices in organizations? List five things that organizations do without error thousands of times in a row (delivering e-mail on an intranet is a good organizational example). Note why they succeed (the process is programmed to be error-free on equipment with back-up capability if a part fails).

List five ways that organizations communicate that are received and understood correctly every time (how much you will be paid as a new employee). Note why they succeed (everyone wants to know the answer, so even if the communication method is poor, people will find out the answer).

List five activities performed less frequently than thousands of times that your organization always does correctly (perhaps you have a money-back guarantee and always honor it). Note why your organization succeeds (customers and employees are both committed to keeping this promise, and any initial error will be corrected in a way that will eventually please the customer).

Extend Theoretical Best Practices Into New Areas

Now that you are beginning to understand the nature of achieving flawless performance, let us see if you can apply it to areas where perfection does not yet exist.

What five places where you personally now make some errors could be made error-free, and what would have to change for this to occur?

In what five places where you personally now make lots of errors could you improve either to be error-free or to make very few errors, and what would have to change for this to happen?

Go over the same questions with regard to your organization.

Spread the Word

Share your questions and answers with members of your family and people you work with. Tell them what you have learned. Coach them in how to answer the questions for themselves. You'll be prepared to take on the role of coach after you have finished the preceding exercises for yourself.

How can you get others interested in pursuing theoretical best practices? Describe your own experiences with the exercises. Explain how you felt when you were first asked to do them and what your concerns were, and then candidly describe what happened during and after you did the exercises. Be sure to explain how large the benefits have been for you compared to the effort required, so that a reasonable expectation will be established. Many people find that thinking along these lines is an important life-changing experience. When that happens, you will have made a lasting impact on that person.

How can you help other people work through the exercises? Encourage them to follow the same process. Remind them of the idea from time to time, and update your experience for them. If you notice that they seem to be having trouble getting started, ask them what problems they are encountering, and then ask how you can help. Some people may simply need a "buddy" to help them. In that case, you could simply suggest that they drop by daily and work on the exercises with you for a while until they get the hang of it.

Applaud those who do pursue the process, and encourage them to share the results with you. Give them lots of genuine praise, especially for their effort in trying and for the things they are doing well. Avoid criticizing. If they need more encouragement, you can ask them questions that they can answer themselves that can lead to improvements.

How can the value of this new way of thinking be spread even further? At whatever point colleagues have found these exercises to be valuable, begin to encourage them to pick some colleagues to coach, as well. Share with them your experiences in doing this type of work with colleagues. If each person takes the time to help just a few others each month, these benefits can quickly be transferred to many people. This is a critical part of the 2,000 percent solution.

Chapter 14
On the Trail of the Holy Grail
Step Six: Pursue the Theoretical
Best Practice

I don't know where I'm going, but I'm on my way.
—Catchphrase

This chapter completes the call to go for the maximum result that can be achieved with reasonable risk and resources, far beyond merely exceeding tomorrow's best practices. This chapter shows you how to set objectives way beyond tomorrow's best practice and implement this new target in a timely and cost-effective way.

After identifying several theoretical-best-practice opportunities in one of your organization's important processes, you need to select which of these opportunities to focus on in combination with your implementation of projects to exceed future best practices. In implementing the pursuit of theoretical best practice in general, you will also need to evaluate your track record for successfully making similar changes and whether you can afford to take several different approaches to designing and pursuing the implementation of each opportunity.

Set Your Sights on the Stars

To select which opportunities to pursue, first set an objective. As described in Chapter 12, make sure the objective is neither too modest nor too aggressive compared to your now well-informed sense of what is practical. And make sure you can frequently realize some benefits along the way to your ultimate goal. Then, with that objective in mind, simply add the theoretical-best-practice choices to the triage table you prepared when analyzing choices for actual best practice (from Chapter 12) and continue your analysis. The apparent best balance of benefits, costs, resources, and time will point to choices you should pursue. Later in this chapter we will return to the shaving cream example to demonstrate how to do this.

In moving toward any theoretical best practice, be sure to use a realistic time frame. Avoid throwing money and resources around in hopes of saving time. Be aware that you are likely to go up a number of blind alleys in various aspects of your quest. It will thus be helpful to pick a theoretical-best-practice target that involves as many as possible of the activities you already know how to do well.

Also be sure to think about what will happen should your project fail. Will you get anything at all out of it should that happen? You should plan so that if the project falls short of its primary goal, you will still end up with most of the benefits you expected to achieve. To that end, organize the work to limit the potentially most costly risks.

Eenie, Meenie, Mynie, Moe

Ideally, in any quest for theoretical best practice, you should try to think of three or four possible ways to reach the goal using problem-solving approaches that you already understand. It is critically important that you hedge your bets by simultaneously pursuing several paths so that you do not end up stuck if the single path you choose does not work.

Independent studies show that if you design four ways to do something, the final cost will usually be about a third less than if you design only one way. If instead you find eight ways of doing the same thing, costs will come down, but only by a maximum of 15 percent more. There is, then, a point of diminishing returns.

And it is always best to begin with the simplest approach. If a process design looks complicated, simplify before implementing it. If it still looks complicated, simplify again. By doing so, you will limit false starts and save much time and money.

When the Sky Isn't the Limit

When pursuing theoretical best practice, you will find that nothing has been tested; the combination of everything is new to everyone. Consequently, each step along the way must be tested against whatever reasonable standard can be developed. These critical implementation steps, of course, cost money. Costs must be held in check, or the budget will be exhausted before the assault on theoretical best practice is completed. Such a constraint is actually an advantage in disguise because it necessitates the use of disciplined decisions and actions in only the most productive areas. Consequently, those with fewer resources are usually more successful in pursuing theoretical best practice. Consider the U.S. program to put a man on the moon as a lesson in the dangers of having too many resources.

When President John F. Kennedy created the "Man on the Moon" objective for the 1960s, he focused primarily on the goal itself and not on the technology needed to achieve that goal. That certainly qualified as a theoretical-best-practice objective then. However, putting a man on the moon and bringing him back safely the way the Americans did it was a singular event that had limited carryover to many other potential areas of space development and thus was of low value as a theoretical best practice.

Nonetheless, the Soviet Union had beaten the United States into orbit, so, in the effort to go one better, cost was no object in achieving the objective through the Apollo program (Exhibit 14-1). The virtually unlimited financial muscle of the U.S. Treasury was used to experiment with exotic fuels and pursue disparate technologies. The Soviet Union had to make do, like a struggling company fighting for its very survival. As it turned out, the constrained but therefore straightforward Soviet space effort bested the United States in some important ways.

With their cost-restrained approach, their best rockets were far ahead of ours in pursuing theoretical best practice; ironically they are being used now to launch some U.S. satellites (Exhibit 14-2). All the Soviet rockets were simple, cheap, and reliable, while ours were complex, expensive, and less reliable. For example, whereas the manned U.S. rockets were fueled with volatile liquid hydrogen, the Soviets used kerosene, the humble propellant that in the United States lit lanterns and cookstoves before gas was piped in. The Soviets perfected higher combustion-chamber pressures and staged combustion in an approach that came close to theoretical best practice for fuel efficiency. By being forced to focus on refining basic rocket technology, the Soviets were able to put Sputnik and large payloads into orbit ahead of the United

Exhibit 14-1   Apollo 11's 1969 Launch to the Moon.
UPI/Corbis-Bettmann. Reproduced with permission.

States and thus had many people convinced that they were much more advanced scientifically.

Russia perfected ten times the number of liquid-fuel rocket engines as the United States did during the Cold War. Its rocket engines led in performance and reliability, too.

Consider some of the advances in rockets that the United States buys from Russia today: Russia uses a single drive shaft and often a single pump to spin both fuel and oxidizer turbopumps, while our rockets, with rare exceptions, use separate shafts and pumps for each of four combustion chambers. NASA's Jan C. Monk says Russia craftily routed kerosene fuel around hot rocket nozzles to cool them, something we just never thought of. It was outside our way of thinking, he told *The New York Times.*

The Soviets perfected higher combustion-chamber pressures, having achieved with kerosene pressures twice as high as with our exotic fuels. It also used every available ounce of energy. U.S. open-cycle engines dumped some fuel that was only half-burned. This sacrificed potential kick. The Soviets used staged combustion, beginning the

Exhibit 14-2   Soviet Rocket, 1986.
© Corbis. Reproduced with permission.

explosive burning of fuel in a preburner that powered the pumps. The blistering gases then hit the main chamber and enhanced performance. As a result the Soviet approach came closer to the theoretical best practice of fuel efficiencies.

Even today in the West only the main rocket engines for the space shuttles use this advanced technique. The seasoned Soviet NK-33 engines, which powered the Soviet Union's secret N-1 moon rocket boasted staged combustion and other advanced features. And the NK-33 used kerosene.

Your costs in moving closer to the theoretical best practice will escalate as you approach your goal. Thus, in addition to keeping in mind the lessons of limited finances, be sure to look for a large ratio of benefits to costs. A good benefit ratio would be 100 times the cost. Then, if costs should rise at an alarming rate and the project turns out to be, say, twenty times as costly as expected, you will still have incurred only a reasonable expense relative to your total benefit.

Whether you are shooting for the moon or simply trying to create something new, you must find out if the resources are available to carry out the project. There will always be a limitation somewhere, especially if you are aiming to be cost-effective. For example, currently there are more biotechnology jobs than qualified candidates to fill them, and it is believed that this scarcity may persist beyond the year 2020. Thus, those who undertake biotechnology-related projects should find out at the start if there are enough qualified people available to help reach their goals. Also, when considering materials and resources you might use, weigh the different costs you will have to pay for each. If a material or resource is scarce, you may drive up the price just by your demand.

Benefiting Along the Way

In any quest for theoretical best practice, you need milestones along the way to mark your progress and indicate if you are on the right track. Part of your game plan should be to have many subgoals. Consider the Apollo scientists who had to figure out how to keep the astronauts alive and healthy while in space, develop new equipment for use on the moon's surface, and design a rocket powerful enough to get to the moon. While all of these goals were subordinate to the goal of landing a man on the moon and returning him safely to Earth, they were nonetheless critical to achieving that ultimate goal. Because of the considerable guesswork involved in the Apollo program, much costly redundancy resulted. However, through redundancy you hedge your bets in the design work and early testing.

Success with subgoals timed so that benefits can be realized about every six months or so also keeps project participants from becoming bored. To its credit, Apollo had a whole series of exciting interim benefits such as the manned space program and the development of semiconductors to power computers. The United States got benefits along the way even without collecting rocks from the moon, a relatively small benefit of the Apollo missions.

Super Strategy

Reaching to improve further and faster requires extraordinary use of change processes. You must be sure to organize your people well to get any novel task done. You should determine what has worked successfully for your organization or others like it in the past. Then set up your program for pursuing the implementation of theoretical best practice on a similar basis, avoiding any plans that have proven ineffectual.

Excitement can have a lot to do with making change easier to accomplish. Consider, for example, that every year at the Super Bowl, a large segment of the audience works together with considerable precision on short notice. On arriving at their seats in the stadium, fans find seat cushions with pockets filled with refreshments and other goodies along with two cardboard placards with different colors on each side and instructions for using them during the half-time show. Two rehearsals, between the first and second quarters, manage to result in about 90 percent of the participants flashing the correct side of the appropriate placard at the right level at the right time. A little extra guidance is provided in the way of someone demonstrating at the front of each section of fans. And, voilà! The implementation level is good enough that the effect works for the tens of millions watching. Not bad for three minutes of training for "volunteers."

The Apollo program had the intellectual, technological, and financial resources the project needed, and when that little extra something was called for, Kennedy could appeal to our patriotism to keep things upbeat. You may want to appeal to some shared value to inspire those on your project, especially if you find you need help from outside organizations (and don't forget to check out government sources). Even if you pay for outside help, you may not get the most for your money if there is no personal interest factor involved.

There's Always Someone Who Doesn't Get the Word

Whenever you want to change the way things are done on a broad scale, you must make sure that absolutely everyone in the organization is fully aware of what you are trying to do. Communication is paramount to managing change.

As it turns out, in most corporations few people actually get the word, and those few generally include the CEO, the board, senior executives, and some middle managers. Roughly two-thirds of those at the top can describe fairly accurately what's going on. Among middle managers, the number drops dramatically. And on the lowest level, a mere handful of entry-level workers will know about the change program. Such lack of communication could be seriously problematic. Suppose the new direction calls for being more helpful to customers? Every employee will have some impact on customers, even the workers who sweep the parking lot or factory floor to make it more pleasant when customers come to visit.

To avoid getting stuck in communications stalls, review Chapter 6. Remember especially that the effectiveness of communication depends greatly on the number of times the message is presented and the number of different ways used to get the message across, as well as on emotional reinforcement and relevance. Find an element of the message that will strike home. In major transformations, the work environment will be altered fundamentally. Tell everyone how the changes affect their personal values, pay, and employment status. That's a grabber!

The average person must have far-ranging new ideas explained for maybe as many as twenty-five times and in as many different ways. For starters, the company might create a video for everyone on the first day.

The company could also stage a live meeting on a television screen and pipe that meeting electronically for everyone in every plant and office to see. To approach theoretical best practice, each employee should attend meetings with several different communicators who explain the idea in their individual styles.

Here's a case study. Consultants were called in to communicate fundamental changes designed to get profits up to a level in line with industry standards at one company's eastern facilities. The consultants scheduled one-on-one meetings. They set up eight different discussions for everyone with eight different people on the task. The words were meticulously scripted so that the message would not be miscommunicated. The consultants also decided to arrange one meeting in the middle of the day. Every employee was assigned a role in a skit. The skit was written so that each person could act out the role that was closest to that person's actual job in the new setup. The sweeper's role in the skit, for example, was to dust the new equipment.

Throughout the day, everyone with a computer was sent an e-mail message. A memorandum on paper was different from the e-mail. Since the change would affect the company's customers, the company arranged to have big customers participate and tell the workers what they could do to help increase customer satisfaction. In all, the eastern division brought ten customers to the facility to play this role.

In addition, several group discussions with different participants were held during the day.

Thus, there were over twenty-five different communications for each worker, and each one was different in style and each came from a different source. Importantly, those twenty-five messages all arrived on that one business day. Presumably, each employee then had a significant understanding of the change. Nevertheless, some people were not clear on the changes and their effects. The message had to be reinforced after that first day to attain the necessary success level. Sound like information overload? No. The goal is for the employees to get the message and know that it is serious.

Are You Still on Track?

While you are implementing your theoretical-best-practice projects, you should periodically reconsider whether your approach remains the most appropriate one. Knowledge may advance so rapidly that you will find you can do a lot better than you had originally planned. However, there are times when considerations of theoretical best practice can hold you back. For example, in the late 1970s the semiconductor industry believed it would soon reach as far as it could with its available technology. As a result, the industry set less aggressive goals because it worried about near-term technical limits. But history has not borne out those fears. The lesson is to remain undaunted by what you might *fail* to accomplish and to focus on a future based on progress by having realistic expectations of your largest areas of potential while carefully avoiding unnecessary risk.

Which companies are run best, and thereby come closest to the theoretical best practice? Opinions differ. Experience with this part of the pursuit of the 2,000 percent solution suggests a surprising conclusion: A new set of measurements is needed to answer the question. Most companies gauge their success in terms of earnings, cash flow, and stock price. A smaller number uses more exotic financial formulas. As Peter Drucker has indicated, all the measurements tell us something and are useful. As we discussed in the last chapter, focus on measures with a history and concentrate on improving on that history. Use the theoretical best practice to reach in practical ways for the stars you can grasp. Let's add the dimension of how a company's success affects the health, happiness, peace, and prosperity of the community at large. By this test, Cadence Design Systems wins big. Cadence makes software that is used to design integrated circuits. Cadence also designs integrated circuits for those who would like to outsource that activity. Cadence Design Systems software or design services are used worldwide.

Cadence's integrated circuit design technology puts state-of-the-art progress in this basic tool of modern society into more types of semiconductors than any other company's competing technology because the software makes the job easier and faster. So we all get benefits much sooner because the chips are available in less time at lower cost.

Further, by providing the service to those who may not be good at designing semiconductors, the worldwide potential for unique new products grows exponentially.

When an organization such as Cadence sets forth in pursuit of theoretical best practice, the path is lonely.

Returning to our shaving cream example, let us imagine that we have three potential theoretical best practices:

1. A shaving cream that slows down hair growth so that the good shave lasts longer
2. A shaving cream that softens the cut ends of the hair so that touching the shaved area is more pleasant
3. A shaving cream that allows the hair to be more easily removed than with a razor and produces a more enjoyable experience than shaving

Let us assume you cannot afford this and that the second theoretical-best-practice opportunity requires the hair end to be rounded off after shaving instead of remaining bluntly clipped. The technology here could involve a genetically engineered microorganism that chews on the hair where the shaving cream touches it. Let us further assume that this second theoretical-best-practice opportunity can be developed faster and cheaper with less risk and resources than the alternatives and that the customer benefits are similar. This approach would then be your selection. If you cannot afford both this and the future-best-practice genetic engineering option, bump the latter. With similar effort, this theoretical-best-practice opportunity is worth more.

That's Not Relevant

Tellabs, Inc., a voice and data communications company, is a good example of a company finding new directions. Since it doesn't know what will be developed in the future, it is very interested in staying abreast of all potentially and remotely relevant technologies. With research projects all over the world, the company has a finger in every imaginable technology pie that could become useful, whether or not it has any current application for its business. Tellabs monitors for breakthroughs and new applications, so if anything should become usable, it will be ready to capitalize on the new development.

Stallbusters

This section provides you with questions, perspectives, and directions for how to locate pertinent theoretical-best-practice information, capture the key insights from that information, and identify how to move ahead of the rest of the world in the most favorable way to you.

Decide Which Theoretical-Best-Practice Opportunities to Pursue

Your first challenge is to decide to which theoretical-best-practice opportunity you want to apply your newfound sense of achievable degrees of perfection. Drawing on the analogy of the Soviet focus on rocket engines and fuel efficiency, you should see where you can create multiple benefits from a single action. As a rule, you will accomplish more with the same resources and time period by looking for multiple benefits from the same action than from randomly trying to be perfect by focusing on a single benefit from each action alone. As was discussed in the shaving cream example, if one genetic engineering product created all of the potential theoretical-best-practice product benefits, that would be your best choice. You need to see if you have some similar opportunity.

A good way to find these potential linkages is to consider the different audiences who might benefit from one or more of these theoretical-best-practice opportunities. If you apply these tests to the shaving cream example in this chapter, you will see that the combined genetic engineering product opportunity meets the necessary tests. Ask yourself the following questions:

Which theoretical-best-practice opportunities for your organization will help which of the following audiences the most? Consider the groups that will be affected by your projects:

Customers	Suppliers
Customers' customers	Suppliers' suppliers
Customers' customers' customers	Suppliers' suppliers' suppliers
Employees	The communities you serve
Employees' families	The rest of humanity
Shareholders	

Keeping in mind the other points made in this chapter, study your answers to the following questions to further narrow your selections to pursue:

Which of these theoretical-best-practice opportunities are the employees most excited about?

Which of these theoretical-best-practice opportunities will provide the most benefits if successful?

Which of these theoretical-best-practice opportunities will cause the least harm if unsuccessful?

How does making the changes required by each theoretical-best-practice opportunity match your historical record of successful changes? What can you do to improve your odds for success?

Which scarce resources needed for developing future best practices will be required to do each theoretical-best-practice opportunity, and what other benefits will be lost, as a result?

Can the theoretical-best-practice opportunity you are considering deliver substantial results every six months, or even more more frequently? What will those results be?

Can you afford to take four or more different approaches to designing the most promising theoretical-best-practice opportunities?

What should the objectives of the most promising theoretical-best-practice opportunities be?

Determine the Best Combination of Projects for Exceeding Future Best Practice and Approaching Theoretical Best Practice

You can use the triage table from Chapter 12 to compare your alternatives. An example of this for the shaving cream company is included in the chapter.

Establish Alternative Process Routes

At this point, you should have selected the theoretical-best-practice opportunities you will implement. Now you need to turn your attention to
how the implementation program should be designed. Here, a lot of
planning can pay high dividends; for example, it can reduce the down-
side risk while expanding the variety of improvements you may enjoy.
Following up on the observation in the chapter about how working
through several ways to implement a solution will normally reduce the
cost and time to achieve the solution, you should be sure that you develop at least four alternative processes for your project at this time.
Note that it is important for you to keep what you do as secret as possible so that competitors will not begin to respond for some time. You
should also give thought as to how to make it harder for competitors to
respond once you have introduced your improvements.

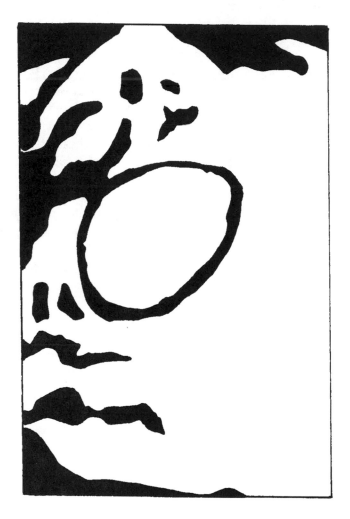

To accomplish a 2,000 percent solution requires involving the right people and using the right incentives. Using inappropriate people or incentives will greatly reduce the benefits. Imagine different shapes (such as circles, squares, triangles, rectangles, and irregularly formed objects) and try to fit them into the various white spaces in this image. Notice the different sizes of the areas that you can cover with these different shapes. Trying to focus the same people on every problem will hinder you in the same way that it would if you tried to fill the white spaces here with the same type and size of shape in each case.

Chapter 15

The Square-Peg-in-the-Square-Hole Opportunity

Step Seven: Identify the Right People and
Provide the Right Motivation

*When Mr. Markel presses button "A," it means that he wants
a copyboy, button "B," that he wants a secretary, button "C,"
that he wants his assistant, and button "D," that he wants a
complete change of staff.*
    —Remark by a copyboy who worked for the late
        Lester Markel, vinegary editor of
        The New York Times Sunday Magazine

*This chapter provides "how to" directions to supplement the search for
the maximum result and exceeding tomorrow's best practices. It develops the sixth of the book's perspectives: creating economic relationships
between organizations and their customers, employees, suppliers, partners, shareholders, and the communities in which they operate to produce a much more effective and affluent result for all these stakeholders.
This chapter breaks new ground in how to combine personal and organizational effectiveness to set new standards of accomplishment for all.*

People are the critical resource in any organization. When a company
tries to improve its processes to beyond future-best-practice and approach theoretical-best-practice levels, it must find the best people to
manage the transition. It is important to keep in mind that few people

function routinely well in a changing environment. Even fewer can act as effective members of the team that institutes changes. Curiously, even close ties among people in your shop can be a negative because one well-connected person who is down on the project can infect others. Also, close ties may mean that it is difficult for people to suggest solutions that they know will be unpopular with someone else on the team whom they have worked with before. The fact that the changes you will be implementing are probably more extreme than usual puts a premium on having the right team.

Change? Over My Dead Body!

It might seem that the best way to implement change is to use the people who know the job best—those who actually work with the problem every day. But if big changes are mandated, this approach isn't always a good idea. Use *only* the old crew and you are likely to run into a very serious foot-dragging stall. Even the best workers lose their perspective over time. You'll recall from Chapter 3 that the freshest ideas are most easily accepted by children, or people who are in a child's world relative to the issues at hand. Experimental evidence shows that people new to the job have a much easier time with understanding and making changes. They can be taught what history they need to know without being stalled by it. The newcomers are not intimately involved in the situation: They can act decisively because they have less or no association with the old mind-set. The current crew can then play devil's advocate—to help keep the new team honest, as it were.

What's more, the people who have worked together in the unit together will have bonded with one another. If they try to initiate major changes under a new strategy, their legitimate commitments to each other based on past performance and promises will have to be violated. For example, promotions may have been promised that can no longer be counted on. Or someone in the group may have worked late for months to save a former project, and so everyone feels it is important for that person to have an easy time now. Rather than trying to force the issue, provide the group with a new challenge in a different part of the company with which they are unfamiliar.

You need very capable, relative strangers to take on a change project, but they don't have to be people from outside the company itself. If the problem to be addressed affects two or more units in your company, you may want to swap people between the two different units so that each person brings a fresh perspective to the table. If both leaders are well qualified, have the one who ran Unit A take over B and vice versa.

Here is an added factor for the equation when you are addressing novel issues: Do not fail to harness all the relevant skills and knowledge. NASA once asked its contractors to reduce the weight of its rockets to limit fuel consumption. Try as they would, the engineers were only able to pare 800 pounds from the gross weight. So one day they shared this weight-reduction goal in a public meeting and a nonengineer spoke up to say, "You'll shave hundreds of pounds if you don't paint the rocket." That may have been the best idea they got. The more heterogeneous the group—psychologically and in terms of skills and experience—the better your chance for success.

Building a Dream Team

There are a number of personal psychological hang-ups that can complicate the change-making process. For one thing, when you recruit your team for the project, you will find that most people are simply unsuited to the task. The vast majority of people are immobilized by more than a little change. You must find people who are energized or excited by change. Your selected workers must see change as a challenge, one that will help them grow personally.

The approach of each member of the team must match the challenges and the hurdles to be overcome in accomplishing the tasks at hand. This is more important than you might think. Let's say you have a diseased finger. If you go to a surgeon, he will operate. An herbalist will offer ginseng, worts, etc., and the physical therapist, massage. Each will see the world in terms of ways they like to do things. Make sure that those whom you choose see the problems in proper heterogeneous ways.

What Do They Know?

Here is an example of what can happen when you fail to get the right people involved. A hotel chain put in a new computer system that cost millions of dollars. But the system failed miserably. It turned out that the hotels for which the computer was designed were not asked to contribute their knowledge and skills. As a result, the computer system did not perform the right tasks. The chain's leaders should have talked to the people at the individual hotels. Looking outside of the organization for help with new software, they might instead have gone to people who had worked on such a hotel project earlier so that they would know what questions to ask the client's people in the hotels.

It's worth noting that the individual who enjoys what he or she is doing will do a better job. Visit the Disney and the Ritz-Carlton organizations and you will find two companies resolved to recruit people who will be positive about their jobs. First, they seek out people who will enjoy certain specific jobs within their companies. When the Ritz-Carlton hires for housekeeping, it looks for people who are almost obsessively neat and tidy. Disney, in choosing guides for Disney World, selects individuals who like to talk and who will enjoy leading people around and explaining things. Both companies also seek out individuals who are excited about the company's values, thus giving the employees two reasons to want to do a good job. These companies approach hiring with the idea that one person's burden is another person's joy.

Disney and the Ritz-Carlton are onto something. There can be little doubt that the degree of excitement that the prospective team member feels about making the change is an important psychological factor. The appropriate candidate will feel that to be chosen to work on your surpassing future best practice or approaching theoretical-best-practice change is the most wonderful thing that ever happened. If you can get that kind of person involved, then you are more likely to succeed. It can be helpful to look for a person from the unit itself who has been frustrated with the way things have been done. The desire to make changes must be the reason the particular person is selected, but every one of the chosen individuals must feel deeply rewarded, psychologically, by being a part of the 2,000 percent solution.

Obviously, you want to avoid persons who are simply inflexible. They do things one way, period. Consider the American in Asia who hired an Oriental boat builder to build a Tahiti ketch, a broad-beamed oceangoing sailboat thirty feet long. He left detailed plans with the builder. The boatbuilder created a boat that was thirty feet long and seaworthy, but it was a Chinese junk. The builder was capable of building in another fashion, but he was too inflexible to do so.

Theoretical-Best-Practice Team Members

When it comes to selecting team members, take a cue from Maslow and his concept of self-actualization; or what a person can be, he or she must be. (See his *Motivation and Personality* [Harper 1954]). Maslow included Lincoln, Thomas Jefferson, Einstein, Eleanor Roosevelt, Beethoven, Thoreau, Walt Whitman, and Albert Schweitzer among the more famous self-actualized persons. He ranked these persons, along with self-actualized friends, for shared characteristics less common among ordinary-performing people. Maslow characterized the highly self-actualized as showing, among other things, more efficient perceptions of reality and more comfortable relations with it; greater acceptance of self, others, and nature; more spontaneity, simplicity, and naturalness; stronger focus on problems outside themselves; a quality of detachment and need for privacy; greater autonomy and independence of culture and environment; continued freshness of appreciation and richness of feeling; more frequent mystical or transcendent experience; a deep feeling of identification with mankind; deeper and more profound interpersonal relations; a more democratic character structure; greater ability to discriminate between means and ends; a philosophical, whimsical, nonhostile sense of humor; and, without exception, creativity, originality, or inventiveness.

Maslow also said these people were not paragons of virtue. They were strong folk and could be vain, irritating, cold, uncritical, and overgenerous. Nor were they free from guilt, anxiety, and conflict. They were more completely individual, and yet also more completely socialized than conventional folk. We know them in our world today among the famous and the friends we have cherished and whom we often seek to emulate. Wise and lucky indeed is the organization that can recruit self-actualized individuals to a change-making team.

Muddling Through

Pooling expertise is useful in situations in which few of the answers are known. Even then, there will be problems that can only be solved through the use of general intelligence, not specific answers to the questions at hand. Echoing the British colonials, we'll have to "muddle through." The phrase has an undeserved, negative connotation today.

To effect major changes, you will be doing a lot of muddling through. You should choose people for the team who understand and enjoy the muddling-through process of finding answers through thought and through trial and error.

Here's a for instance: Trade union electricians become apprentices and learn subtleties on the job that they don't learn in school. Say some master electricians are involved in a novel project, something that hasn't been done before. They don't know what to do at first, but with savvy intuitive skills, they confer in order to muddle through.

More than a generation ago, a master electrician was hired to wire a European-designed monorail at Disneyland, in California, Disney's first theme park. Europe was widely served by monorail trains of this type, but no such project of any size had been attempted in the United States. In addition, European wiring techniques are very different from ours. (We all know you can't plug a U.S.-made hair dryer into a London outlet without a converter.) The monorail company, of course, supplied wiring diagrams designed for European wiring. The Disney electrician was recovering from a heart attack, which may have been helpful in a perverse way. He was forced to sit down and think. He and another master electrician had to learn how to read the new-type (for them) wiring diagrams and then devise new techniques for wiring the monorail. With their skills, native intelligence, and instincts, they muddled through and wired the monorail on time and on budget.

Is There a Leader in the House?

> *Either lead, follow, or get out of the way.*
> —Sign on Ted Turner's desk

Naturally, the key choice in picking your change team is the leader. He or she must share the enthusiasm of each member and know how to harness it. You want someone who has the qualities of a good leader but one who also works well in a team setting. In a team environment, the team leader must be far more interested in the team and in the company's success than he or she is in being the top dog.

You need leaders who can get as many as dozens of people to work well together, to cooperate and help the company and the business succeed. It is not a good idea to borrow leaders from another company (whether they be consultants or outsourced service providers) to serve in this manager function because outsiders usually do not reflect the values of those they are leading. However, if you find that there is no natural leader in your organization—no one capable of making big changes—and you must hire a new person who is an outsider to perform this role, be sure to get someone who will create the excitement necessary to bring off major changes and who matches your company's values as closely as possible.

The kind of person you need must be highly motivated and creative (shades of self-actualization!), like the teacher who couldn't get her fourth-grade class excited about learning. Boldly, she wheedled permission from the principal to set aside the standard curriculum. She had gone to some trouble to determine the basic interests of the children, and discovered that dinosaurs were at the top of the list. That became the backdrop of her teaching plan. She took the class to museums to look at dinosaur bones. They did dinosaur-related artwork and papers. She got them interested in learning by capitalizing on their natural curiosity and excitement about extinct creatures. Thus, a class that was considered to be destined to mediocrity kept up with the best classes who were following the standard curriculum.

Three elements are necessary for leadership to succeed. First, your team leader must understand the problems thoroughly before beginning the mission. Developing such understanding usually means that the leader must visit many locations either within or outside the company, especially places in which workers are dealing with parts of the potential future-best-practice or theoretical-best-practice issue you are facing. Second, the leader will have to prove to people that the project is likely to succeed. For example, the roofing executive who went to Japan to find ways to improve methods in his factory took his key managers to the Japanese plant to prove the changes could be effectuated. People generally have to see it, touch it, feel it. People need to be confident that change is possible. On-the-job training in a successful workplace is one way to convince them of that. If your leader can get your people involved in that way, prospects of success are enhanced. Third, the people being led need to have the right skills. On-the-job training in a successful workplace will also help team members develop the skills they will need to do the job. Because of advanced training taken at the time you are preparing for your change, you won't waste time and resources going in the wrong direction.

Don't Ask Permission, Later Ask Forgiveness (If Necessary)

Count yourself lucky if you can find enough people with enthusiasm for major change. In highly conservative organizations, the word "change" can raise hackles so much that the project can be stopped cold. The "stealth change" method may lead to large improvements that might otherwise stall on the altar of tradition. There was a retail company that was suffering inroads by Wal-Mart and others with more efficient distribution systems. What to do? The CFO called in the company's controller who he knew was quite a remarkable man, able to accomplish much more than most such executives. At age sixty-two, the man was so clever at finding ways to do his job more efficiently that he had time to play golf in midweek. He did this so often that he improved his golf game until he had a single-digit handicap. Controllers rarely have time for this much golf. This controller was so bored he was looking forward to retirement.

However, the CFO managed to recruit him to be the point man in an effort to make the company a better competitor.

The controller sized up the challenge. He knew the ailing company was operating in scores of autonomous regions. His plan was to locate the company's actual best practices within itself and migrate them from the operation in which they were found to the rest of the company's far-flung regions. He was able to scout the actual best practices by visiting each region that was producing unusually good results on the accounting reports that he got weekly. While there, he kept asking questions until he found out what was being done differently that was creating the better performance.

But he faced resistance on the part of regional executives with the internal best-practice knowledge who did not want to take the time to share their special knowledge. So the controller employed a subtle, yet effective psychology. He sought out well-regarded regional executives whose profits were subpar and made them this offer: He would help them obtain special knowledge from other talented executives in the company. In fact, the controller would work with the regional executives to make the knowledge and experience transfer work more smoothly. If this direction helped the executives post more respectable profits (thereby earning them a bonus and keeping their jobs), the executives would agree to share with all the regions that lacked their special knowledge what they had learned about how to adopt the internal best practice from the region that already was doing an outstanding job.

While the newly improved executive was away teaching, the people who ran adjacent regions would handle the absent executive's job. Typically, the executive, away for eighteen months, was eager to return home, so he usually shared rapidly and well.

This was a stealth project. Neither the board of directors nor the CEO, nor anyone else in the senior management group except the CFO, knew of the project. Why? In a similar effort within that company, a project leader had sought permission before proceeding, and the project was delayed for two years.

Create a Hot Foot

Once you find the people and organize the team, you must be sure to tell those chosen for the surpassing future-best-practice or approaching-theoretical-best-practice task what is going to happen to them when this assignment is over. Let them know the assignment is not for the faint of heart. Team members will be betting their careers. If they perform well, they are likely to be asked to solve another business problem or pursue another opportunity of similar magnitude for the company—that's their reward. If they don't execute the changes, they won't have jobs, but you will help them to locate a new position in another company. This is unsettling, even demoralizing information. But this hard-nosed approach is necessary, based on the experiences of companies that have implemented these beyond-future-best-practice and approaching-theoretical-best-practice programs. It develops character, the way boot camp can help an undisciplined teenager become a mature tough-minded adult. Boot camp is admittedly a wrenching experience, but most remember the experience positively. The make or break situation strengthens resolve. Team members will call up inner resources they didn't know they had. It's the burning platform idea. (Recall from Chapter 8 the oil rig worker faced with the burning platform or jumping into the sea.) You must create a burning platform for the team as sufficient incentive for their daunting task. Then they can hotfoot it to the 2,000 percent solution and a more exciting challenge elsewhere in the organization.

Tough Duty

Do not encourage team members to perform their future-best-practice and approaching-theoretical-best-practice assignments, such as a business turnaround or redesigning a research and development process, by promising to promote them. If the participants expect better positions from satisfactory performance, they may not be committed enough to create optimum results. There should be incentives, but the incentives in the special project should in no way mirror the corporation's existing incentives. Success should result in far larger than normal bonuses for team members at their given levels. The incentives can be negotiated, but be sure to build in incentives that will *excite* exceptional effort. If they succeed, there will be a special payment that will be significant and fair to them.

Here's an example of the kind of incentive program that can work. A student had a part-time job as the promotion manager of the university alumni magazine. He was to receive a sum of money each time he raised the magazine's paid circulation. The incentive plan was well structured. It caused the student to focus singlemindedly on achieving the magazine's goal. The student went all out to grow the circulation. He brought in more new circulation in two years than the university had gotten in many prior decades combined. The student thus went from abject poverty to genteel poverty. Incentives are key in getting people to effectively take on hard tasks.

By contrast, a poorly structured plan might encourage a sales force to bring in sales without regard to costs, thus derailing the company's plan to improve profits. Well-structured plans create a strong alignment among the individuals, the team, and the organization to take the right action for the best interests of all involved.

Those who respond to the incentives and enjoy the challenge become an important resource. That's because the process of moving in new directions will be a continuing one in any alert organization. So many on the team can wind up doing this kind of work for you for substantial portions of their time in years to come. In fact, you should be able to develop a special cadre that has this expertise in making changes.

Stallbusters

The following material is designed to help you achieve better implementation results with projects to exceed future best practices and approach theoretical best practices. This will involve changing some of the ways you manage your organization now, finding the best change leaders, preparing them for the task, and motivating change leaders to be at their most effective and enthusiastic.

What to Stop Doing Now

For your new initiatives to exceed future best practices and approach theoretical best practices, you will have to stop doing some things that are important now, such as the processes you want to change and compensation programs that reward behavior you now want to discourage. You will also need to stop doing some things just to create the time to make the change project happen. This action will be especially important to get the time you need from the people who will make good team members and leaders. For help in this area, consider your answers to the following questions:

What are the habits that will push your organization in the wrong direction in making the desired changes? For example, does your organization always rely on providing replacement products when a failure occurs, rather than on designing fault-resisting capabilities (like limited redundancy)? The replacement policy may be making people comfortable with poor designs.

How can you encourage people to abandon those habits? Obviously, you cannot abandon the replacement policy until the designs improve. You could tie a special bonus payment to achieving designs that do not fail in customer locations, with the payment to be a percentage of the reduced cost of providing replacement products.

What incentives do you provide now for those habits that need to be removed? Design people may now be rewarded primarily for finishing the work on time, regardless of whether the design meets the customer's needs for fault tolerance. This incentive needs to be adjusted to reflect being rewarded only for completions that both are on time *and* provide the fault tolerance feature effectively.

What messages need to stop being sent? A message that may be sent to the engineers now concerning the design work could be to "get it out the door" to manufacturing. That message needs to be amended to reflect the new objective.

Find the Best Change Leaders

Who has the best track record in your company for leading the types of changes you are planning? Many human resources departments will not have this information, so it is vital that the company begin to collect it. You can start the process by asking managers to report the most successful change projects in the past, describe what was involved, who the leaders were, and how they organized the change process.

Who else could be an effective contributor to the change process through new ideas, communicating the change, or organizing the change effort? Human resources reviews usually do include this kind of information: the degree to which an individual contributes to the organization and to teams. The search for leaders will also turn up many of these people.

Who are the people who are most excited about the potential to make these changes? A good place to start is by asking if anyone has been pushing for these ideas in the past. You can also interview people who are potential leaders to find out their psychological emotional fit with the assignment.

Prepare the Change Leaders for the Task

What information do the change leaders lack that can be readily provided? How can that be done quickly and accurately? This information is best brought out by having the leader visit sites where the most similar activities are being done, and by asking people there to help the leader assess her or his information currency and adequacy. These people should also have suggestions for getting the information. The leader should bring along someone who is familiar with information development and the information that your organization has now.

What skills or training will they need to be effective? How can this training be timed to help them when it will be most relevant to the task at hand?

What resources will they need? How can these be made available in a timely way?

Motivate the Change Leaders

What combination of desires for recognition, reward, and feedback is right for each leader to help him or her reach the highest level of performance? Remember that creativity researchers have found that rewards for being creative often backfire, while rewards for accomplishing a predefined task usually work well. The best way to begin is by talking to the person about what motives him or her.

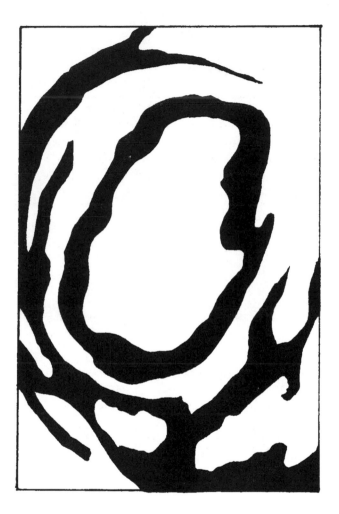

Repeating the steps you have been reading about in Part Two of *The 2,000 Percent Solution* will provide most of the benefits that your organization will receive in creating new processes. Imagine that the dark object in the center is a path that you have followed in a valley to examine your process the first time. Then imagine that the other dark object around the edges is the second path you will follow. This second path allows you to explore much more territory both by branching into many different areas and by allowing you to go higher up in the hills around the valley, from which the perspective will be different. Each time you repeat the steps outlined in Part Two, you will widen and elevate your perspective on the process you arc improving.

Chapter 16

Mustard Repeats!

Step Eight: Repeat the First Seven Steps

If at first you don't succeed, try, try again.

—Anonymous

This chapter further develops ways in which to create economic relationships between organizations and their customers, employees, suppliers, partners, shareholders, and the communities in which they operate to produce a much more effective and affluent environment for all these stakeholders. In this chapter, we see how repetition of the process described at the beginning of Part Two builds a powerful new habit that is the foundation for a continually expanding level of exponential success.

"Practice makes perfect." We learned to walk by taking more and more steps each time before we fell. We learned how to write by copying each letter many, many times. So we learn by doing. Achieving twenty times progress also requires repetition. Through the eight-step stall-busting process you will uncover new and better ideas with each repetition of the fundamental process. The first success will generate more success again and again. Outcomes will occur: Earnings will grow, cash flow will be higher, the company will be able to raise more money and move into more kinds of opportunities. Over time, the process gets easier, more productive, and faster. It will become a part of your corporate culture. You will develop lasting good habits. As new opportunities open up, you will be automatically pursuing them. You will have your 2,000 percent solution to improving your organization. If we were all to learn to use this process, then everyone would be far more effective in working with each other. The potential to multiply progress in your organization will leap forward in an exponential way.

The Grey Poupon Odyssey: He Really Cuts the Mustard!

When the executives began working on the problems of Grey Poupon mustard for Heublein, a leading consumer products and service company in the early 1970s, there wasn't much mustard to cut. Grey's was a premium brand doing only $100,000 a year in sales. Some corner newsstands do more business. When the company looked at where it should be spending its time, Heublein, which had sales of hundreds of millions of dollars a year, decided the company had to either grow this tiny business by orders of magnitude or bail out.

The situation truly called for a 2,000 percent solution. It's interesting to see how they applied the process we have been talking about in the previous chapters. As you can well imagine, the issue of having tiny sales was altered as the executives worked it, like clay in a sculptor's hands.

When Heublein reviewed the market, it asked consumers to compare a number of mustards for taste. Good news! Mustard-eaters liked Grey Poupon mustard best. They would buy it, if available. But with only $100,000 coming in, Heublein couldn't afford to spend much on advertising, promotion to supermarkets, or free samples so people could try it and taste how good it was.

So Heublein adopted a plan to sell the product to intermediaries who would then make it available to consumers. In this way, many people could sample the product at little cost to Heublein. Heublein's research indicated that current and potential Grey Poupon customers mostly had college educations. They also traveled a lot. Heublein was already packaging small bottles of liquor, which were sold on commercial airlines. The airlines that flew those jets could possibly be persuaded to buy the mustard in individual packets and distribute them to passengers along with sandwiches and some main courses.

But there was a problem. Mustard contains vinegar. It is acidic. The Grey Poupon vinegar ate through the packaging. Eventually Heublein found the proper multilayered packaging materials to hold their mustard, and the mustard packages took to the air. Soon thereafter sales in stores rose smartly as Grey Poupon-smitten eaters sought to continue enjoying this taste treat.

Heublein was also forced to alter the formula. Grey Poupon was a lot spicier right out of the vat than it was after sitting on the shelf for weeks. In fact, it would make people's eyes water, and they would eat less. By the time it was put on the plane, the small quantity had mellowed significantly. In the jar, Grey Poupon retained its high level of spiciness for many days until it aged properly. Heublein needed a recipe and a manufacturing process that offered the same spiciness over time. The problem solvers at the factory changed the process for more consistent spice levels and reformulated the mustard to make it consistently more mellow to appeal to a broader customer base.

Meantime, Heublein's financial people had realized that even if sales grew tenfold, the company still wouldn't make much money selling Grey Poupon at retail. Grey Poupon bottles were quite small—to emphasize value by keeping the price per bottle low, a perfumer's trick. But the cost of the packaging accounted for most of the wholesale price. People wouldn't pay much more money for the small quantity of mustard the small bottle offered. The cost per ounce was enormous. So Heublein put Grey Poupon in a much bigger container (the current small-sized jar), so the package itself represented a modest fraction of the former cost per ounce to the retail customer. In doing so, the price that consumers paid per ounce for the mustard could also be dropped significantly. (Eventually it would be sold in jars fifteen times larger than the original standard.)

Also, the perfume-bottle version of Grey Poupon had been sold in that special section in the supermarket where imported and very expensive condiments are displayed. Few shoppers went there, and fewer purchased in those days. So after adopting the new size jar, Heublein's marketers persuaded the supermarkets to put Grey Poupon in the section where all the best-selling mustards were sold. This is where the mustard buyers were usually making their decisions about which brand to purchase. Often, Grey Poupon turned out to be the one high-priced alternative to the cheaper, plain yellow mustards on the shelf. After this fourth change in the business, supermarket sales were growing at a rapid rate.

On the next pass, Heublein's marketers focused on overcoming the hurdle that many people simply didn't know about Grey Poupon. Heublein had to find a way to tell them effectively and inexpensively.

Some corporate planning people attended a Heublein presentation for Smirnoff Vodka, one of Heublein's most successful and profitable brands, and talked to the people there. The vodka marketers said people like a product with a heritage. Smirnoff used medals and artifacts from the nineteenth century that were associated with Smirnoff. One result: The public paid more for Smirnoff than many other brands and made it the number one vodka in the United States.

The corporate planning people shared this concept with the mustard marketers who then wondered if Heublein could sell more mustard if they created a heritage-based image for Grey Poupon. They turned to Madison Avenue. Some bright copywriters studied the heritage game plan and eventually created the famous ad with two snooty guys in Rolls Royces rolling down their windows so one could ask the other for some Grey Poupon (Exhibit 16-1). Sales blossomed, and once sales were burgeoning, Heublein budgeted money to invest in national advertising campaigns. Sales grew even more.

Grey Poupon was a pioneer in this evolving process to come closer

Exhibit 16-1   Grey Poupon Advertisement.
Copyright © Nabisco, Inc. Used by permission.

and closer to the theoretical best practice of profiting from a small food brand. The executives continually recycled through the first seven steps, each time finding at least one more new breakthrough idea to implement. The executives went through the repeat process like someone on a rowing machine, building muscle along the way. In all, the various initial steps to implement what emerged from the eight-step process took about twenty months from 1973 to 1975.

Grey Poupon has since become the best-selling mustard in the United States as measured by dollar volume, and by far the most profitable. Today, the brand continues its spicy success under the excellent leadership of Nabisco Holdings, which years earlier acquired Heublein's food businesses.

Repeating the process is, for example, something that you can adapt to your own life—say, cooking. How might repetition of a process that leads you in new directions affect your cooking?

Let's say you do want to be a better cook. As a first step, you prepare a rice recipe from a cookbook, no changes. The rice seems a bit bland. As a second step of improvement in your cooking, you add onion, some Grey Poupon, or some curry powder à la Jacques Pepin, the sardonic master chef who appears on public television with his daughter. As follow-up steps, you experiment even more after getting ideas from watching the Food Channel, taking a course at the Cordon Bleu, or simply cooking, tasting, and experimenting. To implement what you have learned, you buy new pots and a food processor and learn the microwave way to prepare quick meals.

Eventually you are ready for the big leagues. You go to dirty rice (pork-fried) and are making turduckqualen, à la Emeril Lagasse, the famed New Orleans chef. You stuff your boned quail with the pork-fried dirty rice. Now you're cooking with gas, Cajun style. The quail is pushed into a boned duck stuffed with onion and seedless raisins. The duck, in turn, is thrust into a chicken stuffed, perhaps, with bread and piñole. The chicken is stuffed into a turkey that already contains your traditional Christmas dressing.

Your turduckqualen is now ready for the oven. When you start this process, you think you have only one bird to bone, but in fact, you are dealing with turduckqualen, multiple issues, lots of meat to chew. Even using the same recipe, you find you can improve the process. You learn to debone each bird better, doing it over and over again, and putting the entire fowl thing together faster. The more times you perform the process overall, the better you get at it and the better chef you become.

Every Day in Every Way, I'm Getting Better and Better

As you pursue the eight-step process in your own business or organization, you'll find that the people who work on the problem-solving process learn and their ideas change repeatedly as they get to know more and more. You stretch people each time you go through the process. You also have a different mix of people because workers leave, and you want fresh people on the implementation teams. If one employee is good at product differentiation, involve him or her in one of the product cycles. You go through the process again to find, say, that you are lacking some manufacturing knowledge you need to improve the performance of your various products. You need to go out and hire someone who is good at your type of manufacturing, maybe a consultant or engineer, to be part of your team.

Each time you repeat the process, you are not necessarily answering the same question. Let's say you have just discovered the theoretical-best-practice limits and are trying to see how close you can get to them. One reason for repeating the process is to get answers to different questions. In many fast-changing areas today, it is necessary to repeat the process again and again. In fields such as semiconductors or software development in which there are major advances in knowledge literally every two weeks, if it takes weeks to do the exercise, you need to repeat the process continually just to stay up with what is the potential to be best in the field. That potential is constantly in flux.

Obviously, you don't usually repeat that process monthly. By contrast, microprocessor chip speeds have been doubling in less than two years' time. If you are a microprocessor manufacturer, you can't wait for a doubling of speed before you refine *that* process. If chips are working at a 400 megahertz rate, start trying to come much closer to theoretical best practice by aiming ahead of the regular development time frame by a wide margin. Find a way to jump from 400 megahertz to 1,600 megahertz during the normal eighteen-month improvement cycle, in effect, doubling the effectiveness and speed of the normal cycle. You can be working on this improvement even as the 400-megahertz chip is still being developed. In fact, the theoretical-best-practice opportunity may be to increase by four- or eightfold the rate of improvements in microprocessor chips in each eighteen-month cycle.

Thus we now have two reasons to repeat the process: (1) You get new ideas each time through, as with the Grey Poupon story, and (2) it helps you to identify new and faster ways to grow, as with microprocessor chips in which you should aim to dramatically shrink development time. There's a third reason: Like any process that requires thinking, the more you do it, the more skill you develop. You'll find yourself getting better at identifying the right questions to ask, while improving at how well you answer the questions. You'll get better at identifying theoretical best practice, a hard concept for some people to learn. You'll be better at implementing the solution that gets you closer to theoretical best practice.

The Balanchine Practice

The theoretical best practice can be, and has been, applied in many walks of life. For example, let's consider the late George Balanchine. This genius master of dance might have invented theoretical best practice by continually pushing for better and better results. He used every element at his disposal in his implacable search for the best. He picked the finest young ballerinas and pushed them to new limits of achievement with their bodies through the choreography he created to take advantage of their skills. In so doing, he moved dance into a new era.

In choreographing *The Nutcracker* (a perennial holiday favorite around the world), he had to train and recruit lots of child dancers and get them to repeat, repeat, repeat until the lessons became as familiar as tying their shoes. The company became a unit, with the dancers synchronized with each other despite the vast differences in maturity and skill.

The dancers learned and practiced the various techniques, the many leaps and pirouettes separately and together, until a Balanchine culture emerged. The Balanchine culture was institutionalized, not only the dance movements, but the emotion and the expectation for the future quality of the Balanchine ballet. Younger dancers were brought along to learn the basics and then echo the steps of the mature dancers to give the company staying power.

Balanchine is gone now, but the culture he established, now in the hands of successor dance masters, continues to advance the state of dance art, pushing ever forward toward theoretical best practice as Balanchine did in his time. In this way, the process continues to repeat to the delight of all who love the exciting world of dance that we have inherited as a result of his initiatives. You, too, should seek to use repetition to create and reinforce this wonderful improvement process as part of your organization's current and future culture.

More Stately Mansions: Build a Culture of Change

For greatest effectiveness, this eight-step process should become part of your organizational culture, related to an organizational value of seeking the maximum possible rate of improvement. By using this process, you can create a common language, thought process, culture, and capability that will be strengthened by the fact that you focus on approaching theoretical-best-practice limits. People will say that your organization is serious about improvements because everyone operates in the same way. From the CEO down, this process can be used to hurdle over stalls to make faster progress. As more people use this process, it becomes institutionalized. The CEO must create the expectation by setting the example and telling everyone that the 2,000 percent solution process is the new standard. These words become thoughts throughout the organization. The thoughts become ideas. The ideas become actions. The actions become new habits. The new habits are reinforced and improved by learning, experience, and success. The habits remake the culture. Repetition strengthens, deepens, and widens the impacts of each of these reinforcing mechanisms.

Stallbusters

The main issue for you here is planning to reinforce the potential for repetition of the process. Skip this step, and you will lose almost all of the benefit of using what you have learned in this book.

Here is your assignment:

* Make everyone aware that the eight-step process will be repeated in the same area, again and again.
* Set dates to start repeating the process at the time the process is begun.

* Set dates to begin the eight steps in other important management processes.
* Set dates to begin repeating the eight steps in those other important management processes.
* Add to your ability as an organization to use the eight-step process through improved capabilities like:
  —More measurement capabilities to spot more ways to improve
  —Better ability to identify cause and effect
  —Better access to organizations with best practices in subprocesses
  —Faster ability to capture learning from other organizations
  —Better forecasting of the likely rate of process improvement in the future
  —Improved conceptualization of the theoretical best practice
  —Better planning to approach the theoretical best practice rapidly with contained costs, while obtaining an ability to expand rapidly into new opportunities as a result of having approached the theoretical best practice

Make a copy of the above assignment and put it somewhere near your office telephone so that you will see it every time you make or receive a call. Doing this will remind you to communicate these critical points.

If you would like a free copy of the eight-step process list and this assignment to post at your office, please call (781)466-9500 in the United States twenty-four hours a day and leave your name and address. Or you can send an e-mail requesting this along with your name and address to donmitch@fastforward400.com.

By now, you should be an expert at noticing opportunities and ways to overcome obstacles, and at seeing both positive and negative in the same circumstances. To use this drawing, first make a larger copy of it. Then label each part of this image twice, once as an opportunity and once as an obstacle (use different-color pencils or ink if that helps you). Next, write down your ideas for how to get started in order to seize the benefits and overcome the obstacles. Write down what you need to do in the white spaces in the image. Then post your marked-up copy of the image in your working area where you will see it frequently every day. Add new ideas to the image as they occur to you.

By the way, can you see the dark shape in the center of the left edge as a person blowing their obstacles away? What else do you see?

Epilogue

The Route to Your 2,000 Percent Solution

An Evolution Revolution of Continuing Challenge

Here you will learn about the danger of complacency stealing back into your organization as you become adept at creating 2,000 percent solutions. Your marvelous success will create even greater risks of complacency. This Epilogue completes the book's treatment of the sixth perspective: creating economic relationships between organizations and their customers, employees, suppliers, partners, shareholders, and the communities in which the organization operates to provide much more effective and affluent results for all these stakeholders. This wider, more successful population will in turn continually open up more opportunities for your organization to achieve exponential success through locating and implementing more 2,000 percent solutions.

Keep Your Feet to the Fire . . . Even If You Have to Start the Fire Yourself

Once you have $200 million in liquid net worth, you cannot spend or give the money away as fast as you make it. I don't know what to do next.
—A successful entrepreneur

You should now understand how to make rapid progress by overcoming stalls and adopting new, more effective habits. What you probably do not yet appreciate is how rapidly change can occur, and how large the change can be. This Epilogue provides you with that perspective by describing how fast evolutionary changes occur when survival is at issue using examples from nature and business.

When Is It Time for a Change?

We have learned in the classroom that evolution takes millions of years, but there are examples of the fact that this needn't be so. The biological rate of change in species can be more than a million times faster than that. A study reported in the journal *Nature* ("Natural Selection Out on a Limb," Ted J. Case, Volume 387, pp. 15–16, May 1, 1997) tells about an experiment in which common lizards indigenous to the Caribbean were introduced to fourteen islands near the Exumas in the Bahamas.

Exhibit E-1   Rapidly Evolving Caribbean Lizard.
© Joe McDonald. Reproduced with permission of Animals Animals/Earth Scenes.

Some of the islands were smaller than a football field. Terrain ranged from barren to lush.

The object of the exercise as originally conceived was to study extinction. The researchers were convinced that if they moved the lizards to small islands, they would not survive for long because the new habitats were very ill-suited for them. But instead of dying out, most of the lizard colonies thrived, defying the researchers, because the bodies of the lizards quickly and dramatically changed in their new environments. Fourteen years after arrival in their new homes, the lizards were as different from their ancestors as a jockey and a basketball center (Exhibit E-1).

Their original home, Staniel Cay, is wooded. But most of the adoptive islands are almost treeless, the better to bring the species to extinction—or so the researchers had believed. Lizards introduced to islands with scrub vegetation kept their stubby legs and darted about more quickly. Speed is essential for success in the ground lizard world—both to catch insects and to elude predators. Lizards placed on islands with more trees than Staniel Cay developed longer legs and learned to jump from branch to branch. This adaptation made it easier for them to find food and to escape from predators.

The rate of evolutionary change in a species' wing or leg or beak (remember Darwin's finches mentioned in Chapter 1?) is assessed in degree-of-physical-change units called darwins. Physical changes detected in a single species after millions of years in the fossil record typically amount to one darwin or less. *The New York Times* reported in a review of the *Nature* article on the lizards that the transplanted lizards evolved at daredevil speeds of up to 2,000 darwins.

What this experiment demonstrated is that a species can evolve vastly faster if it is placed in the most challenging environment imaginable, where it has little chance to survive. This evolution will occur both because of developing existing capabilities (like the lizards that learned to scurry faster on the ground), and because of natural selection favoring variations in the next generations that are the best adapted to that environment (like the tree lizards). Undoubtedly, environmental pressures can affect human beings as well since almost all our DNA is the same as in all other animals. Potentially, we could change even more rapidly than other animals because through our minds we can adapt mentally more than animals can. Our mental adaptations allow us not only to physically adapt to our environment but to actually change that environment in ways that suit us. Further, we can use the tools we design. The question before us now is: How can a challenging environment make a difference for us in achieving a 2,000 percent solution?

Creating the Environment for a 2,000 Percent Solution

Let's turn to the experience of a corporate loser facing extinction and see what happens when the decision is made to make the changes needed to approach the theoretical best practice. This situation is the business equivalent of the lizard colonies being relocated onto the new islands.

At the time of the decision to create as much of the 2,000 percent solution culture as it could, this company had the lowest profit margin (after-tax earnings divided by sales) in the industry, the second to lowest market share (company sales divided by industry sales), the highest debt-to-equity ratio; poor stock-price growth; and it was forced to charge the lowest prices for its products. Its officers decided they wanted to become an industry leader, to have the highest profit margin, a normal amount of debt on the balance sheet, and a more rational pricing strategy (hopefully including higher prices).

Within a year of making the decision to improve, the company increased its market share by more than 50 percent, more than doubled its profit margin to become the second highest in the industry, improved its balance sheet to reach normal debt ratios, and increased its prices to customers substantially. Stock price grew by more than 50 percent in a year when the overall stock market was relatively flat.

After seven more years, its profit margin was the highest in the industry. It had almost tripled its market share, slashed its debt to very low levels, and saw its stock price grow impressively by more than ten times the market growth rate. All of this improvement occurred in a commodity industry in which the annual growth rate in units was less than 4 percent. Companies achieve this kind of growth in profits and stock price fairly often in rapidly growing industries where annual expansion in industry sales is over 50 percent, but in slow-growth industries the results normally take decades.

How were these changes possible in a dull, laggard industry by a company that had been losing ground? Here is what happened in that company in less than one year. The company measured the profits it could expect to earn by serving its existing customers as well as the profits it might earn if it could land any other potential customer in its universe compared to the profits that its competitors could earn in the same accounts. The company quickly learned which customers and potential customers were the most promising. Then, following a key acquisition to create the potential to slash manufacturing and shipping costs, the company directed marketing and sales efforts at the best potential customers for its cost and performance strengths versus competitors, and shifted production to more rationally exploit the narrowly focused needs that new customer base required. (Prior to these changes, the company had higher costs because of providing whatever anyone wanted, whether or not it could be done efficiently.) Then the business instantly turned around.

If we test this company's changes relative to our eight steps, we'll find that the company probably reached no more than the fourth step during that first year. It learned the importance of new measurements and applied them to important marketing and manufacturing processes. It identified the potential future best practice—getting the right mix of customers and products for higher profit margins than their competitors would enjoy. It approached that potential future best practice and speeded up the results with an acquisition that fit the strategy. That is quite a lot to do in one year.

The executives enjoyed the entire experience. The company didn't have to lay off anyone after that, though it had been laying off workers before it started in this new strategic direction. The senior executives all live far more rewarding and fulfilling lives today, as do many of the employees. Shareholders were ecstatic. Little information is available about the company's customers.

However, imagine what the company could have done using all eight steps. It fell victim to one of the greatest afflictions that can affect an organization pursuing 2,000 percent solutions: It became so successful so quickly that it developed a complacency stall. Like the lizards on the other islands, after they successfully adapted to each new island, the rate of change quickly went back to the usual slow pace. The momentum of the brief spurt of adaptation caused prosperity to expand for some time to come, however, which decreased the incentive to adapt.

You should apply stall-busting techniques to overcome the dangerous barrier of too much success too soon, and constantly re-create the environment most conducive to avoiding stalled thinking so that you can experience the exponential success that the 2,000 percent solution so readily provides . . . and can continue to provide with each repetition.

Conclusion

What, then, should be your goals for your organization? By now you should see that an organization is a way for all people to help each other lead more effective, challenging, rewarding, and balanced lives. By eliminating stalls, we can get on to the more important things in life, whatever they be for each organization and each individual. We do want to keep and build on all of the benefits of effective human cooperation in the process. Together, we can approach the theoretical best practices all around us and create exponential success not only now but also in generations to come, by preparing future generations to take on the proper mantle of focused searching for large opportunities to improve to near the theoretical-best-practice-level.

You are now ready to start creating 2,000 percent solutions (if you have begun already—good for you!). Here are the questions you need to answer and consistently act on:

What habits does your organization have now that could lead it to be derailed by success from creating a permanent 2,000 percent solution organizational culture?

How can you introduce the 2,000 percent solution to overcome those habits?

Who in your organization should you begin teaching about this process and how to overcome stalled thinking in order for you and the organization to get the most benefit from your learning?

Where in your organization is the best process to use to begin using what you have learned?

What are your organizational and personal objectives for helping others in your organization to use these ways of thinking?

What are your personal objectives for the benefits you will enjoy as a result of overcoming stalled thinking and using the eight-step process outside of your work?

We must each evolve into self-actualized individuals, who can recognize stalls and the stall mind-set, both personal and corporate, and then guide companies and organizations to overcome specific stalls to become self-actualized. We can use the eight-step stall-busting process to help us make that evolution occur much more rapidly as we pursue our opportunities to improve health, happiness, peace, and prosperity *for all* at a much faster pace. We, our loved ones, family, friends, neighbors, colleagues, those we serve, and descendants will be enormously glad we did.

Afterword

As you read in the Foreword, the purpose of this book is to shock you out of your complacency, to get you to think, and to get you to act. This Afterword shows you what actions you need to take now.

To get the most benefit for your organization:

1. Write down where your organization is performing well in relation to your needs for tomorrow.
2. Write down where your organization needs to improve now in light of tomorrow's potential.
3. Write down those areas where your organization must change in order to perform close to its future potential, and set deadlines for when those changes need to occur.
4. Share what you have written down with those who will have to make the changes. Give them this book, and set a time limit for them to develop their plans for how they are going to meet these deadlines for change.
5. Begin training everyone in your organization to identify stalls, overcome them through stallbusting, and create many 2,000 percent solutions by using the management process described in Part Two of this book.
6. Put measurements in place within each key activity to track the rise and fall of complacency throughout your organization.
7. Reread this book annually.

Index